Knowledge Quest

Myths, Legends and Folk Tales

Celtic mythology provides a rich tapestry of stories and colourful characters, including Brendan the Navigator who is best-remembered for his epic sea voyage.

Knowledge Quest

Myths, Legends and Folk Tales

Published by
The Reader's Digest Association Limited
London • New York • Sydney • Montreal

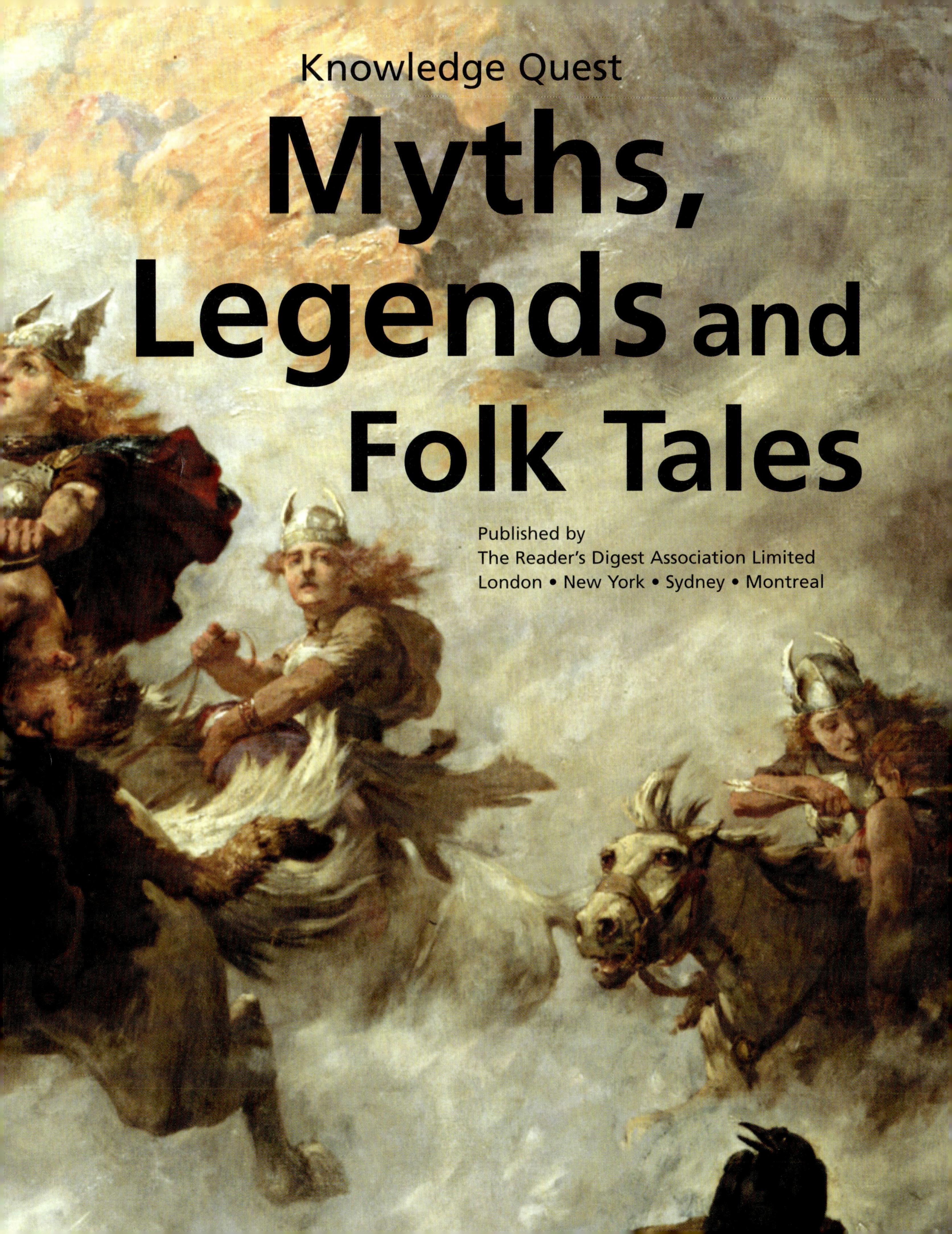

Contents

How to use Knowledge Quest

Knowledge Quest: Myths, Legends and Folk Tales is a uniquely interactive reference book that brings you a wealth of information and stories from mythology and folklore around the world.

Knowledge Quest will make adding to your store of knowledge both interesting and fun. It builds into a highly illustrated reference series, with each volume delivering authoritative facts and many other significant things to know about a particular branch of knowledge.

Myths, Legends and Folk Tales is packed with accessible information about world mythology and our rich heritage of folk takes, all contained within the core reference section (pages 39 to 145). If you want to use the book as a straightforward source of information the contents page lists the major topics covered, while the detailed index (starting on page 153) allows you to look up specific subjects. If you simply like to browse, you will find that each fascinating piece of information leads you to discover another, and another, and another . . .

What's so special about Knowledge Quest?

The unique feature of **Knowledge Quest** is the set of quiz questions that can be used as an entertaining way to get into the reference information. You can use these to test out what you already know about mythology, legends and folk tales, and to lead you eagerly into finding out more.

How do the questions link to the reference section?

There are 100 quizzes of 10 questions each, which are graded and colour-coded for levels of difficulty (see right). Each question is accompanied by a page number, which is the page in the reference section where you will find both the answer and more information on that subject generally.

The answers to all questions relating to the topic of the spread – which will come from several quizzes – are listed by question number in the far-left column. A number (or sometimes a star) following each answer refers you to the box containing the most relevant additional information elsewhere on the spread. More than one box may be indicated, and sometimes none are especially relevant, in which case an additional detail is given with the answer.

The questions in each quiz lead you to several different pages and topics in the reference section, which is great for finding out more, but is not so convenient if you want to use the quizzes as straightforward quiz rounds. So, for all keen quizmasters, we also list the answers to all the questions in each quiz in the 'Quick answers' section which starts on page 146.

Each question in the quizzes at the front of the book is linked by a page number (given immediately below the question number) to a page in the reference section, where you will find the answer, plus additional information on the subject. In this example, question 72 is linked to page 132.

The answers to all the questions relevant to the overall topic of a reference spread are listed by question number in the left-hand column. Each answer is followed by a box reference showing where more information can be found. Sometimes, instead of a box reference, additional information is given with the answer.

Each box on the rest of the reference spread contains information about an aspect of the overall topic. In this example, the topic of pages 132-33 is magical objects and box ❼ provides information on the symbolism of different kinds of fruit. Sometimes more than one box will be relevant to an answer.

From question . . . to answer . . . to discovering more

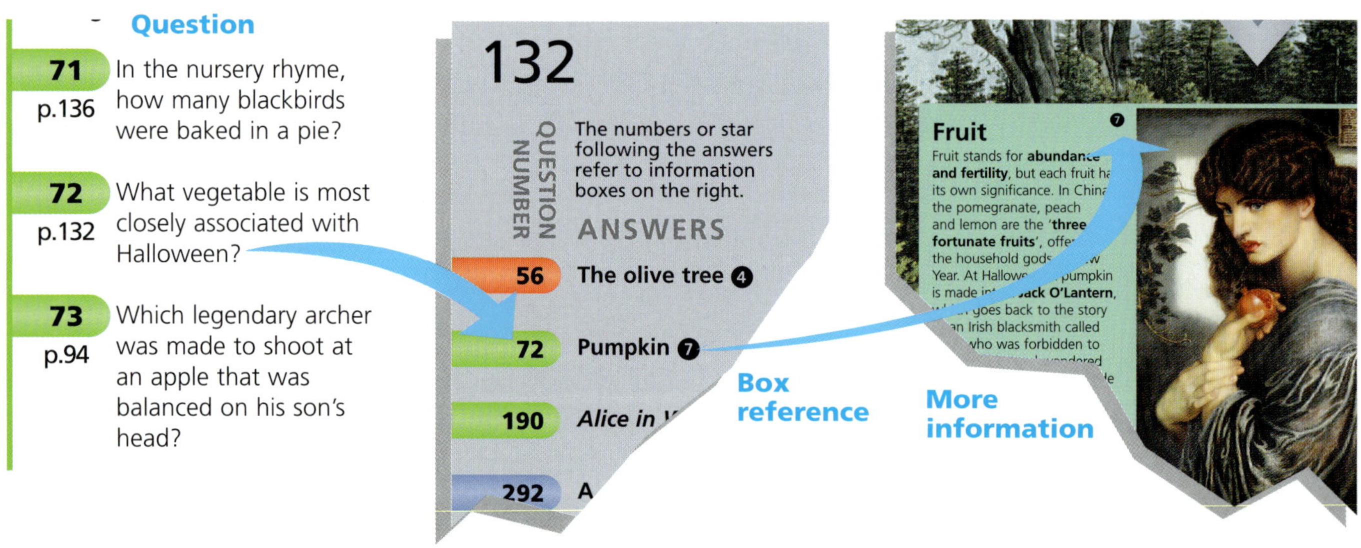

Colour-coding for quizzes of different levels of difficulty

A thousand questions are provided in a hundred themed quizzes. There are three levels of difficulty – **Warm Up**, **In Your Stride** and **Challenge**:

QUIZ 64 WARM UP

Warm Up quizzes feature easy questions to get you into the swing. Children may enjoy these quizzes as much as adults.

QUIZ 46 IN YOUR STRIDE

In Your Stride questions are pitched at a more difficult level than 'Warm Up' quizzes, requiring a little more knowledge of the subject.

QUIZ 5 CHALLENGE

Challenge quizzes are the most difficult, often requiring in-depth or specialist knowledge. But have a go anyway – you never know what information may be tucked away in the recesses of your brain!

Two other categories, **All Comers** and **Multiple Choice**, include mixed-level questions, ranging from 'warm-up' level to 'challenge', and generally becoming harder as a round progresses.

QUIZ 91 ALL COMERS

All Comers quizzes cover a range of levels of questions, from easy to hard. Everyone should be able to join in and see how they get on.

QUIZ 39 MULTIPLE CHOICE

Multiple Choice quizzes offer four possible answers to each question, only one of which is correct. They feature mixed-ability questions, generally arranged to become harder as a quiz progresses.

Special features

Star answers

One answer on each two-page spread is marked with a **star** in the answer column. This indicates a subject of special or unusual interest within the spread topic. (Occasionally, more than one answer in the answers column refers the reader to the star answer box.)

★ 114 Confucius

★ 114

Reluctant deity

According to legend, when Confucius was born a unicorn appeared and spat out a piece of jade on which was written that

Tie-breaker questions

Some spreads, but not all, feature tie-breaker questions:

Tie-breaker

These questions can be used by quizmasters in a quiz in the event of a tie, but they also contain information that expands on the answer for the interested reader.

Keeping score

The most straightforward **scoring method** is simply to award one point – or if you prefer, two points – for every correct answer.

If you are using the quizzes as rounds in a competition, you may find it easiest to look up the answers in the **Quick Answers** section at the back of the book.

For readers who would like to use this book as an information source for setting quizzes, a blank **Question sheet** and **Answer sheet** are provided at the back of the book. Quizmasters can photocopy the question sheet for their own use, and the answer sheet for distribution among contestants.

QUIZ 0 WARM UP

Animal magic

Ten questions about animals, real and imagined.

1 p.118 In the race between the hare and the tortoise, who won?

2 p.68 What kind of creature was Cerberus?

3 p.86 What is the name of the mythical creature said to have the head of an eagle and the body of a lion?

4 p.62 What pipe-playing Greek god of pastures is usually depicted with the horns and legs of a goat?

5 p.140 In Tchaikovsky's *The Nutcracker*, who do the toys do battle with?

6 p.56 Which day of the week is generally regarded by Roman Catholics as a 'fish day'?

7 p.86 According to medieval books of animals, which bird is inclined to sing itself to death?

8 p.96 The manatee is a large sea mammal, believed to have given rise to tales of which mythical creature?

9 p.68 The Minotaur was said to be the offspring of the queen of Crete and which animal?

10 p.140 What is the name of the dog that looks after the children in *Peter Pan*?

QUIZ 1 WARM UP

Time out

A quiz based on time and the calendar.

11 p.134 How many years' bad luck are said to result from breaking a mirror?

12 p.112 In Sleeping Beauty, how many years does the princess sleep before being awakened by the prince?

13 p.144 What is the name of Dr Who's time machine?

14 p.130 Which saint's day is celebrated on February 14?

15 p.112 By what time, at the very latest, must Cinderella leave the ball?

16 p.106 On which night of the year (hinted at in the title of a Shakespeare play) is it said that fairies can be seen dancing under the Moon?

17 p.72 Thursday is named after the Norse god of thunder. Who was he?

18 p.120 Who was warned by a soothsayer to beware the Ides of March?

19 p.54 Of the 12 creatures representing the years in the Chinese astrological calendar, all are real animals except one. What is the one mythological creature?

20 p.134 Which day of the week, in combination with which date in the month, is said to be particularly unlucky?

QUIZ 2 IN YOUR STRIDE

The name game

Test your knowledge about who is who.

21 p.94 Who was the partner in crime of Bonnie Parker?

22 p.62 Who was the Greek god of wine?

23 p.144 Which 1982 film was based on the novel *Do Androids Dream of Electric Sheep?* by Philip K. Dick?

24 p.138 What is the name of the Dark Lord in *The Lord of the Rings*?

25 p.108 Who played the vampire in the 1992 film *Bram Stoker's Dracula*, directed by Francis Ford Coppola?

26 p.116 Which famous teller of fairy tales was the son of a poor shoemaker and worked in a tobacco factory while still a boy?

27 p.142 What is the name of the girl with whom Spider-Man is secretly in love?

28 p.120 According to the Bible, which prophet survived the lions' den?

29 p.82 Which Native American chief of the 18th century – whose name is recalled nowadays in a famous American car – united the Indians of the Great Lakes against the European invaders?

30 p.118 In Ovid's story, what is the name of the boy who falls in love with his own reflection?

QUIZ 3 IN YOUR STRIDE

Hooray for Hollywood

A round of questions about the movies.

31 p.76 In which film does Sir Robin the Not-Quite-so-Brave-as-Sir-Lancelot join a band of other knights?

32 p.116 In the 1952 movie *Hans Christian Andersen*, who played Andersen?

33 p.110 In what film did Yul Brynner play a recreational cowboy android who runs amok?

34 p.144 What film featuring a boy android is based on a short story by Brian Aldiss entitled *Supertoys Last All Summer Long*?

35 p.108 Bela Lugosi played which character in numerous films in the 1930s and 1940s?

36 p.96 In the film *Splash*, what kind of creature does Daryl Hannah play?

37 p.112 Which Neil Jordan film is a Freudian interpretation of the story of Red Riding Hood?

38 p.122 Which 1975 film is based on the true story of the haunting of the Lutz family at their home in New York State?

39 p.88 Who played the Spanish hero El Cid in the 1961 film of the same name?

40 p.52 Qing China is the backdrop for which high-voltage movie about two warriors in search of a stolen sword?

For answers and more facts go to the page given below each question number.
For quick answers to complete quizzes 0 to 6 go to page 146.

QUIZ 4 ALL COMERS

Travellers' tales

A set of questions about real and mythical journeys.

41 p.84 Which saint, the patron of travellers, is said to have carried the infant Christ across a river?

42 p.138 In which film do two children and their flying car fight a child-hating king and his child-catcher?

43 p.74 Which Irish saint is said to have gone on a sea journey in search of the Land of Promise?

44 p.78 Which Russian witch sails through the air in a mortar and pestle?

45 p.144 In which H.G. Wells novel does a traveller go to the 800th century?

46 p.80 What English term describes the Aborigine custom of making treks into the bush for extended periods every once in a while?

47 p.106 In the lore of RAF pilots, what type of creature makes things go wrong with aircraft?

48 p.100 Which 16th-century English explorer went on two expeditions in search of the fabled land of El Dorado?

49 p.50 Which 1997 film is based on the true story of an Austrian climber who became friends with the Dalai Lama?

50 p.114 Which 19th-century adventurer and traveller produced an acclaimed translation of *The 1001 Nights*?

QUIZ 5 CHALLENGE

Mixed bag

A round of questions on a range of topics.

51 p.114 Which fairy-tale dwarf challenges a queen to guess his secret name?

52 p.48 Which Hindu god is said to have appeared in ten incarnations?

53 p.90 In Greek myth, what remains in Pandora's box when all the evils have flown out?

54 p.74 According to Irish legend, how many eyes did the giant Balor have?

55 p.114 What is the Perrault fairy tale *La Barbe-Bleue* called in English?

56 p.132 What kind of tree, common in Greece, was sacred to the goddess Athena?

57 p.142 What is the name of Batman's butler?

58 p.140 Who wrote the tale on which the ballet *The Nutcracker* is based?

59 p.82 Which civilisation came first: the Toltecs, or the Aztecs?

60 p.44 Which Egyptian god was credited with inventing hieroglyphs?

QUIZ 6 MULTIPLE CHOICE

Pot luck

Select the correct option from the four possible answers.

61 p.58 What is the name of the Greek god of sleep?
A Hypnos B Reclinus
C Orpheus D Thanatos

62 p.54 The first astrological prediction to be published in a newspaper was written for whom?
A Queen Victoria B Adolf Hitler
C Princess Margaret D Oscar Wilde

63 p.72 What is the Edda?
A A Norse epic B A Chinese dragon
C An African cult D A Celtic book

64 p.78 In what year did the Russian state of Rus convert to Christianity?
A AD 888 B AD 988
C AD 1088 D AD 1188

65 p.82 What is sometimes called the bird of Washington?
A The kite B The falcon
C The bald eagle D The vulture

66 p.50 What in Buddhism is dharma?
A Spiritual truth B Spiritual falsehood
C Spiritual conflict D Spiritual muddle

67 p.84 Who is the patron saint of Norway?
A St Olgin B St Odin
C St Olaf D St Oslo

68 p.58 In Greek mythology, what are the Elysian Fields?
A A kind of heaven B The birthplace of Zeus
C A famous battleground D A garden in Athens

69 p.48 According to Hindu mythology, how long is a Brahma day and night?
A 8640 years B 86 400 years
C 864 000 years D 8 640 000 years

70 p.56 The Norse festival of Yule took place in which season?
A Spring B Summer
C Autumn D Winter

QUIZ 7 WARM UP

Food for thought

A quiz round all about foods and eating.

71 p.136 In the nursery rhyme, how many blackbirds were baked in a pie?

72 p.132 What vegetable is most closely associated with Halloween?

73 p.94 Which legendary archer was made to shoot at an apple balanced on his son's head?

74 p.136 What was Little Miss Muffet eating when she had her scary encounter?

75 p.136 Which nursery-rhyme character tries to buy a pie from a pieman on his way to the fair?

76 p.74 In Irish mythology, Finn MacCool gains spiritual insight when he tastes a magic fish. Was it the Salmon of Knowledge, the Trout of Truth or the Mackerel of Wisdom?

77 p.136 According to the rhyme, who are made of sugar and spice and all things nice?

78 p.108 If you were faced with a vampire, what would be more useful: a string of garlic or a string of onions?

79 p.112 Who is given a poisonous apple to eat by her wicked stepmother?

80 p.136 Which nursery-rhyme character sticks his thumb in a plum pie?

QUIZ 8 IN YOUR STRIDE

True or false?

Decide whether these statements are correct.

81 p.108 Vampires' reflections do not show up in mirrors.

82 p.124 Eschatology is the magician's art of escaping from chains.

83 p.84 St Patrick is the patron saint of postal workers.

84 p.104 In *Gulliver's Travels*, Gulliver is a ship's surgeon.

85 p.74 The mythical Irish warrior Cuchullain is known as the Hammer of Donegal.

86 p.72 Tyr is the Norse god of sunshine.

87 p.124 According to the Koran, there are eight portals of Hell.

88 p.94 William Wallace is a fictional character invented in the 19th century as the Scottish answer to Robin Hood.

89 p.144 NASA's space shuttle was called *Enterprise* in honour of the fictional starship.

90 p.134 Walking under a ladder is said to bring good fortune.

QUIZ 9 IN YOUR STRIDE

Add it all up

Ten questions loosely involving numbers.

91 p.56 Which month takes its name from the Latin for 'eighth'?

92 p.62 According to the ancient Greeks, how many Muses were there?

93 p.68 How many eyes did the giant Argus Panoptes have: 10, 100 or 1000?

94 p.92 In Jesus's parable, how many 'wise virgins' are ready to meet the bridegroom?

95 p.42 According to the Bible, how many plagues did God visit upon Egypt before Pharaoh released the Israelites?

96 p.46 How many sides does the Great Pyramid at Giza have?

97 p.54 How many signs are there in the Chinese astrological system?

98 p.90 According to folklore, how many ranks of angels are there: 9, 99 or 999?

99 p.70 In Roman times, for how many years did a Vestal Virgin serve in the temple: 3, 23, or 30?

100 p.64 How many labours did Hercules perform in expiation for the murder of his family?

QUIZ 10 ALL COMERS

It's a classic

A round of questions about the ancient world.

101 p.66 Which Greek hero led the expedition to seize the Golden Fleece?

102 p.70 Who is the Roman god of beginnings, worshipped at New Year, and usually depicted with two faces?

103 p.68 In Greek mythology, what was the many-headed dragon which grew two new heads if one was cut off?

104 p.70 Who is the Roman god of business?

105 p.40 What word, now used to mean total disorder, is the Greek term for the void that existed before the creation of the world?

106 p.68 In Greek myth, what fate befell people who looked directly at the gorgon Medusa?

107 p.66 Which Trojan prince did Achilles kill and then drag behind his chariot for 12 days?

108 p.70 Who are the twin brothers said to have founded Rome?

109 p.120 In Greek myth, which prophetess foresaw the fall of Troy?

110 p.68 According to legend, which Greek inventor built the labyrinth that held the Minotaur?

**For answers and more facts go to the page given below each question number.
For quick answers to complete quizzes 7 to 13 go to page 146.**

QUIZ 11 ALL COMERS

Pot luck

Ten mixed questions on a range of topics.

111 p.114 What is the Perrault fairytale *Belle au bois dormant* called in English?

112 p.78 In which North European country are stories told of a sky god named Jumala?

113 p.56 What month and weather did Guns N' Roses sing about?

114 p.52 Which Chinese philosopher, born in the 6th century BC, was declared a god in 1907?

115 p.96 What name is given to the figure who is said to have mocked Christ on the way to Calvary, and so is condemned to walk the Earth until the Second Coming?

116 p.74 By what name is the mythological Irish hero Fionn MacCumal better known in English?

117 p.80 Which Polynesian god is said to have fished up the islands with a fish-hook and given fire to mankind?

118 p.82 On which continent did the native people believe in a Great Spirit called Manitou?

119 p.88 In the *Saga of the Nibelungen*, who or what are the Nibelungen?

120 p.48 Which Hindu god is sometimes called 'the Destroyer'?

QUIZ 12 CHALLENGE

Books and bookmen

A round with a literary theme.

121 p.120 Which book in the Bible contains an account of a vision of the end of the world?

122 p.44 What nationality was Plutarch, the historian who first wrote down the Egyptian myths of Osiris?

123 p.88 Which Irish poet published a prize-winning translation of the Anglo-Saxon epic *Beowulf* in 2000?

124 p.100 Who wrote *Lost Horizon*, the story of an Englishman who discovers paradise in the Tibetan valley of Shangri-La?

125 p.74 According to the *Red Book of Hergest*, which of King Arthur's knights is the husband of Enid?

126 p.92 In *The Pilgrim's Progress*, what does Christian carry on his back?

127 p.46 In ancient Egypt, what book was thought to help the souls of the dead in the afterlife?

128 p.94 Which Australian writer recently revived the story of Ned Kelly in a novel purporting to be 'the true history…'?

129 p.80 Who wrote *Songlines*, a book that explores the myths of the Australian aborigines?

130 p.48 Which Hindu epic contains Krishna's 'Bhagavad Gita' – the Song of the Lord?

QUIZ 13 MULTIPLE CHOICE

Mixed bag

Select the correct option from the four possible answers.

131 p.98 According to legend, the holy mountain of Croagh Patrick is where St Patrick drove what animals out of Ireland?
A Cockroaches — B Snakes — C Spiders — D Rats

132 p.46 Which of these pairs were the tokens of kingship in ancient Egypt?
A A feather and a sword — B A crook and a flail — C A crown and a cat — D An eagle and a beard

133 p.52 What does the word tao in Taoism mean?
A Service — B Way — C Life — D Choice

134 p.90 On which day of the year is Lady Day?
A January 25 — B February 25 — C March 25 — D April 25

135 p.64 In what form did the god Zeus first seduce his sister Hera?
A As a cloud — B As a cuckoo — C As a horse — D As an eagle

136 p.78 In Russian myth, what was Bannik the spirit of?
A The bakery — B The brewery — C The bathhouse — D The belfry

137 p.72 In Norse mythology, what form does the bridge called Bifrost take?
A A rainbow — B A giant snake — C A golden sword — D A cloud

138 p.126 What is a havhest?
A A magic Viking helmet — B A sea monster — C A Swedish pixie — D A Danish festival

139 p.62 Where, according to the Greeks, does a dryad reside?
A In an animal — B In a lake — C In a rock — D In a tree

140 p.112 Who directed the 1946 film *La Belle et la bête*?
A Jean-Paul Sartre — B Jean Cocteau — C Jean Renoir — D Jean Marais

QUIZ 14 WARM UP

Pot luck

Ten questions on a range of topics for everyone to try.

141 p.140 In *The Nutcracker*, who greets Clara when she arrives in the Land of Sweets?

142 p.106 What three-letter word describes a type of fairy?

143 p.92 According to Aesop's fables, the wolf disguised itself in whose clothing?

144 p.124 Which saint is said to stand at the gates of Heaven?

145 p.90 What device, commonly used in board games and in gambling, is sometimes called the 'devil's bones'?

146 p.50 Hermann Hesse's 1922 novel *Siddhartha* is about which great religious figure?

147 p.92 Who told the story of 'the pearl of great price'?

148 p.138 In *Through the Looking-Glass*, what is a jabberwock?

149 p.128 Which Middle Eastern country features a star of David on its national flag?

150 p.142 What is Batman's real name?

QUIZ 15 IN YOUR STRIDE

Mixed letters

Unravel the anagrams with the help of the clues.

151 p.94 ETHNOL JILT was the name of Robin Hood's very tall comrade-in-arms (two words).

152 p.90 DONA RAP was the woman who opened a box containing all the woes of the world.

153 p.144 RATE AX LITTERS ERR describes a visitor from another planet.

154 p.88 AT RUB HYMN is a form of endlessly circulated modern story (two words).

155 p.70 SOUL RUM, according to legend, was a twin founder of Rome.

156 p.46 SPRAY UP was an ancient writing material.

157 p.98 A TYBURNS LOG is a town in Somerset where Joseph of Arimathea is said to have begun the conversion of the English.

158 p.126 A MANNA BINE LOB MOWS is the name for an elusive creature, coined after a British-led expedition to Everest in 1951 (two words).

159 p.54 A GORY SLOT is to study the stars.

160 p.76 LIMNER was imprisoned in a tree by his lover Nimue.

QUIZ 16 ALL COMERS

Fabulous fauna

A mixed round on the theme of animals.

161 p.114 What is the Perrault fairy tale *Le Chat Botté* called in English?

162 p.70 In Roman mythology, which wild animal is said to have suckled the twins Romulus and Remus?

163 p.68 After the Greek giant Argus was killed, the goddess Hera bestowed his many eyes on which bird?

164 p.126 In which film does a monster parasite form inside a person?

165 p.80 The trickster god known in the West Indies as Anansi Spider originated on which continent?

166 p.138 In the trilogy *His Dark Materials*, who are the animal companions that people have by them at all times?

167 p.44 Thoth, the Egyptian god of learning, was often depicted as which animal?

168 p.52 Which mythical Chinese animal is said to have the horns of a deer, the head of a camel, the claws of an eagle and the feet of a tiger?

169 p.82 Which Mexican people worshipped a god in the form of a plumed serpent?

170 p.44 Which Egyptian god presides over funeral rites and has the head of a jackal?

QUIZ 17 CHALLENGE

Greece is the word

A round of questions on the theme of ancient Greece.

171 p.64 Which Greek hero was the son of the nymph Thetis?

172 p.120 To which god was the Delphic Oracle dedicated?

173 p.62 By what name are Clotho, Lachesis and Atropos collectively known?

174 p.64 What was the 12th Labour of Hercules?

175 p.60 Who is the Greek goddess of the hearth?

176 p.68 Which Cyclops was blinded in his cave by Odysseus?

177 p.56 Who is the Greek goddess of the dawn?

178 p.120 By what title was the priestess of the Oracle at Delphi known?

179 p.62 By what name are the three companions of Aphrodite – Aglaia, Thalia and Euphrosyne – collectively known?

180 p.64 Which king of Thessaly was condemned by Zeus to roll a boulder uphill for ever?

**For answers and more facts go to the page given below each question number.
For quick answers to complete quizzes 14 to 18 go to page 146.**

QUIZ 18 WARM UP

Every picture tells a story

Match the pictures with the stories.

- ***Alice in Wonderland***, Lewis Caroll
- ***Puss in Boots***, Charles Perrault
- ***Le Petit Prince***, Antoine de Saint-Exupéry
- ***Thumbelina***, Hans Christian Andersen
- ***Frankenstein***, Mary Shelley
- ***Goblin Market***, Christina Rossetti
- ***Struwwelpeter***, Heinrich Hoffmann
- ***The Wizard of Oz***, L. Frank Barnum
- ***Animal Farm***, George Orwell
- ***Uncle Remus***, Joel Chandler Harris

181
p.138

182
p.116

183
p.106

184
p.136

185
p.114

186
p.110

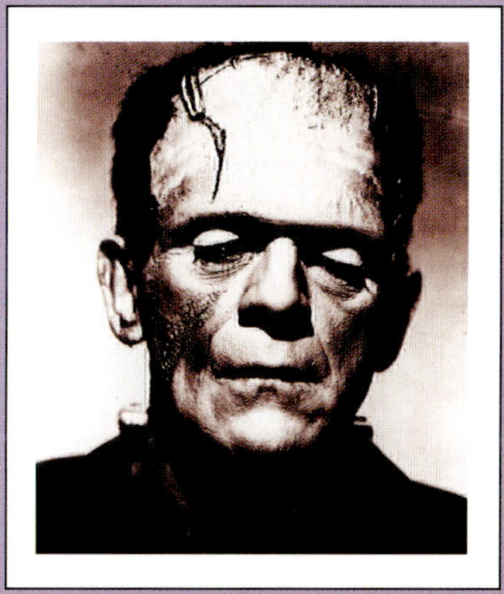

187
p.110

188
p.114

189
p.92

190
p.132

QUIZ 19 WARM UP

Pot luck

Ten questions on a range of topics for everyone to try.

191 p.102 What name is given to the spooky night before All Hallows' Day?

192 p.112 Which fairy tale heroine breaks into the house of the three bears?

193 p.100 Which biblical leader was promised by God that his people would one day come to a 'land of milk and honey'?

194 p.102 What is the name of the good wizard and friend of Frodo in *The Lord of the Rings*?

195 p.140 Who, in J.M. Barrie's play, is the little boy who never grew up?

196 p.54 The name of which star sign means 'water carrier'?

197 p.112 In which fairy tale is a hideous monster transformed into a prince by the love of a captive girl?

198 p.142 What is the name of the younger and more excitable member of the Dynamic Duo?

199 p.76 In Arthurian legend, what name is given to the cup from which Jesus drank at the Last Supper?

200 p.100 'There we wept when we remembered Zion …' By the rivers of which ancient city did the psalmist weep?

QUIZ 20 IN YOUR STRIDE

Climb every mountain

A set of questions about mountains and climbers.

201 p.98 True or false: women and female animals are banned from Mount Athos, or Holy Mountain, in Greece?

202 p.98 By what name is the Never-Dying Mountain, a sacred place in Japan, better known to the wider world?

203 p.42 On which mountain did Moses receive the Ten Commandments?

204 p.84 Who is the patron saint of mountaineers?

205 p.64 On which mountain was Prometheus chained by Zeus: Mount Caucasus or Mount Olympus?

206 p.74 In which country will you find the rock formation known as The Giant's Causeway?

207 p.42 On which mountain is Noah's ark said to have come to rest?

208 p.68 In which Mediterranean volcano did Zeus imprison the monster Typhon?

209 p.80 Oldoinyo Oibor – 'white mountain' in Masai – is also known by what name?

210 p.98 Which massive, man-made Neolithic mound – the largest in Europe – is situated near Avebury in Wiltshire?

QUIZ 21 ALL COMERS

Mixed bag

A quiz round on a range of topics.

211 p.56 According to the rhyme, Wednesday's child is full of … what?

212 p.112 Which Israeli duo sang the hit song 'Cinderella Rockefella'?

213 p.114 What is the Perrault fairy tale *Petit Chaperon Rouge* called in English?

214 p.124 In Catholic belief, where do souls go to be cleansed before they enter Heaven?

215 p.58 What word meaning 'hall of the slain' denotes the Viking heaven?

216 p.58 'Babe' was a romantic hit for which US band?

217 p.70 In Roman mythology, what were the gods of particular places or people called?

218 p.140 What important possession did Peter Pan lose in Wendy's nursery?

219 p.88 What term describes a mystery play dealing with the death and resurrection of Christ?

220 p.56 Who was the Roman goddess of springtime, flowers and fruit, whose name is now used to mean vegetation in general?

QUIZ 22 ALL COMERS

First letter clues

Each answer starts with the letter provided.

221 p.82 What 'S' is the more proper term for a 'medicine man'?

222 p.106 What 'L' is an Irish fairy?

223 p.90 What 'B' means 'lord of the flies' and is one of the names of the devil?

224 p.88 Mystery plays are also known by what other two-word term beginning with 'M'?

225 p.122 What 'P' is a ghost or spirit that throws or moves objects?

226 p.124 What 'L' in Catholic belief is the abode of good people who have died without being baptised?

227 p.130 What 'R' is a Japanese form of healing through laying-on of hands?

228 p.40 Which Greek god, whose name begins with 'P', is said to have fashioned mankind from earth and his own tears?

229 p.46 Which 'N' is the name of an Egyptian queen who was the wife of Akhenaten?

230 p.84 What 'H' means the life story of a saint?

**For answers and more facts go to the page given below each question number.
For quick answers to complete quizzes 19 to 25 go to pages 146 and 147.**

QUIZ 23 CHALLENGE

The dogs of war

A set of questions about wars and warriors.

231 p.144 Who wrote the science fiction fantasy *The War of the Worlds*?

232 p.72 In Norse mythology, which beautiful maidens select the warriors to be slain?

233 p.56 Which month is named after the Roman god of war?

234 p.72 Which Norse god was said to adopt all warriors killed in battle?

235 p.74 The mythical Irish warrior Cuchullain fell in battle against which queen?

236 p.60 Who is the Greek god of war?

237 p.88 Of which Spanish Mediterranean city was El Cid de facto ruler from 1094 until his death in 1099?

238 p.104 In the Bible, the boy David's opponent, Goliath, belonged to which nation?

239 p.66 Who killed the Greek hero Achilles?

240 p.80 Which warlike African people acknowledges a creator god called Unkulunkulu?

QUIZ 24 CHALLENGE

Culture vulture

A quiz round drawn from poetry and art.

241 p.88 Which Greek epic poem describes the wanderings of a hero returning from the Trojan war?

242 p.100 Which Dutch master painted a picture of the pleasures of the land of Cockaigne?

243 p.84 Who is the patron saint of artists?

244 p.120 Under what title were Nostradamus's volumes of prophecies and predictions originally published?

245 p.124 Which medieval Dutch painter is known for his nightmarish paintings of the torments of Hell?

246 p.62 Which painting by Sandro Botticelli depicts a mythological version of the coming of spring?

247 p.124 In Dante's *Inferno*, which type of sinners occupy the ninth circle of Hell?

248 p.62 Which sculptor created the statue known as 'The Three Graces'?

249 p.120 Which Old Testament character interpreted Nebuchadnezzar's dream of a statue with feet of clay?

250 p.72 Where did the 13th-century poet and historian Snorri Sturluson live?

QUIZ 25 MULTIPLE CHOICE

Pot luck

Select the correct option from the four possible answers.

251 p.56 According to the rhyme, what new gift did 'my true love send to me' on the third day of Christmas?

A Gold rings | B French hens
C Turtle doves | D Colly birds

252 p.68 What did the three Gorgons have instead of hair on their heads?

A Gold | B Cats' tails
C Rope | D Snakes

253 p.58 What is the name of the Greek goddess of the harvest?

A Persephone | B Artemis
C Demeter | D Cornucopia

254 p.40 Which of these is the Egyptian god of the Earth?

A Geb | B Deb
C Feb | D Seb

255 p.54 According to the Bible, how many wise men came to visit the baby Jesus?

A Two | B Three
C Four | D It does not say

256 p.74 What, in Irish mythology, is the Fianna?

A A screaming witch | B A royal bodyguard
C An enchanted sword | D A festival

257 p.82 What is peyote?

A An hallucinogenic drug | B A magic wand
C An accursed coyote | D A heraldic emblem

258 p.64 In Greek mythology, what is Moros?

A The food of the gods | B The concept of destiny
C A crown worn by Zeus | D A one-eyed monster

259 p.118 The story of Echo and Narcissus was originally told by?

A Plutarch | B Aesop
C Ovid | D Virgil

260 p.102 Which of these is said to be a magic word?

A Abulafia | B Abracadabra
C Alhambra | D Abecedarian

QUIZ 26 WARM UP

Pot luck

Ten questions on a range of topics for everyone to try.

261 What four-word phrase is usually used to begin fairy tales? p.112

262 Their name, according to the author who invented them, means 'hole-dwellers'? Who or what are they? p.138

263 Which biblical hero derived his strength from the fact that he never cut his hair? p.130

264 Which female saint was martyred on a wheel, and is remembered in the name of a firework? p.84

265 What term refers to a board, inscribed with the letters of the alphabet, used to receive messages in seances? p.122

266 What vegetable is transformed into a carriage by Cinderella's fairy godmother? p.112

267 According to Aesop's fable, what kind of animal did the shepherd falsely claim was attacking his sheep? p.118

268 What phrase is sometimes used to refer to a sighting of an alien spaceship? p.144

269 According to the Bible, what kind of animal persuaded Eve to eat the forbidden fruit? p.90

270 According to folklore, what household object does a witch use for transport? p.102

QUIZ 27 IN YOUR STRIDE

Book club

Test your knowledge about books and writers.

271 Who wrote the original story of Frankenstein? p.110

272 Which book of the Bible, the name of which has come to mean 'departure', tells the story of the Israelites' escape from slavery in Egypt? p.42

273 Who wrote the satire of tiny people and great giants, *Gulliver's Travels*? p.92

274 What is the name of the novel by Arthur Conan Doyle about a spectral dog? p.126

275 What is the name of the narrator in the Brer Rabbit stories of Joel Chandler Harris? p.114

276 Who wrote the religious allegory *The Pilgrim's Progress*? p.92

277 In T.H. White's *The Once and Future King*, who is the king in question? p.76

278 In which famous book will you read of a monster called a behemoth? p.86

279 Which member of Slytherin house is Harry Potter's main rival? p.138

280 What is the name of the devil who writes instructive letters to his demon nephew in the book by C.S. Lewis? p.138

QUIZ 28 IN YOUR STRIDE

The love bug

See if you know who was in love with whom.

281 Which Greek god is said to shoot arrows that cause people to fall in love? p.130

282 What is the name of the woman loved by Robin Hood? p.94

283 What is the name of the intrepid newspaper reporter loved from afar by Clark Kent? p.142

284 Which 1982 film stars Catherine Deneuve as a vampire and David Bowie as her lover? p.108

285 Who is the Greek goddess of love and desire? p.60

286 Who is Flash Gordon's girlfriend? p.144

287 In which Hans Christian Andersen tale does a toy melt in a fire, leaving a little metal heart in the ashes? p.116

288 In Ovid's story, who is the girl who pines away for love of Narcissus, leaving only the faint sound of her voice behind? p.118

289 In Greek myth, who falls in love with a statue he has created? p.110

290 In the *commedia dell'arte*, who is Harlequin's lover? p.140

QUIZ 29 ALL COMERS

Trees and flowers

A quiz with a horticultural theme.

291 Which spirit of mines and quarries is now more often seen in the form of garden statuary? p.106

292 In Chinese myth, which kind of fruit tree can be climbed to heaven: a peach tree, or a pear tree? p.132

293 In the children's rhyme, whose garden grows with silver bells and cockleshells? p.136

294 Which English folk figure is usually depicted wreathed in foliage or oak leaves? p.96

295 Which flower symbolised the Nile to the ancient Egyptians: the tulip, lotus or rose? p.46

296 Which Celtic priests performed their sacred rites in oak groves and revered mistletoe? p.102

297 Which of the knights of the Round Table is sometimes called 'the flower of the knights'? p.76

298 Which country's monarch is traditionally said to govern from the 'Chrysanthemum Throne'? p.52

299 According to the rhyme, what do we all do at the end of Ring-a-ring o' Roses? p.136

300 According to the rhyme, roses are red, violets are _____? p.136

**For answers and more facts go to the page given below each question number.
For quick answers to complete quizzes 26 to 32 go to page 147.**

QUIZ 30 ALL COMERS

United nations

Ten questions about countries real and mythical.

301 Who is the patron saint of Scotland?
p.84

302 In which country will you hear a myth of the earth goddess Papa and the sky god Rangi?
p.40

303 The epic tales of which country are recounted in *The Mabinogion*?
p.74

304 In which modern country is Mount Ararat, where Noah's ark is said to have come to rest?
p.42

305 The *Kalevala* is the national epic of which country?
p.78

306 In *Gulliver's Travels*, which country is populated by tiny people?
p.104

307 The poem *Beowulf* is a founding work of English literature, but is set in which country?
p.88

308 According to the Bible, in which country did Joseph become a high government official?
p.42

309 If you were to catch sight of Bigfoot, which continent would you be on?
p.126

310 Who is the patron saint of England?
p.84

QUIZ 31 CHALLENGE

Word games

A round about the invention and meaning of words.

311 Sir Thomas More called his imaginary ideal society Utopia. What does Utopia mean?
p.100

312 Which writer coined the word 'robot'?
p.110

313 By what name is the symbol sometimes called a fylfot or a gammadion better known?
p.128

314 Which north-western cape of Spain means 'end of the earth'?
p.98

315 What English term is used to translate the aboriginal word *alchera*?
p.80

316 What is the name of the monastic order which was founded by St Robert de Champagne in 1098?
p.84

317 The Last Judgment is sometimes referred to by which Latin phrase?
p.124

318 What is the more common term for a lycanthrope?
p.108

319 God sent a diversity of languages to the world to confound which over-ambitious biblical building project?
p.124

320 Which battle of 1836 is sometimes called the 'Thermopylae of America'?
p.82

QUIZ 32 MULTIPLE CHOICE

Pot luck

Select the correct option from the four possible answers.

321 Nostradamus's predictions are expressed in poems of how many lines?
p.120

A Four B Six C Eight D Ten

322 In Egyptian mythology, who was the evil brother of Osiris?
p.44

A Sam B Seth C Steph D Saul

323 Where is the mythical monster, the leviathan, said to live?
p.86

A In the sea B On land C In the air D In the sky

324 On which day did God create the sea creatures and birds?
p.40

A Day three B Day four C Day five D Day six

325 Who wrote *Moby Dick*?
p.92

A Mark Twain B Herman Melville C Henry James D Nathaniel Hawthorne

326 Which French poet wrote about the love of Sir Lancelot and Queen Guinevere?
p.76

A Gérard de Nerval B Pierre de Ronsard C Chrétien de Troyes D Alfred de Vigny

327 Which saint lived on Holy Island (Lindisfarne)?
p.98

A St Augustine B St Brendan C St Cuthbert D St David

328 What fruit did Hades give to Persephone to bind her to him in the Underworld?
p.132

A An apple B A fig C A pomegranate D A peach

329 In Norse mythology, what are the Havfine?
p.96

A Winged horses B Mermaids C Giants D Goblins

330 What in Russia are bylini?
p.78

A Pancakes B Mushrooms C Sprites D Folk tales

QUIZ 33 WARM UP

Film fantasy

A round of questions on the silver screen.

331 p.104 In the Disney version of Snow White, who is the only dwarf whose name is not an adjective?

332 p.108 In which video does Michael Jackson lead an army of zombies?

333 p.110 Who played the Terminator in the film of the same name?

334 p.122 In which film do Dan Ackroyd and Bill Murray play scientists who set up a company to deal with infestations of spectres?

335 p.126 What is the name of the giant mutated Tyrannosaurus Rex that first appeared on screen in Japan in 1954?

336 p.94 Which actor played Robin Hood in the 1991 film *Robin Hood: Prince of Thieves*?

337 p.110 In *Star Trek: The Next Generation*, what is the name of the android who serves on the starship *Enterprise*?

338 p.144 What is the name of the Jedi knight played on screen by Alec Guinness?

339 p.138 In what film do nightmarish creatures harvest children's screams?

340 p.126 Which fictional giant ape was first seen on screen in 1933?

QUIZ 34 IN YOUR STRIDE

Pot luck

Questions on a range of topics for everyone to try.

341 p.128 Which disciple of Jesus was said to be crucified upside-down?

342 p.106 What is the word for the demon of Arabian myth, sometimes imprisoned in a lamp?

343 p.76 Which band recorded the album *Avalon* in 1982?

344 p.56 According to the rhyme, Saturday's child does what for a living?

345 p.110 What is the literal meaning of the word android?

346 p.116 Which of Hans Christian Andersen's tales was parodied in a burlesque entitled 'Once Upon A Mattress'?

347 p.132 In the Harry Potter stories, what is the name of the mirror which shows anyone who looks into it what their heart most desires?

348 p.116 Which Hans Chrisian Andersen story inspired the famous bronze statue overlooking Copenhagen harbour?

349 p.46 In Egyptian mythology, what type of creature is the sacred animal Apis?

350 p.110 Which hit musical, made into a film in 1964, was based on George Bernard Shaw's version of the Pygmalion myth?

QUIZ 35 IN YOUR STRIDE

Power dressing

Ten questions on items of clothing.

351 p.134 Who should wear something old, something new, something borrowed, and something blue?

352 p.68 What property did Hades' helmet confer upon its wearer?

353 p.112 From what material were Cinderella's shoes made?

354 p.136 In the rhyme 'Ride a cock-horse to Banbury Cross', what does the lady wear on her toes?

355 p.142 Who is the Caped Crusader?

356 p.140 What is the name of the *commedia dell'arte* figure who wears a mask and a silken suit with a diamond pattern?

357 p.42 Who in the Bible was given a magnificent robe, described in the King James Version as 'a coat of many colours'?

358 p.102 What items of clothing are the object of desire for the wicked witch in the Wizard of Oz?

359 p.138 In the Harry Potter stories, what item of clothing decides who goes into which house at Hogwarts?

360 p.116 Which tale ends with a royal person parading naked through the streets?

QUIZ 36 ALL COMERS

Can you place it?

The questions in this round are all about towns and cities.

361 p.98 In which city was the prophet Muhammad born?

362 p.76 According to legend, in which Cornish town was King Arthur born?

363 p.98 Which city is the spiritual centre of Tibetan Buddhism?

364 p.70 Which river runs through Rome?

365 p.50 In which town did Buddha sit under the bodhi tree and wait for enlightenment?

366 p.98 In which city in northern Spain is the apostle St James said to be buried?

367 p.88 In which Bavarian town has a play depicting the Easter story been performed since 1633?

368 p.98 Mecca is one of Islam's two most holy cities: what is the other?

369 p.48 The name of which Indian city is a corruption of the phrase Kali Ghat, meaning 'steps of Kali'?

370 p.82 Which South American civilisation built Machu Picchu?

**For answers and more facts go to the page given below each question number.
For quick answers to complete quizzes 33 to 39 go to page 147.**

QUIZ 37 ALL COMERS

Shine on

These questions are loosely based on the theme of light.

371 What is the Hebrew word for the Festival of Lights, celebrated every December?
p.132

372 In the movies, which order of knights fight using light-sabres?
p.144

373 According to Genesis, on which of the six days of creation did God create light?
p.40

374 Which Greek god stole a spark of fire and made a gift of it to mankind?
p.64

375 Which country's flag has a red sun on a white ground?
p.52

376 In *Northern Lights*, the first book in Philip Pullman's trilogy, who is the beautiful witch, clan-queen of the witches of Lake Enara?
p.102

377 Who wrote the opera *Götterdämmerung* (*The Twilight of the Gods*)?
p.140

378 A menorah – a candlestick with seven branches – is a symbol of which religion?
p.128

379 On which saint's day do Swedish girls wear crowns of candles?
p.132

380 What is the name of the Hindu festival of lights, celebrated in October or November?
p.48

QUIZ 38 CHALLENGE

Zoo time

A set of brainteasers on the animal world.

381 What does the word 'zodiac' mean?
p.54

382 According to aboriginal myth, the blood of which animal caused the evening colour of Uluru?
p.98

383 Sekhmet, the Egyptian goddess of war, had the head of which animal?
p.44

384 In Greek legend, what animal was Actaeon transformed into by Artemis?
p.60

385 In ancient Tahiti, what creatures were euphemistically called 'long-legged fish'?
p.80

386 Orion the Hunter seems to be aiming his arrow at which animal constellation?
p.104

387 According to medieval legend, which animal gave birth to twins, only one of which it loves?
p.86

388 Who were the companions of the wine god Dionysus?
p.62

389 Name the political allegory, written by Karel Čapek, in which ants represent labour?
p.92

390 The year 2005 is represented by which creature in the Chinese zodiac?
p.54

QUIZ 39 MULTIPLE CHOICE

Pot luck

Select the correct option from the four possible answers.

391 By what name was the Greek hero Heracles known to the Romans?
p.64

A Mercury — B Apollo — C Horace — D Hercules

392 In Scandinavian myth, what is the word for a warrior who fights ferociously and without armour?
p.72

A A beefeater — B A berserker — C A bluffer — D A bullethead

393 Which of these is an Egyptian god?
p.40

A Nun — B Not — C Nub — D Nat

394 In Russian myth, Volos was the god of what?
p.78

A Music — B War — C Farming — D The family

395 In Buddhism, what is a boddhisattva?
p.50

A A Buddhist monk's robe — B An incense burner — C A buddha-to-be — D A kind of demon

396 On which day of the year is Walpurgis Night?
p.122

A June 1 — B October 31 — C May 1 — D December 31

397 Which birds are said by sailors to embody the souls of dead mariners?
p.134

A Albatross — B Cormorants — C Puffins — D Stormy petrels

398 What nationality was the astronomer Copernicus?
p.54

A German — B Polish — C Dutch — D Swedish

399 In Hindu myth, Yama rules over how many hells?
p.58

A 12 — B 21 — C 121 — D 211

400 What is the Edessa Cloth also known as?
p.132

A The Holy Mandrake — B The Holy Magdalene — C The Holy Mandylion — D The Holy Madras

QUIZ 40 WARM UP

Answers count

Each answer or question involves a number?

401 p.54 How many signs of the zodiac are there?

402 p.104 How many dwarves live in the house where Snow White comes to stay?

403 p.136 How many men, according to the rhyme, did the grand old Duke of York have?

404 p.68 In Greek legend, how many eyes did the Cyclopes have?

405 p.40 According to the Bible, what did God do on the seventh day of Creation?

406 p.112 How many stepsisters does Cinderella have?

407 p.62 According to the ancient Greeks, how many seasons were there in a year: three, four or five?

408 p.92 In the Bible, how many parables does Jesus relate: 4, 14, or 40?

409 p.102 According to myth, how many witches are there in a coven: three, six or twelve?

410 p.128 How many points does a pentagram have?

QUIZ 41 IN YOUR STRIDE

Calling cards

A round of questions on names.

411 p.136 Which nursery rhyme character is known as Boule Boule in France?

412 p.70 What is the Roman name for the god of war known to the Greeks as Ares?

413 p.140 In *Peter Pan*, what is Wendy's surname?

414 p.142 By what name is Diana, princess of the Amazons, known when she is in her superhero guise?

415 p.138 What is the name of the dragon who is slain at the climax of *The Hobbit*?

416 p.142 Which jungle character was created by Edgar Rice Burroughs in 1912?

417 p.94 Which Australian bushranger and folk hero is famous for wearing home-made armour?

418 p.40 In which religion is the creator god called Brahma?

419 p.138 By what name is the writer Charles Lutwidge Dodgson better known?

420 p.122 What is the first name of Scrooge, the curmudgeon of a Dickens' novel who is haunted by a series of ghosts?

QUIZ 42 ALL COMERS

All in a name

Ten questions on a range of topics for everyone to try.

421 p.104 Happy, Dopey, Playful, Sneezy: which of these is not one of the seven dwarves?

422 p.96 If you came across a bogle in Scotland, would you run away from it, eat it, or play a tune on it?

423 p.70 What is the Roman name for the Greek god Hermes?

424 p.76 'How to Handle a Woman' was sung by Richard Harris in which 1967 film?

425 p.58 In Greek mythology, who was abducted by Hades, god of the Underworld?

426 p.82 The novel *The Plumed Serpent* is a vivid evocation of Mexico by which author?

427 p.60 In Greek mythology, who is the mortal who judges Aphrodite to be the most beautiful of the goddesses?

428 p.50 By what name is Siddhartha Gautama better known to history?

429 p.70 Who is the Roman goddess of the hearth? Her name has been used in modern times on a brand of matches.

430 p.140 What is the name for Peter Pan's gang of children?

QUIZ 43 CHALLENGE

Poets' corner

Test your knowledge of legends in literature.

431 p.106 What is the name of the spirit who serves Prospero in Shakespeare's *The Tempest*?

432 p.42 In which Babylonian tale does Utnapishtim escape a great flood?

433 p.124 Which epic poem begins with the words: 'Of man's first disobedience ...'?

434 p.76 Which 12th-century English author wrote the first known account of the deeds of King Arthur?

435 p.94 Which 15th-century poet wrote a romantic account of the life of William Wallace?

436 p.110 In which Shakespeare play does what appears to be a statue of the long-dead Queen Hermione come to life?

437 p.70 Virgil's *Aeneid* is an account of the founding of which ancient state by Aeneas after the fall of Troy?

438 p.58 The mythical poet Orpheus descended into Hades to seek his dead wife Eurydice. How did she die?

439 p.74 Who is the son of Finn MacCool, said to be the greatest poet in Ireland?

440 p.62 Who wrote the poem 'Endymion' about a Greek shepherd's love for Cynthia, the Moon?

**For answers and more facts go to the page given below each question number.
For quick answers to complete quizzes 40 to 44 go to page 148.**

QUIZ 44 ALL COMERS

Animal features

Use the list of names to identify the mythological creatures illustrated here.

- Horus (Egyptian)
- Ganesha (Indian)
- Hanuman (Indian)
- Taweret (Egyptian)
- Sebek (Egyptian)
- Anubis (Egyptian)
- Bast/Bastet (Egyptian)
- Cernunnos (Celtic)
- Simorgh (Persian)
- Nandi (Indian)

QUIZ 45 WARM UP

Beginning with…

Each answer starts with the letter provided.

451 p.90 What 'S' is one of the names of the Devil?

452 p.46 What 'S' is the name of a beetle that was sacred to the Egyptians?

453 p.126 What 'Y' refers to a large, man-like creature said to inhabit the Himalayas?

454 p.76 What 'C' is the legendary site of King Arthur's court?

455 p.122 What 'E' means the practice of expelling spirits or demons?

456 p.108 What 'V' is the name of a real historical person who inspired the vampire myth?

457 p.122 What 'M' refers to a person who can communicate with the spirit world?

458 p.52 Which fish, beginning with 'C', symbolises strength and endurance in China, and the samurai virtue of fortitude in Japan?

459 p.90 What 'A' is a messenger from God?

460 p.42 Which biblical character, whose name begins with 'N', had sons named Shem, Ham and Japheth?

QUIZ 46 IN YOUR STRIDE

Myths and music

Test your musical knowledge with this set of questions.

461 p.78 Who wrote the music for *The Firebird* ballet, first performed in 1910?

462 p.40 In which country will you find sacred trails called 'songlines'?

463 p.96 Which legendary musician led away all the rats, then all the children?

464 p.68 Which Greek hero played music to get past Cerberus, the guard-dog of Hades?

465 p.114 According to the fairy tale, which German town had animal musicians?

466 p.94 Which rock star portrayed the outlaw Ned Kelly in a film of the 1960s?

467 p.50 Kurt Cobain was the lead singer with which heavenly band?

468 p.140 In which Shakespeare play is music described as 'the food of love'?

469 p.40 Which Austrian composer wrote the oratorio *The Creation*, first performed in 1798?

470 p.110 Which German group had a hit with a remix of 'The Robots' in 1991?

QUIZ 47 ALL COMERS

Relative values

Can you identify these family connections?

471 p.136 In the song 'Summertime', momma is said to be good-looking, but what is daddy?

472 p.142 What are the names of Superman's adoptive human parents?

473 p.60 In Greek myth, who is the god of the sky and father of the Titan Cronus?

474 p.66 Which Greek hero is the husband of Penelope?

475 p.44 Which Egyptian goddess is the sister of Osiris?

476 p.102 What is the name of the witch who is the half-sister of King Arthur?

477 p.50 Who was the royal mother of the Buddha?

478 p.72 Tyr, the Norse god of war, is the son of which even more warlike god?

479 p.58 Which brother of Zeus is the Greek god of the Underworld?

480 p.72 In Norse mythology, who is Odin's wife?

QUIZ 48 ALL COMERS

Water all around

These questions all have a watery theme.

481 p.126 In which body of water was a large, dinosaur-like creature supposedly spotted in 1933?

482 p.66 What is the name of the ship in which Jason and his heroes sailed to Colchis?

483 p.68 Which two Greek monsters guard the narrow Strait of Messina?

484 p.46 Which river, according to the ancient Egyptians, ran through the centre of the Universe?

485 p.96 What is the name for a female creature who is half-human, half-fish?

486 p.138 What ship features in the title of one of C.S. Lewis's Narnia tales?

487 p.82 Which northern people once revered a goddess named Sedna?

488 p.104 In Greek myth, which hunter was so tall that he could walk on the seabed with his head above the waves?

489 p.100 What legendary civilisation, mentioned by Plato, is said to have been submerged by a catastrophic flood?

490 p.60 Who was the Greek god of the oceans?

**For answers and more facts go to the page given below each question number.
For quick answers to complete quizzes 45 to 51 go to page 148.**

QUIZ 49 ALL COMERS

All Greek

The answers in this round all relate to ancient Greece.

491 p.64 Which hero, famed for his strength, was the son of Zeus and Alcmena?

492 p.64 Which divine charioteer drove the Sun across the heavens?

493 p.60 Which mad Roman emperor came to believe he was the Greek god Zeus?

494 p.62 Who had himself tied to the mast of his ship so that he could hear the song of the Sirens without being lured away?

495 p.40 Which race of gods ruled before the Olympians?

496 p.68 How many Gorgons are there?

497 p.66 Which German archaeologist excavated the site of Homer's Troy in the 1870s?

498 p.62 Polyhymnia, Terpsichore or Erato: which of these is the muse of love poetry?

499 p.62 Which monsters had the head of a woman and the body of a bird?

500 p.64 In Greek mythology, to which place below Hades were the wicked sent for eternal punishment?

QUIZ 50 CHALLENGE

Of ghosts and gods

Ten questions on a range of topics.

501 p.98 Which island in the North Sea is sometimes known as Holy Island?

502 p.52 In which oriental belief system will you encounter the Eight Immortals?

503 p.122 In the 1984 movie *Ghostbusters,* Drs Venkman, Stantz and Spengler are professors of which branch of psychology?

504 p.84 What are the two stages in the process of becoming a saint?

505 p.78 Characters in the *Kalevala* had a powerful influence on which composer?

506 p.58 Which Egyptian god is often depicted wrapped in mummy's bandages?

507 p.118 Name the pompous schoolteacher hero of *The Legend of Sleepy Hollow*.

508 p.106 In which poem by Christina Rossetti are two sisters tempted to eat forbidden fruit by the call of 'fruit-merchant men'?

509 p.82 Which Central American people worshipped a god named Itzamna?

510 p.90 John Berendt's 1994 tale, *Midnight in the Garden of Good and Evil*, is set in which US city?

QUIZ 51 MULTIPLE CHOICE

Pot luck

Select the correct option from the four possible answers.

511 p.40 What is Adam's ale?
- A Beer
- B Water
- C Milk
- D Apple juice

512 p.92 Someone who helps a person in distress is a good what?
- A Sumerian
- B Sybarite
- C Samaritan
- D Somalian

513 p.134 What kind of cat is associated with good or bad fortune?
- A A Siamese cat
- B A black cat
- C A white cat
- D A polecat

514 p.50 What in Buddhism is a mantra?
- A A sacred insect
- B A sacred text
- C A sacred word
- D A sacred bell

515 p.44 In ancient Egypt, which animal was sacred to the god Hathor?
- A The crocodile
- B The cow
- C The lion
- D The dog

516 p.126 What is ogopogo?
- A A spell
- B A dance
- C An evil spirit
- D A lake monster

517 p.132 What is a vadjra?
- A An altar
- B A Buddhist staff
- C Japanese wind chimes
- D A pilgrimage

518 p.44 What was the name of the ugly dwarf god of Egyptian mythology?
- A Des
- B Bes
- C Res
- D Les

519 p.62 Thalia was the Muse of what?
- A Comedy
- B Literature
- C Agriculture
- D Astronomy

520 p.114 In *The 1001 Nights*, what is the name of the hero who discovered the magic password?
- A Sesame
- B Aladdin
- C Ali Baba
- D Abou Hassan

QUIZ 52 WARM UP

In the library

A quiz round all about books, poems and writers.

521 p.40 What book of the Bible tells the Creation story?

522 p.88 The *Odyssey* is credited to which Greek poet?

523 p.118 Who wrote a story called 'How the Camel Got His Hump'?

524 p.84 Which four saints are traditionally regarded as the authors of the gospels?

525 p.96 Who got their names in a poem that begins with the words: ''Twas the night before Christmas'?

526 p.110 The tin man first appeared in a book by L. Frank Baum. What was the book's title?

527 p.110 Which famous wooden character was created by an Italian journalist in 1881?

528 p.110 In Mary Shelley's famous novel, who is Frankenstein: the monster, or its maker?

529 p.100 In Coleridge's poem, who built a 'stately pleasure dome' in Xanadu?

530 p.138 What is the English name for the fictional character known as Bilbon Sacquet in French, Bilbo Bolsón in Spanish and Zsákos Bilbó in Hungarian?

QUIZ 53 IN YOUR STRIDE

Body of evidence

All these questions are about parts of the body.

531 p.66 A person's fatal weakness is said to be his or her Achilles' … what?

532 p.44 According to Egyptian mythology, when a person died which body organ was weighed against the feather of truth?

533 p.60 In Greek mythology, the goddess Athena was born from which part of her father Zeus's body?

534 p.112 Which fairy-tale character declares 'Grandmother, what big teeth you have'?

535 p.134 In which profession is the expression 'break a leg' commonly used to wish a person luck?

536 p.130 What part of the body is examined in the form of divination known as chiromancy?

537 p.130 Which body organs have been called 'the windows of the soul'?

538 p.130 The 'funny bone' is part of which jocular-sounding bone in the body?

539 p.130 What are you doing if you 'speak with a forked tongue'?

540 p.46 When pharaohs were mummified, how were their brains removed?

QUIZ 54 ALL COMERS

Royal flush

A round about kings, queens and emperors.

541 p.66 Who was the Greek queen whose face is said to have launched a thousand ships?

542 p.70 Which Roman emperor was declared a god in AD 14?

543 p.144 What is the name of the evil emperor opposed by Flash Gordon and his friends?

544 p.60 Who is the king of the Greek gods?

545 p.114 In the Grimm fairy tale, who is the princess with extraordinarily long hair?

546 p.106 According to folklore, who is the queen of the fairies?

547 p.116 In the Hans Christian Andersen tale, what present does the Emperor of Japan send to the Emperor of China: a diamond lizard, a golden fish, or a clockwork nightingale?

548 p.138 In the Narnia stories, what is the name of the castle where the four children rule as kings and queens?

549 p.64 Which Phoenician princess does Zeus abduct while disguised as a bull?

550 p.114 In *The 1001 Nights*, what is the name of the storyteller?

QUIZ 55 CHALLENGE

Pot luck

Ten challenging questions on a range of topics.

551 p.112 Which Italian composer turned the Cinderella story into the opera *La Cenerentola* in 1817?

552 p.90 What common objects are sometimes called the 'devil's picturebook'?

553 p.108 Which 1922 vampire film was remade in 1979, starring Klaus Kinski?

554 p.40 Which people of the world tell a story of a giant called Pangu who smashed his way out of a black egg?

555 p.64 What is the name of the son of Helios who lost control of the chariot of the Sun and nearly destroyed the Earth with fire?

556 p.102 Matthew Hopkins was responsible for the execution of more than 200 supposed witches. What was his official title?

557 p.56 The ancient Greeks invented the week: true or false?

558 p.100 Which English composer wrote the 'Cockaigne Overture'?

559 p.42 Which Old Testament character interpreted a pharaoh's dream about seven fat cows and seven thin cows?

560 p.124 Name the four horsemen of the Apocalypse.

For answers and more facts go to the page given below each question number.
For quick answers to complete quizzes 52 to 56 go to page 148.

QUIZ 56 IN YOUR STRIDE

My hero

Can you identify these ten superheroes?

- Achilles
- Thor
- Lancelot
- William Wallace
- Robin Hood
- Hercules
- Perseus
- Jason
- William Tell
- Spider-Man

561 p.66

562 p.142

563 p.64

564 p.94

565 p.66

566 p.76

567 p.68

568 p.72

569 p.94

570 p.94

QUIZ 57 WARM UP

Mixed bag

Ten questions on a range of topics.

571 p.110 In which film does Arnold Schwarzenegger play a cyborg?

572 p.40 In the Book of Genesis, what is the name of the garden where the first man and woman lived?

573 p.54 Which star sign comes before Libra?

574 p.56 Which day of the week is named after the Norse god Thor?

575 p.76 According to legend, which wizard was friend and adviser to King Arthur?

576 p.142 What is the substance that can deprive Superman of his superpowers?

577 p.128 In Chinese thought, which male force opposes and complements the female yin force?

578 p.82 What was the term for the pipe smoked by the North American Plains Indians in honour of the Great Spirit?

579 p.142 What is the name of the woman who meets Tarzan in the jungle?

580 p.112 What was Walt Disney's first full-length animated feature film, based on a Grimms' fairy tale?

QUIZ 58 IN YOUR STRIDE

True or false?

Decide whether these statements are correct.

581 p.108 In myths about werewolves, the creatures take on animal form only on moonless nights.

582 p.82 Navajo mythology has a creature called Spider Woman who fights the power of evil.

583 p.118 The story 'The Town Mouse and the Country Mouse' was written by Rudyard Kipling.

584 p.86 It was once believed that the horn of a unicorn could detect poison.

585 p.128 The swastika is an ancient symbol of good luck.

586 p.144 Alien spacecraft are sometimes called flying soup-plates.

587 p.40 Gaia was the Greek name for Mother Earth.

588 p.80 The statues on Easter Island all face out to sea.

589 p.108 In Bram Stoker's novel, Dracula has his body shipped to America.

590 p.122 In the Bible, the Gadarene Swine were possessed by demons.

QUIZ 59 ALL COMERS

Birds of a feather

Myths about birds are the topic of these teasers.

591 p.64 To seduce Leda, Zeus transformed himself into what bird?

592 p.60 Which bird symbolised Athena, the Greek goddess of wisdom?

593 p.86 Which large flightless bird was once believed to eat red-hot horseshoes?

594 p.42 What was the first bird Noah released to check that the waters of the Great Flood were receding?

595 p.86 According to medieval legend, which large bird with a capacious beak fed its young with its own blood?

596 p.86 Which mythical bird consumed itself by fire every 500 years, then rose renewed from its own ashes?

597 p.44 The Egyptian god Horus was usually depicted with the head of which bird?

598 p.84 Who preached to a flock of birds, with the words: 'My brothers, birds, you should praise your Creator very much and always love him'?

599 p.66 Which Greek youth was given wings, but flew too near to the Sun and perished?

600 p.86 In medieval times, which bird was said to be a protector against the plague?

QUIZ 60 ALL COMERS

Dead right

The chilling theme of this round is ... death.

601 p.74 Which Irish fairy foretells a death?

602 p.116 In which Hans Christian Andersen story does a young girl freeze to death on New Year's Eve?

603 p.88 By what more descriptive term are the medieval ravages of plague known?

604 p.84 According to Christian tradition, which martyred saint was burned to death on a gridiron?

605 p.76 What is the name of King Arthur's nephew, who wounds him mortally in battle?

606 p.92 In Jesus's parable, which poor beggar dies and is carried by angels to 'Abraham's bosom'?

607 p.144 'Exterminate, exterminate!' was the constant refrain of which aggressive aliens?

608 p.108 Which Caribbean cult features a god of the dead named Baron Samedi?

609 p.72 Who is the Norse god of the Underworld, whose name has come to mean the place of damnation?

610 p.122 In which film starring Bruce Willis does he help a boy who can 'see dead people'?

For answers and more facts go to the page given below each question number.
For quick answers to complete quizzes 57 to 63 go to pages 148 and 149.

QUIZ 61 ALL COMERS

Quote unquote

Test your knowledge of rhymes and quotations.

611 p.144 What is Buzz Lightyear's warcry?

612 p.136 In which book does Humpty Dumpty declare: 'It's very provoking to be called an egg – very'?

613 p.104 In which fairy tale will you hear the words: 'Fe, fi, fo fum, I smell the blood of an Englishman'?

614 p.56 According to the rhyme, on what day of the week is the child who is 'full of grace' born?

615 p.130 What part of the body did Aristotle call 'the tool of tools'?

616 p.70 Which Roman emperor declared on his deathbed, 'I feel myself becoming a god': Vespasian, Hadrian or Claudius?

617 p.126 Which mountaineer once remarked, 'There is precious little in civilisation to appeal to a yeti'?

618 p.136 In the rhyme that begins 'Hush little baby…', what is the first thing that momma's going to buy?

619 p.124 According to Dante, where will you see a sign reading 'Abandon all hope ye who enter here'?

620 p.136 Who 'picked a peck of pickled pepper'?

QUIZ 62 CHALLENGE

Who, where, what?

A round on gods, saints and objects sacred and magical.

621 p.84 Who is the patron saint of lawyers?

622 p.42 In the Bible, what was the final and most terrible plague to afflict the Egyptians?

623 p.52 What is the Japanese religion whose name means 'the way of the gods'?

624 p.78 In Slavic and Russian tales, what type of musical instrument entertains the wizard Koshchei?

625 p.132 Whereabouts in a Jewish home would you be likely to see a mezuzah?

626 p.64 What form did Zeus assume in order to seduce Danaë, daughter of the king of Argos?

627 p.62 Who were Alecto, Megara and Tisiphone?

628 p.116 In a Hans Christian Andersen tale, a soldier steals a magic object with which he can summon fierce dogs. What is the object?

629 p.84 Who is the patron saint of accountants?

630 p.72 What type of creature do the Valkyries ride?

QUIZ 63 MULTIPLE CHOICE

Pot luck

Select the correct option from the four possible answers.

631 p.72 What name is given to the abode of the Norse gods?
A Bogard | B Asgard | C Raitgard | D Selegard

632 p.134 What would you touch if you wanted to avert bad luck?
A Wood | B Your head | C Metal | D The ground

633 p.110 What is a golem?
A A straw man | B A clay man | C A kind of hobbit | D A marsh-dwelling fairy

634 p.54 What were the astrologers of Babylon known as?
A The Assyrians | B The Chaldeans | C The Pythagoreans | D The Varangians

635 p.94 In some versions of the Robin Hood myth, Robin is an aristocrat. What is his title?
A Duke of Nottinghamshire | B Earl of Lincoln | C Earl of Huntingdon | D Lord Sherwood

636 p.132 Which country celebrates the Bon Festival?
A Indonesia | B France | C Japan | D Turkey

637 p.48 What is an avatar?
A A Swedish fairy tale | B An incarnation of Vishnu | C A Greek priestess | D A ceremonial bowl

638 p.70 Who was the legendary queen of Carthage?
A Helen | B Dido | C Leda | D Minerva

639 p.92 In *Animal Farm*, what kind of animal is Napoleon?
A A cock | B A horse | C A pig | D A sheep

640 p.90 Who, according to the Bible, was the first murderer in history?
A Cain | B Aaron | C Adam | D Joshua

QUIZ 64 WARM UP

Alphabet soup

Use the clues to help you to unravel the anagrams.

641 p.106 THOTO What children leave under their pillows in order to receive a coin from a fairy.

642 p.102 ASIANAFT The Disney film in which Mickey Mouse plays the sorcerer's apprentice.

643 p.134 ROSHEHOSE It is believed to bring luck.

644 p.104 SLEDGE GONG Laid by the little brown hen that Jack steals from the giant (two words).

645 p.46 TAX PINGHERS A giant monument in Egypt.

646 p.98 GET ONES HEN A circle of standing stones near Salisbury said, mistakenly, to be a Druid temple.

647 p.122 MINTS YE CRY A gang consisting of Scooby Doo and four human friends that is dedicated to unmasking false ghosts (two words).

648 p.70 PRUJITE The Roman name for the Greek god Zeus.

649 p.124 LOAH The golden disc that circles the head of saints.

650 p.118 NEW PINK RIVAL In Washington Irving's story, this character falls asleep and wakes to find that many years have passed (three words).

QUIZ 65 IN YOUR STRIDE

Pot luck

Mixed questions covering a range of topics.

651 p.78 *En Saga* and *Finlandia* are works by which composer?

652 p.58 In Greek mythology, what is the name of the river that loops nine times round Hades?

653 p.102 What Old English word meaning 'wisdom' also means the practice of witchcraft?

654 p.40 According to Bishop James Ussher, what momentous event occurred in 4004 BC?

655 p.100 Which US female group had a hit in 1965 with the song 'Leader of the Pack'?

656 p.142 In the original novel by Edgar Rice Burroughs, Tarzan is an English lord: what is his title?

657 p.144 Who is the French captain of the USS *Enterprise* in *Star Trek: the Next Generation*?

658 p.144 Who played Flash Gordon in the 1930s serial?

659 p.52 In the mythology of which country is the supreme god known as the August Personage of Jade?

660 p.54 What is the fifth sign of the zodiac?

QUIZ 66 ALL COMERS

Money matters

Ten questions about money, riches and wealth.

661 p.120 Traditionally, whose palm would you cross with silver?

662 p.130 On which country's banknotes will you see the ancient symbol of an eye inside a triangle?

663 p.66 In Greek mythology what golden object did Jason have to steal?

664 p.136 'The king was in his counting house, counting out his money…' What pre-decimal coin is mentioned in the first line of this nursery rhyme?

665 p.100 What legendary country, whose name means 'the gilded one' in Spanish, was believed to be filled with gold?

666 p.96 Who is the patron saint of pawnbrokers?

667 p.92 In Jesus's parable, who wastes his inheritance?

668 p.66 In Greek myth, which greedy king turns everything he touches to gold?

669 p.60 What title of the god Hades, also the name of one of the planets, means 'giver of wealth'?

670 p.90 According to St Paul in the Bible, the love of the money is the root of what?

QUIZ 67 ALL COMERS

Either/or

In each pair of alternatives, which one is correct?

671 p.134 Is an owl said to be lucky, or unlucky?

672 p.44 In Egyptian mythology, was Horus god of the sky, or of the sea?

673 p.58 What is an *obolus*: a silver coin placed in the mouth of a dead person, or a long shield used as a coffin lid?

674 p.48 The Hindu god Sesha, also known as Ananta or 'the Infinite', takes what animal form: a snake, or a sea lion?

675 p.52 Who was born first: Jesus, or Buddha?

676 p.58 Who is the Greek god of death: Mortos, or Thanatos?

677 p.48 According to Hindu legend, was the young Krishna raised by cowherds, or boatmen?

678 p.78 Is Perun a Slavonic god of thunder, or an Hawaiian god of volcanoes?

679 p.52 The title Lao Tzu was given to the founder of Taoism. Does it mean Old Master, or Wise Prince?

680 p.96 Is a buggane a goblin or a giant?

For answers and more facts go to the page given below each question number.
For quick answers to complete quizzes 64 to 70 go to page 149.

QUIZ 68 ALL COMERS

Makers and shapers

A round about objects and their makers or origins.

681 p.42 What do these four have in common: Noah; Manu in Hindu myth; Deucalion in Greek myth; and Utnapishtim in Babylonian myth?

682 p.106 What Scandinavian fairies are renowned for their skills at metalwork?

683 p.84 St Joseph is the patron of which craftsmen?

684 p.60 Which Greek sculptor made a huge gold and ivory statue of the goddess Athena for the Parthenon in Athens?

685 p.76 Which English city has a round table claimed to have been King Arthur's?

686 p.98 Which Himalayan city has a temple, built, according to myth, over the heart of a demoness?

687 p.98 In Muslim myth, the angel Gabriel gave the Black Stone of Mecca to which patriarch, revered alike by Muslims, Jews and Christians?

688 p.128 'Solomon's seal' was used in mystical Jewish texts in the Middle Ages. By what name is it now generally known?

689 p.46 Until the construction of the Eiffel Tower, which ancient building was the tallest in the world?

690 p.50 Which Japanese city is famous for the Todai Temple, housing the Daibutsu, a 15 m (50 ft) statue of the Buddha?

QUIZ 69 CHALLENGE

Between the covers

Challenging questions with a bookish theme.

691 p.52 By what alternative name is the Chinese book called the *I Ching* also known in English?

692 p.108 Who wrote the novel *Interview with the Vampire*?

693 p.114 Who published a collection of stories called *Household Tales*?

694 p.94 Which German dramatist wrote a play based on the story of William Tell?

695 p.124 Which Swedish mystic wrote a detailed account of the afterlife entitled *Heaven and Hell*?

696 p.60 Who, in the 6th century BC, wrote the genealogy of the Greek gods known as the *Theogony*?

697 p.110 'The Modern Prometheus' is the subtitle of which famous horror novel?

698 p.120 Which English writer is sometimes called 'The Immortal Dreamer'?

699 p.54 Which Greek astronomer wrote the *Tetrabiblios*, or Four Books?

700 p.62 Calliope, Clio, Euterpe, Thalia: which of these is the muse of history

QUIZ 70 MULTIPLE CHOICE

Mixed bag

Select the correct option from the four possible answers.

701 p.134 Which of these objects is said to be lucky?
A A pig's ear | B A cat's tail | C A rabbit's foot | D An elephant's trunk

702 p.62 Naiads, nereids and oceanids are all female nymphs. Where do they live?
A In fire | B In the air | C In water | D In the ground

703 p.68 Who is the monstrous Gorgon slain by Perseus?
A Redusa | B Medusa | C Sedusa | D Dedusa

704 p.60 In Greek myth, what was the food of the gods?
A Elixir | B Panacea | C Epicure | D Ambrosia

705 p.78 In Russian myth, what is a rusalka?
A A magic sailing boat | B A water nymph | C An axe | D A doll

706 p.128 What would you do with a pentacle?
A Wave it | B Wear it | C Eat it | D Blow on it

707 p.68 In Greek legend, the Cyclopes giants were ...?
A Horsemen | B Wheat-growers | C Metalworkers | D Minstrels

708 p.72 In Viking mythology, the Universe rests on the branches of what kind of tree?
A An oak | B An elm | C An ash | D A yew

709 p.82 In Aztec myth, who is the brother of Queztlcoatl?
A Zozotl | B Cocotl | C Xoxotl | D Quazi

710 p.86 What is the heraldic term for an animal that is lying down?
A Couchant | B Dormant | C Courant | D Mordant

QUIZ 71 WARM UP

Pot luck

Ten questions covering a range of topics.

711 In Roald Dahl's fairy tale, what is the BFG?
p.104

712 What word beginning with 'P' is a kind of fairy particularly associated with Devon and Cornwall?
p.106

713 What is the Perrault fairy tale *Cendrillon* called in English?
p.114

714 Who is the scourge of evil created by American writer Joss Whedon?
p.142

715 Who is the alter ego of Dr Jekyll?
p.108

716 Which medieval prophet and astrologer wrote hundreds of predictions about future events?
p.120

717 Who is the orphaned young hero of the first *Star Wars* film?
p.144

718 Which day of the week is named after the Moon?
p.56

719 In which city does Batman fight crime?
p.142

720 What is the meaning of the word 'brer', as in Brer Rabbit and Brer Fox?
p.114

QUIZ 72 IN YOUR STRIDE

Animal magic

Questions involving animals, some mythical, some real.

721 What kind of animal is the beast of Exmoor?
p.126

722 The Hindu god Ganesha is depicted with the head of which animal?
p.48

723 In Greek myth, what was the name of the monster, part-woman and part-lion, which killed all who failed to solve her riddles?
p.68

724 What kind of animal is the legendary basilisk?
p.86

725 In La Fontaine's fable of two insects – one hard-working, the other lazy – what kind of insect is the lazy one?
p.118

726 In *The Wizard of Oz*, what is the name of Dorothy's dog?
p.110

727 The Hindu god Hanuman takes what form?
p.48

728 Bast, the Egyptian goddess of pleasure, is portrayed with the head of which animal?
p.46

729 What is the name for the mythical creature which is half-man, half-horse?
p.86

730 Who wrote the political fairy tale *Animal Farm*?
p.92

QUIZ 73 ALL COMERS

In the library

This round of questions has a literary theme.

731 Who wrote *The Interpretation of Dreams*, published in 1900?
p.120

732 Which 19th-century English poet wrote a version of 'The Pied Piper of Hamelin'?
p.96

733 Steerpike is the villain of which fantasy fiction trilogy published in the 1940s and 50s?
p.138

734 What are the first three words of the first book of the Bible?
p.40

735 What is the more correct title of the collection of stories sometimes called *The Arabian Nights*?
p.114

736 In which Charles Kingsley novel does a child chimney sweep run away and fall into a river?
p.106

737 Which Irish-born playwright wrote *Man and Superman*?
p.142

738 What title did Rudyard Kipling give to his set of fables which he published in 1902?
p.118

739 Who wrote the original Dracula novel, published in 1897?
p.108

740 'One for sorrow, two for joy …' Which bird does this rhyme refer to?
p.134

QUIZ 74 CHALLENGE

Eat, drink, be merry

The delights of the table are the subject of this round.

741 What is the meaning of the name Avalon, the island on which King Arthur is said to rest?
p.74

742 Who was the Greek sorceress who turned Odysseus's greedy companions into swine?
p.102

743 What is the medieval fantasy world where fences are made of sausages and the streets paved with pastry?
p.100

744 In Greek mythology, what fruit symbolises marriage?
p.132

745 According to legend, which god taught the ancient Egyptians how to bake bread?
p.44

746 'A little old lady once took a flat pan, and made for her husband a gingerbread man …' What were the gingerbread man's eyes and buttons made of?
p.112

747 What proverbial expression derives from the Aesop story of a fox who could not reach some fruit on a vine?
p.118

748 In Greek mythology, what is a cornucopia?
p.42

749 Who is the hedonistic Greek god said to have invented wine-making?
p.62

750 Whose feast was interrupted when a mysterious hand wrote the words 'Mene, Mene, Tekel, Parsin' on the wall?
p.120

**For answers and more facts go to the page given below each question number.
For quick answers to complete quizzes 71 to 75 go to page 149.**

QUIZ 75 ALL COMERS

Gods and goddesses

Match the divinities illustrated below with the names in the list.

- Diana
- Amaterasu
- Bes
- Vishnu
- Apollo
- Avalokitesvara
- Shou Lao
- Odin
- Venus
- Dionysus

QUIZ 76 WARM UP

What's in a name?

A round about the names of people and other beings.

761 p.144 In *Star Trek*, what is the name of Captain Kirk's Vulcan first officer?

762 p.100 What was the name of the pilgrim in Bunyan's *The Pilgrim's Progress*?

763 p.142 What is Spider-Man's real name?

764 p.40 According to the Bible, who was the first man?

765 p.116 In the Hans Christian Andersen tale, what is the name of the tiny heroine who is a female Tom Thumb?

766 p.142 What is the real name of The Hulk?

767 p.136 Which arachnophobic girl sat on a tuffet?

768 p.138 What does the 'J' in J.K. Rowling stand for?

769 p.114 In the Grimm fairy tale, which two children find a gingerbread house in the woods?

770 p.106 Who is Peter Pan's fairy companion?

QUIZ 77 IN YOUR STRIDE

Wondrous weapons

A quiz on weapons of myth and legend.

771 p.76 What is the name of King Arthur's magical sword?

772 p.72 The Norse god Baldur was killed by a spear made from which plant?

773 p.60 What is the name of the three-pronged spear traditionally associated with the Greek god Poseidon?

774 p.108 Name one of the two things that can kill a werewolf?

775 p.80 According to legend, what weapon was invented by the snake named Bobbi-Bobbi?

776 p.54 Which is the only star sign depicted by a person armed with a weapon?

777 p.90 Which place, according to the Bible, is guarded by an angel with a flaming sword?

778 p.72 The Norse god Thor carries a weapon called Mjollnir. What is it?

779 p.60 What is the traditional weapon of Zeus, which he used to strike down his father?

780 p.144 What is the name for the glowing sword-like weapon of the Jedi knights?

QUIZ 78 ALL COMERS

Taking the stage

Ten questions with a theatrical theme.

781 p.140 Who composed the music for the 1935 ballet *Romeo and Juliet*?

782 p.102 What is the name of the sorcerer who rules the island in Shakespeare's *The Tempest*?

783 p.94 Which Italian composer wrote an opera based on the story of William Tell?

784 p.122 In which Shakespeare play does a prince see the ghost of his father?

785 p.78 Which Czech composer wrote an opera entitled *Rusalka*, first performed in 1901?

786 p.88 Which German composer turned the 12th-century epic *Das Niebelungenlied* into a cycle of operas?

787 p.102 In which Shakespeare play will you encounter the 'weird sisters' huddling round a cauldron?

788 p.122 Which 19th-century Norwegian dramatist wrote a play named *Ghosts*?

789 p.76 Which modern English composer has written an opera based on the story of Gawain and the Green Knight?

790 p.140 In which opera by Mozart would you encounter the Queen of the Night, Pamina and Sarastro?

QUIZ 79 ALL COMERS

The good book

Test your knowledge of the Bible and its stories.

791 p.130 In the Bible, Eve was fashioned from which part of Adam's body?

792 p.132 In Exodus, Moses demonstrates God's power by turning his staff into an animal, then back into a staff. What animal?

793 p.130 Which temptress deprived Samson of his strength?

794 p.42 A swarm of frogs, a swarm of bats, a swarm of gnats: which is not a biblical plague?

795 p.90 Which righteous man did Satan, with God's permission, deprive of all his blessings?

796 p.104 While still a boy, the future King David fought which giant?

797 p.132 What happened to Uzzah when he touched the Ark of the Covenant with unconsecrated hands?

798 p.42 In the Old Testament, what famous object was 450 ft long, 75 ft wide and 45 ft high (137x23x13.7 m)?

799 p.132 Branches from which trees were laid before Jesus when he rode into Jerusalem on a donkey?

800 p.124 What miracle did Jesus perform on his friend Lazarus?

For answers and more facts go to the page given below each question number.
For quick answers to complete quizzes 76 to 82 go to pages 149 and 150.

QUIZ 80 CHALLENGE

Word play

Words and phrases are the theme of this quiz.

801 Kissing which stone in Ireland is said to impart the gifts of eloquence and flattery?
p.74

802 In astrology, what word meaning a pointed end denotes the time when one star sign passes into the next?
p.54

803 The Christian Hell is said to be a place of fire and brimstone. What is brimstone better known as today?
p.124

804 Triskaidekaphobia is an irrational fear of which number?
p.134

805 In Hinduism and Buddhism, what word denotes the idea that a person's deeds are rewarded or punished in the circumstances of a future reincarnation?
p.90

806 What word meaning 'accepted by tradition' refers to a mystical Jewish system of theology and metaphysics?
p.128

807 What is the Japanese term for 'the way of the Buddha'?
p.52

808 The word planet derives from the Greek for what?
p.54

809 What is the Buddhist term for the cycle of birth, death and rebirth?
p.50

810 The 17th-century English philosopher Thomas Hobbes wrote a book named after which mythical sea monster?
p.86

QUIZ 81 CHALLENGE

Pot luck

Ten challenging questions on a range of topics.

811 Which British group had a hit in 1983 with the song 'Karma Chameleon'?
p.90

812 In Greek mythology, what is the name of Mother Earth?
p.40

813 In some Christian circles, what term describes the transport of righteous people directly to Heaven at the Second Coming?
p.124

814 What term, derived from the Middle English for 'silent', referred to a group of actors who went from house to house at Christmas performing playlets?
p.140

815 What is the Hebrew term for Hell?
p.124

816 Which Hindu hero is believed to be the eighth incarnation of Vishnu?
p.48

817 Which Scottish fairy does housework while everyone is asleep?
p.106

818 In Greek mythology, which giant was held aloft by Heracles until he died?
p.130

819 In the *commedia dell'arte*, what is the name of the doddery old man?
p.140

820 Who is the Irish goddess of death in battle?
p.74

QUIZ 82 MULTIPLE CHOICE

Gods, calendars and superstitions

Select the correct option from the four possible answers.

821 What is the Roman name for the Greek god Poseidon?
p.70
A Neptune — B Thor — C Osiris — D Mercury

822 In the Chinese calendar 1977, 1989 and 2001 were the years of the what?
p.54
A The rat — B The snake — C The monkey — D The dog

823 Which arch-enemy of Batman was played by Jim Carrey?
p.142
A The Fiddler — B The Diddler — C The Riddler — D The Middler

824 Who wrote *A Connecticut Yankee in King Arthur's Court*?
p.76
A F. Scott Fitzgerald — B Ernest Hemingway — C Jack London — D Mark Twain

825 If you smile broadly are you grinning like a what?
p.138
A A Wiltshire cat — B A Yorkshire cat — C A Cheshire cat — D A Berkshire cat

826 In Greek myth, who ferries the dead to Hades?
p.58
A Terracy — B Charon — C Hypnos — D Pluto

827 The Russian folk figure Grandfather Frost is known in Britain as what?
p.96
A Old King Cole — B Jack Frost — C Father Christmas — D The Green Man

828 The fairytale heroine Briar Rose is better known as what?
p.112
A Sleeping Beauty — B Snow White — C Cinderella — D Goldilocks

829 Ra was the Egyptian god of what?
p.44
A The Moon — B The Sun — C The Nile — D The Earth

830 Which of these birds is said to be unlucky?
p.134
A The sparrow — B The robin — C The albatross — D The eagle

QUIZ 83 WARM UP

Animal crackers

A round about animal myths, tales and other antics.

831 In the rhyme that begins 'Hey diddle diddle…', what does the cow jump over?
p.136

832 In *The Ugly Duckling*, what type of bird does the 'duckling' grow up to be?
p.116

833 In Egypt, which animal was worshipped in the temple at Crocodilopolis?
p.46

834 In the Middle Ages it was believed that lions never sleep: true or false?
p.86

835 Which star sign is represented by a ram?
p.54

836 What kind of animal was the legendary Python, slain by the god Apollo?
p.68

837 The males of which type of whale grow a spiral tusk up to 2-3 m (7-10 ft) long?
p.86

838 According to Christmas folklore, what kind of animals are Dasher, Comet and Cupid?
p.96

839 'How the Leopard Got His Spots' is a story written by Rudyard Kipling: true or false?
p.118

840 What mythical animal looks like a deer or horse with a single horn growing from its forehead?
p.86

QUIZ 84 IN YOUR STRIDE

Pot luck

Ten questions covering a range of topics.

841 What are the geometric designs Buddhists and Hindus sometimes use as an aid to meditation?
p.128

842 In Bram Stoker's *Dracula* novel, what is the name of the professor who pursues and kills Dracula?
p.108

843 Which celestial feature was called the World Tree or White-Boned Serpent by the Maya of Central America?
p.82

844 Which Scottish highlander is the hero of a novel by Walter Scott and a film starring Liam Neeson?
p.94

845 According to Christian legend, what kind of mythical animal was defeated by St Michael, and also by St George?
p.86

846 What word, derived from the Old English for 'to know', means a woman who can perform magic?
p.102

847 What 'T' links the song 'Africa' with a canine character in *The Wizard of Oz*?
p.80

848 Who is the irascible ship's doctor serving alongside Captain Kirk on the USS *Enterprise*?
p.144

849 Two of Santa's reindeer have names that mean 'thunder' and 'lightning' in German: what are their names?
p.96

850 A crescent is the symbol of which world religion?
p.128

QUIZ 85 ALL COMERS

Colour coded

In this round, it's all a question of colour.

851 What colour does The Hulk turn when angry?
p.142

852 Who is Harry Potter's red-headed friend and classmate?
p.138

853 Which fairy-tale heroine has hair as black as ebony and lips as red as blood?
p.112

854 Who was the Russian writer of fables whose stories included *The Multi-Coloured Sheep*?
p.118

855 According to tradition, Robin Hood and his men wore clothes of what kind of green?
p.94

856 The pyramids were originally faced with stone of what colour?
p.46

857 What is Black Shuck: a headless knight seen in Edinburgh; a ghostly hound seen in Norfolk; or a thick and eerie fog seen in Ireland?
p.126

858 Which of the knights of King Arthur was challenged to a beheading contest by the Green Knight?
p.76

859 What is the name of the reddish stone at the centre of Stonehenge?
p.98

860 The Slavic people originally had two gods: Byelobog was the 'white god'; who was the 'black god'?
p.78

QUIZ 86 CHALLENGE

Who did what?

Name the person, real or mythical.

861 Who wrote *The Legend of Sleepy Hollow*?
p.118

862 Who is the Hindu king of the dead?
p.58

863 Who was the sorceress, and daughter of the king of Colchis, who aided Jason in his quest?
p.66

864 In the Bible, who was 'weighed in the scales and found wanting'?
p.120

865 In Greek mythology, who was the twin of Pollux?
p.64

866 Who is the Hindu goddess of death?
p.48

867 Who is the Greek god of the west wind?
p.56

868 According to legend, which lover of Aphrodite was killed by a wild boar?
p.66

869 Who wrote the poem 'Ode to Psyche'?
p.58

870 Who did Monica Bellucci portray on screen in 2004?
p.88

For answers and more facts go to the page given below each question number.
For quick answers to complete quizzes 83 to 87 go to page 150.

QUIZ 87 CHALLENGE

Cross word puzzle

Match the types of cross illustrated with the names in the list.

- St Andrew's cross
- Cross of Lorraine
- Tau cross
- Latin cross
- Greek cross
- Ankh cross
- Russian cross
- Maltese cross
- Papal cross
- Celtic cross

871
p.128

872
p.128

873
p.128

874
p.128

875
p.128

876
p.84

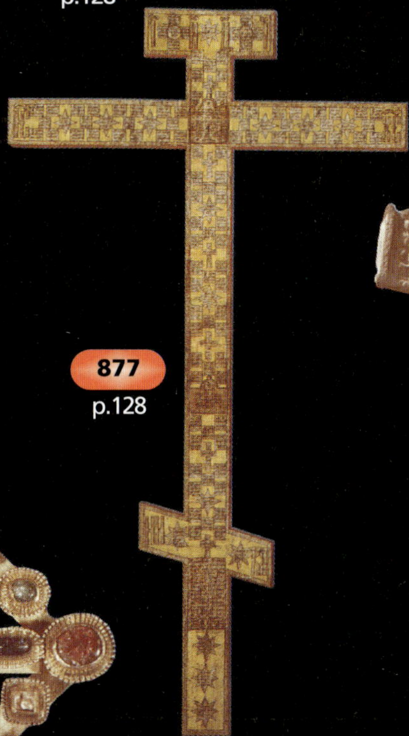

877
p.128

878
p.128

879
p.128

880
p.74

QUIZ 88 WARM UP

Pot luck

Ten questions on a range of topics.

881 (p.144) What does the acronym UFO stand for?

882 (p.98) Which legendary wizard is said in one old tale to have built Stonehenge?

883 (p.54) Which star sign are you born under if your birthday is on New Year's Day?

884 (p.144) What is the name of the space-ranger doll who is one of the heroes of the film *Toy Story*?

885 (p.56) Which day of the week is named after the Norse god Woden?

886 (p.94) Who is the rotund priest in Robin Hood's band of merry men?

887 (p.140) Which traditional plays, usually with fairytale themes, are performed in theatres during the Christmas period?

888 (p.102) Who is the wizard headmaster of Hogwarts School?

889 (p.104) In the fairy tale, which tiny boy is carried away by a bird, swallowed by a fish, and returned to his adopted mother when she buys the fish to eat?

890 (p.134) What is said to be the consequence for a person who catches the bride's bouquet at the end of a wedding?

QUIZ 89 IN YOUR STRIDE

The spirit world

A round of questions on gods, ghosts and spirits.

891 (p.106) Robin Goodfellow is another name for which Shakespearean fairy?

892 (p.70) What is the Roman name for the Greek goddess Hera?

893 (p.122) In which Shakespeare play does the ghost of Banquo appear?

894 (p.122) In Noël Coward's play *Blithe Spirit*, what sort of character is Elvira?

895 (p.82) *Inti Raymi* was a feast dedicated to a god in which civilisation?

896 (p.78) In Slavonic myth, what is a leshy?

897 (p.78) In Russian mythology, where would you find a spirit called a polevik: in a field or a town?

898 (p.102) What was the first name of the suburban witch played by Elizabeth Montgomery in the TV comedy *Bewitched*?

899 (p.134) Is a rabbit's foot considered lucky or unlucky?

900 (p.122) In which book does Tiny Tim appear?

QUIZ 90 IN YOUR STRIDE

Family matters

These questions are based on family ties.

901 (p.138) What relation to Bilbo Baggins is Frodo Baggins?

902 (p.138) What is the name of Tweedledee's twin brother?

903 (p.66) Who was the mother of Oedipus?

904 (p.136) In the nursery rhyme, what was the name of the old mother who went to the cupboard to fetch her poor dog a bone?

905 (p.110) Who is Pinocchio's kindly 'father'?

906 (p.42) In the Bible, who was sold into slavery by his jealous brothers?

907 (p.60) In Greek mythology, what was the name of the child of Hermes and Aphrodite, who was both male and female?

908 (p.62) Which Greek hero killed his own mother, Clytemnestra, in vengeance for the death of his father?

909 (p.66) Who was the husband of Helen of Troy?

910 (p.60) Which of the Greek gods is the twin brother of Artemis?

QUIZ 91 ALL COMERS

Around the world

Nations and nationality are the theme of this round.

911 (p.84) Who is the patron saint of Ireland?

912 (p.132) Which Middle Eastern country was famed for its cedars?

913 (p.96) In which country is Hamelin, where a piper led away all the children?

914 (p.104) Which country is populated by giants in Swift's *Gulliver's Travels*?

915 (p.84) Who is the patron saint of both Greece and Russia?

916 (p.60) The ancient culture of which country is described by the word 'Hellenistic'?

917 (p.50) Which country is the home of the Buddhist practice sometimes called Lamaism?

918 (p.116) What nationality was Hans Christian Andersen?

919 (p.66) Which country on the Black Sea is sometimes identified with Colchis, the land of the Golden Fleece: Bulgaria, Georgia or Turkey?

920 (p.84) Who is the patron saint of Wales?

For answers and more facts go to the page given below each question number.
For quick answers to complete quizzes 88 to 95 go to page 150.

QUIZ 92 ALL COMERS

Four of a kind

What word or phrase best describes all four examples.

921 Gawain, Lancelot, Galahad, Bedivere. p.76

922 The hare, the tiger, the ox, the snake. p.54

923 Boreas, Zephyrus, Eurus, Notus. p.56

924 'The Elephant's Child', 'The Cat That Walked By Himself', 'The Butterfly That Stamped', 'How the Camel Got His Hump'. p.118

925 Columbine, Harlequin, Pantaloon, Scaramouche. p.140

926 Legolas, Gimli, Boromir, Pippin. p.138

927 Cronus, Oceanus, Tethys, Mnemosyne. p.60

928 *Das Rheingold*, *Die Walküre*, *Siegfried*, *Götterdämmerung*. p.72

929 Tane, Papa, Rangi, Tangaroa. p.80

930 Cobweb, Moth, Mustardseed, Peaseblossom. p.106

QUIZ 93 ALL COMERS

Royal allegiance

Kings, queens and princes – some real, some mythical.

931 In the nursery rhyme, which king was 'a merry old soul'? p.136

932 In Arthurian legend, who is King Arthur's father? p.76

933 According to folklore, who is the king of the fairies? p.106

934 Which prince of Thebes unwittingly murdered his father and then married his mother? p.66

935 The Scottish national hero William Wallace fought against which English king? p.94

936 According to the legend, which future king of Scotland took heart from seeing a spider spin its web? p.94

937 What allegorical poem by Edmund Spenser extols the reign of Elizabeth I? p.92

938 In the Welsh epics, is the hero Pwyll the prince of Dyfed or of Powys? p.74

939 Which English king is said to have 'burnt the cakes'? p.94

940 Who was the proverbially wise ruler of Israel? p.92

QUIZ 94 CHALLENGE

The sky's the limit

A quiz about the heavens and heavenly bodies.

941 What astronomical body is sometimes called 'the eye of heaven'? p.130

942 In Greek mythology, which hunter was accidentally killed by Artemis, and then immortalised among the stars? p.104

943 According to the ancient Greeks, who carried the world on his shoulders? p.104

944 Which Old Testament character had a vision of angels on a ladder between Heaven and Earth? p.120

945 If you were born between June 23 and July 23, what would be your sign of the Zodiac? p.54

946 In Shinto, is Amaterasu the goddess of the Sun, of the Moon, or of the stars? p.52

947 Which constellation is named after a beautiful princess rescued from a sea monster by the Greek hero Perseus, who then married her? p.68

948 What synonym for heaven is derived from the Persian for 'walled garden'? p.124

949 How many heavens are there in Islamic theology: 7, 17 or 7000? p.124

950 Shamash was the god of the Sun in which ancient civilisation? p.54

QUIZ 95 CHALLENGE

Naming names

Answers include the names of people, gods and places.

951 In *Gulliver's Travels*, what is Gulliver's first name? p.104

952 Which of King Arthur's knights was said to be the only one virtuous enough to see the Holy Grail? p.76

953 By what name was Camp David known under President Franklin D. Roosevelt? p.100

954 Four of the five rivers of the classical underworld were Acheron, Styx, Phlegethon and Cocytus. What was the fifth? p.58

955 By what name is the Spanish hero Rodrigo Díaz de Vivar better known to history? p.88

956 In the gospels, Jesus exorcises a man who explains his name with the words 'For we are many'. What is the name? p.122

957 What is the name of the cynical English vampire who is on the fringe of Buffy's circle? p.142

958 Which Toltec and Aztec god was represented by a plumed serpent? p.82

959 In the Bible, to what did Jacob change his name after wrestling through the night with a strange angelic opponent? p.120

960 What is the Roman name for the Greek goddess Athena? p.70

QUIZ 96 WARM UP

Can you place it?

Identify the city, mountain or other landmark.

961 p.126 Which famous building does King Kong climb at the climax of the 1933 film?

962 p.98 The sacred heights of Mount Fuji look down on which city?

963 p.142 In which town does Buffy slay vampires and other demons?

964 p.94 Robin Hood's arch enemy is the sheriff of which town?

965 p.74 The head of the mythical Celtic warrior Brân is reputed to be buried at which ancient London landmark?

966 p.66 According to legend, which city was captured by a band of warriors hiding in the belly of a large wooden horse?

967 p.128 Which biblical town, the birthplace of Jesus, is sometimes called 'the city of David'?

968 p.140 Who was told by the bells of London to 'turn again'?

969 p.142 What is the name of Superman's home planet?

970 p.100 In John Newton's hymn, 'glorious things ... are spoken' of which city?

QUIZ 97 IN YOUR STRIDE

First letter

Ten questions with an alphabetical theme.

971 p.102 What word beginning with 'W' means an evil wizard?

972 p.86 What 'B' is a legendary snake?

973 p.122 What 'S' means a meeting where people try to get in touch with the spirits of the dead?

974 p.86 According to medieval legend, which reptile beginning with 'S' lives in fire?

975 p.136 In the rhyme that begins 'Pat-a-cake, pat-a-cake…', which letter of the alphabet is the cake marked with?

976 p.138 What name beginning with 'E' does Aragorn take when crowned King of Gondor in *The Lord of the Rings*?

977 p.106 What 'G' is a little demon that can curdle milk by smiling at it?

978 p.126 What 'S' is a large ape-like creature which has supposedly been sighted in the forests of north-west America?

979 p.88 What 'P' meant a wagon or wheeled stage in medieval times, but is now used for a spectacular parade or procession?

980 p.90 What 'A' denotes the last great battle between good and evil, as described in the book of Revelation?

QUIZ 98 ALL COMERS

Naming names

Who or what is the person, being or place described?

981 p.70 What is the Roman name for the Greek goddess Aphrodite?

982 p.72 In Norse mythology, what is the name of the trickster god who is a friend of Thor?

983 p.84 Who is the patron saint of Belgium: St Joan, or St Joseph?

984 p.102 According to the Bible, which king of Israel consulted the witch of Endor?

985 p.100 Which mythical land is said to have formed a bridge between Cornwall and the Scilly Isles?

986 p.50 What is the title of the Tibetan spiritual leader believed to be an incarnation of the boddhisattva Avalokiteshvara?

987 p.122 Who is Scrooge's old business partner, who appears to him in ghostly form?

988 p.56 What is the Greek name for the Moon?

989 p.100 Who stars as hired gun fighter Cole Thornton in the 1966 Howard Hawks Western *El Dorado*?

990 p.110 In *Star Wars*, who is the droid companion of C-3PO (See-Threepio)?

QUIZ 99 CHALLENGE

Pot luck

Ten challenging questions on a variety of topics.

991 p.52 According to legend, what age will you live to if you climb China's holy mountain of Tai Shan?

992 p.48 Who are the three main gods in the Hindu triad?

993 p.132 In which novel by Oscar Wilde does a portrait become the reflection of the sitter's soul?

994 p.44 Taweret, the Egyptian goddess of childbirth, was depicted as which animal?

995 p.66 Which Cretan princess gave Theseus a ball of string to help him find his way out of the Minotaur's labyrinth?

996 p.122 Which Henry James ghost story was turned into an opera by Benjamin Britten?

997 p.114 By what title is Charles Perrault's collection of fairy tales, *Contes de ma mère l'oye*, known in English?

998 p.84 Which saint is said to have shared his cloak with a beggar who turned out to be Jesus?

999 p.112 Which Stephen Sondheim musical is a retelling of several fairy tales, including Cinderella and Little Red Riding Hood?

1000 p.66 What is the Latin name for the city of Troy?

For answers and more facts go to the page given below each question number.
For quick answers to complete quizzes 96 to 99 go to page 150.

MYTHS, LEGENDS AND FOLK TALES

A wealth of fascinating information and
stories from mythology and folklore
around the world

The story of creation

QUESTION NUMBER

The numbers or star following the answers refer to information boxes on the right.

ANSWERS

QUESTION NUMBER	ANSWERS
105	**Chaos** ❷
228	**Prometheus** ❷
254	**A: Geb** ❸
302	**New Zealand** ❹
324	**C: Day five** ❽
373	**The first** ❽
393	**A: Nun** ❸
405	**He rested** ❽
418	**Hinduism** ❼
462	**Australia** ❺
469	**Joseph Haydn** (1732-1809)
495	**The Titans** ❷
511	**B: Water** – 'Adam's ale is the best brew', proverb
521	**Genesis** ❶ ❽
554	**The Chinese** ❾
572	**The Garden of Eden** (described Genesis 2) ❶ ❽
587	**True** ❷
★ 654	**The creation of the world**
734	**'In the beginning ...'** ❽
764	**Adam** ❶ ❽
812	**Gaia** ❷

Core facts ❶

◆ Creation myths are known as **cosmogonies**. Most cultures and religions have stories about the creation of the world and of mankind.

◆ The **Hebrew** story of creation, also part of the **Christian** tradition, is told in Genesis, the first book of the Bible. The account of Adam and Eve (who also feature in the **Muslim** tradition) is told afterwards and seems to be a separate story.

◆ There are patterns in creation myths. Most start with the idea of darkness, emptiness or a black and endless sea. Into this is introduced some creative impulse which sets creation in motion and introduces order – often beginning with the separation of **Earth and sky**.

Greek ❷

According to the writer **Hesiod**, there was once nothing but the void called Chaos. Into this came **Gaia** (Mother Earth) who gave birth to **Uranus**, the sky. Uranus sent rain to Gaia, which filled her hollows to make lakes and seas, and caused her to be covered with greenery and bring forth animals. Gaia subsequently mated with Uranus and bore the **Titans**, who later overthrew Uranus and were in turn overthrown by the **Olympian gods**. One of the Titans, **Prometheus**, made mankind. The goddess **Athene** later breathed life into his creations.

SKY GODDESS
The Egyptians believed Nut actually formed the sky, held up by her outstretched arms and legs.

Egyptian ❸

The Egyptians believed that creation began when the Sun god **Atum** rose up out of a dark and endless sea called **Nun**. Atum brought forth **Shu**, the god of air, and **Tefnut**, the god of water. The offspring of this pair were the Earth god **Geb** and the sky goddess **Nut**. These two were for a long time locked in an incestuous embrace until Shu parted them – pushing Nut upwards to form the firmament, and Geb downwards to make the Earth.

Maori ❹

The Maori creation myth contains a striking parallel to the Egyptian. The Earth goddess **Papa** and the sky god **Rangi** were so in love that they could not let go of each other, and no light could enter the world. They bore several children, who were trapped between their bodies. One of these children, with great effort, forced the parents apart. Light flooded the world and plants grew. Rangi's bitter tears became the rivers and seas.

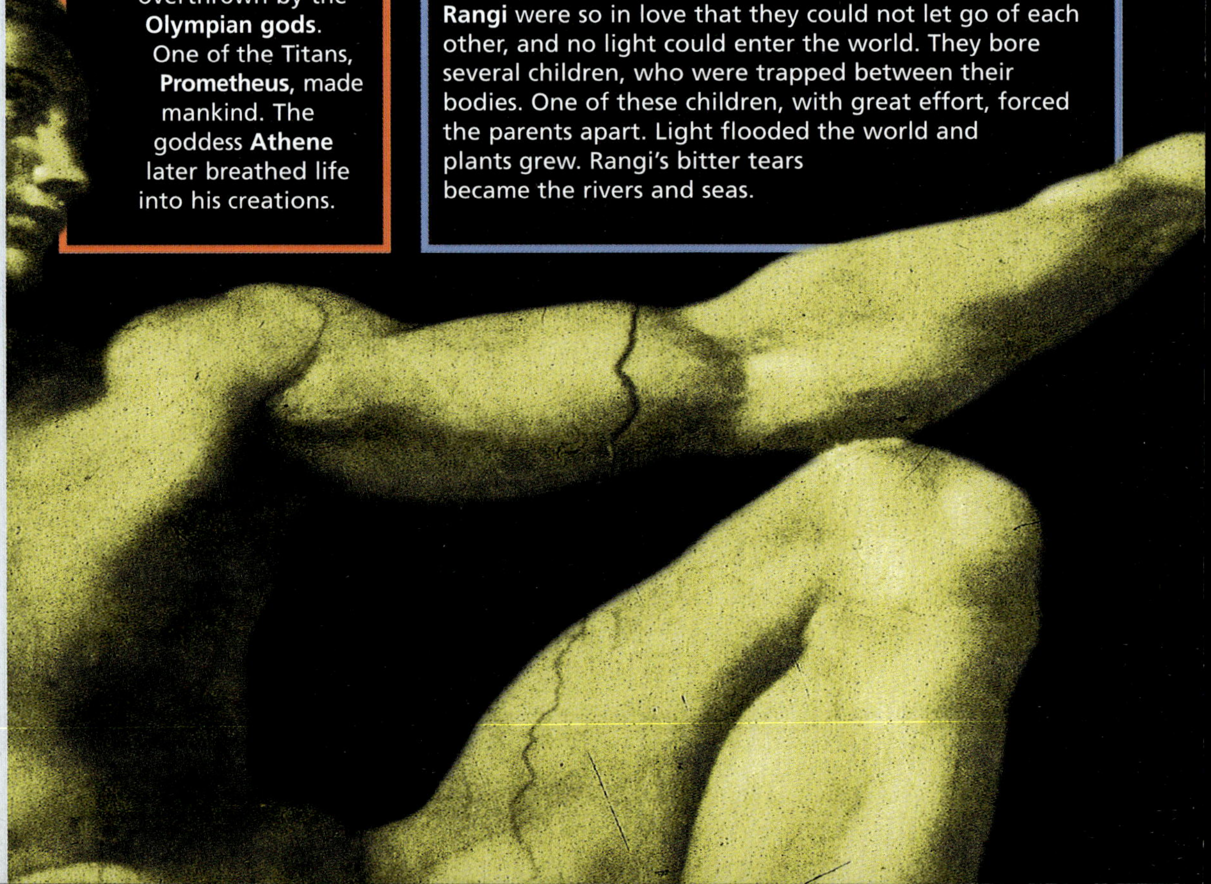

SPIRIT WORLD Ancient rock paintings depict the spirits that wandered the Earth.

Aboriginal 5

According to the Aborigines, the Earth was once a vast, flat plain. Everything slept. Then the eternal ancestors arose and wandered the Earth. The trails they walked became the sacred **songlines**. On their travels the ancestors found humans half-made from animals and plants. They took these not-quite-men, and moulded them into finished specimens.

Japanese 6

In Japanese mythology, the goddess **Izanami** gave birth to the 'eight-island country' of Japan after she and her husband **Izanagi** descended on to the island of Onogoro-Jima from the **Floating Bridge of Heaven**. The Sun goddess **Amaterasu** was made from Izanagi's bronze mirror and sent by him to rule over the heavens.

FIRST LAND According to legend, the god Izanagi and goddess Izanami stirred the ocean with a jewelled spear, creating the island Onogoro-Jima from the drips that fell from its tip.

654

Day one

In the 17th century, **James Ussher**, an Irish bishop, **calculated the exact day of creation** by correlating the family chronologies given in the Bible. He concluded that the Universe came into being on Sunday, October 23, 4004 BC. Later, John Lightfoot, one of Ussher's contemporaries, worked out the precise time on that day – 9 am.

Hindu 7

In Hindu thought the Universe, like human life, goes through cycles of being. It is generally held that the present Universe was once a primeval ocean, into which the Divine Will set a golden egg. Out of that egg came the creator god **Brahma**. Taking the form of a boar, he dived beneath the waters and lifted up the Earth with his tusks. Some Hindus believe Brahma was created not from an egg but from the god **Vishnu**'s navel.

The Bible story 8

The first words of the Bible are 'In the beginning…'. Chapter 1 of Genesis tells how God created the world in a week.

GOD MAKES MAN The Biblical story of creation has inspired numerous works of art, including this, Michelangelo's *Creation of Adam*.

Day	What happened
One	God said 'Let there be light', and created day and night
Two	God divided the waters from the sky
Three	God created dry land and the seas
Four	God created the Sun, Moon and stars
Five	God created sea creatures and birds
Six	God created land creatures and mankind
Seven	God rested

Chinese 9

All the Universe was contained inside an egg, which also held the giant **Pangu**. After 18 000 years, Pangu broke out of the egg. The lighter part rose to form the sky and the heavier part sank to become the Earth. For 18 000 years Pangu held the Earth and sky apart but at the end of that time he died, his eyes becoming the Sun and Moon, his breath clouds, his limbs mountains and his hair vegetation. The fleas on his body became the first men.

QUESTION NUMBER

The numbers or star following the answers refer to information boxes on the right.

ANSWERS

QUESTION NUMBER	ANSWERS
95	**Ten** ❼
203	**Mount Sinai** – after the Israelites had left Egypt
207	**Mount Ararat** ❷
272	**Exodus** (Greek *ex* = out + *hodos* = way) ❼
304	**Turkey** (Turkish Agri Dagi, in extreme east) ❷
★ 308	**Egypt**
357	**Joseph** ★
432	***The Epic of Gilgamesh*** ❸
460	**Noah** ❶ ❷ ❸
559	**Joseph** ★
594	**A raven** ❷
622	**Death of the firstborn** ❼
681	**They all built arks** ❶ ❷ ❹
748	**A horn of plenty** ❻
794	**A swarm of bats** ❼
798	**Noah's Ark** ❷
906	**Joseph** ★

Flood, famine and plague

Core facts ❶

◆ Many mythologies have stories that recount **ecological disaster**. Ancient peoples were well aware that drought, flood or epidemic rendered their lives precarious.
◆ More than 200 **flood myths** have been recorded around the world. Often these floods are seen as punishment for wickedness. Usually, some righteous person or group is spared.
◆ The Bible story of **Noah** and his ark fits this pattern. Eight people are saved: Noah and his wife, together with his three sons and their wives. Noah is also commanded to save the world's animal life: the ark is to house birds, animals and creeping things, 'two of every sort'.

Noah's flood ❷

In the Bible, God determines to make 'an end of all flesh', apart from Noah and his family. The **ark** is built to God's precise blueprint. When the flood comes, its waters cover the Earth for 40 days. It is 110 days more before the waters abate. The ark comes to rest on **Mount Ararat** and Noah sends out, at intervals, a **raven**, then a **dove**, then another dove. When the second dove returns with a fresh olive leaf, Noah knows the land is once more habitable. God declares that he will never again send a flood to destroy mankind, and makes the **rainbow** a token of this promise.

PRECISE INSTRUCTIONS God told Noah to build an ark from gopher wood 137 m (450 ft) long, 23 m (75 ft) wide and 13.7 m (45 ft) high.

The Babylonian flood ❸

The Epic of Gilgamesh tells how **Utnapishtim** is warned by the god Ea of a flood. Like Noah, he is told to build a ship, where he and his family take refuge with animals. The storm rages for six days, after which the ark comes to rest on a mountaintop. In a final echo of Noah's tale, Utnapishtim releases three birds to see if the waters have receded.

ANCIENT HERO Utnapishtim told his tale to Gilgamesh, depicted here between two bull-men.

Other flood stories ❹

The **Egyptians** believed that the creator god **Ra** would one day grow tired of mankind and reinstate the primeval ocean. The **Greeks** had a myth in which **Zeus** sends a flood to destroy mankind. In this tale the role of righteous man is played by **Deucalion**, who is advised by **Prometheus** to build a boat. In **Hindu** myth, there is a character called **Manu** who spares the life of a tiny fish. The fish grows rapidly to the size of a whale, and in its gratitude warns Manu of an impending flood. Manu builds a boat, which the now huge fish tows through the flood waters. When Manu says he is lonely, the gods grant him a wife. Their children are the ancestors of mankind.

WEIRD AND WONDERFUL 5

Flood myths occur in many cultures. Although the events in these myths are usually sudden, they are thought by most scholars to have been inspired by the **rising sea levels** that occurred at the end of the last Ice Age.

308

Famine story

The **Bible** tells the story of **Joseph**, who was sold into Egyptian slavery by his jealous elder brothers. In Egypt, Joseph's gift for interpreting dreams brought him to the attention of the pharaoh. Joseph told him that his dreams were a warning of seven years of famine, which would come after seven years of plenty.

SIRENS HOLDING THE CORNUCOPIA According to one Greek myth, the cornucopia was formed from one of the horns of the river god Archelous, after it was broken off in combat with the hero Heracles. 6

Cornucopia

The idea of a **horn of plenty**, a vessel which provides limitless food and drink, is bound to appeal to any culture that is subject to drought or famine. In **Greek mythology**, the cornucopia, as it is called, was a gift from **Zeus** to **Amalthea**, the nymph who nursed him in his infancy. The horn is sometimes seen as an attribute of **Pluto**, the god of riches. In **Irish mythology** there is a god named **Dagda** who owns a cauldron of plenty, which is always full to the brim with meat.

Egypt's plagues 7

The book of Exodus relates that God visited ten plagues on Egypt to persuade the pharaoh to release the Israelites. They were:

Plague	Description
First	Nile waters turn to blood
Second	Swarms of frogs
Third	Swarms of gnats
Fourth	Swarms of flies
Fifth	Cattle pestilence
Sixth	Boils 'on man and beast'
Seventh	Hailstorms
Eighth	Swarms of locusts
Ninth	Darkness over the land
Tenth	Death of the first-born

ILL WIND According to the Bible, Moses stretched his rod to raise the south wind, which brought the locusts to Egypt.

QUESTION NUMBER

The numbers or star following the answers refer to information boxes on the right.

ANSWERS

60	Thoth 7
122	Greek 1
167	A baboon 7
170	Anubis 9
322	B: Seth 2 4
383	A lion 8
443	Anubis 9
446	Horus 1 5
447	Tawaret 8
450	Sebek 8
475	Isis 1 2 3
★ 515	B: The cow
518	B: Bes 8
532	The heart 9
597	A falcon 5
672	The sky ★
745	Osiris 2
760	Bes 8
829	B: The Sun 1 6
994	A hippopotamus 8

Egyptian gods

Core facts 1

- There are countless carvings and paintings of the Egyptian gods, but we know relatively little about the myths surrounding them.
- The gods in the Egyptian pantheon were **originally local deities**, represented as animals. These developed into the many animal-headed gods that we see in Egyptian art.
- Sometimes, the gods seem to overlap. **Horus**, god of the sky, and **Ra**, the Sun god, are sometimes so similar as to be indistinguishable.
- Much of what we do know about the gods of Egypt is due to the Greek historian **Plutarch**, who wrote a book about the cults of **Osiris** and **Isis** at the very end of the Egyptian era.

Osiris 2

The god Osiris is the founding deity of the Egyptian pantheon. As a young deity he became king of Egypt, and installed his sister Isis as his queen. His reign was wholly benevolent: he taught mankind how to make bread, build cities and practise religion. He then set out on a journey to civilise other nations. On his return he was murdered by his younger brother, Seth, who cut his body into 14 pieces. Isis retrieved the pieces, reconstructed her husband and restored him to life.

TWICE KING After Isis restored him to life, Osiris ruled the Underworld.

Isis 3

The sister and consort of Osiris, Isis shares in his civilising work. She taught women to **spin**, **weave** and **cure illness**. She also introduced the Egyptians to the custom of marriage. Her cult grew over the centuries, gradually absorbing nearly all the other female deities. In some images, she is shown on a throne, wearing wings which are spread in a protective gesture over Egypt.

ISIS AND HORUS Isis eventually became the supreme mother goddess. She is often depicted suckling her son Horus.

Seth 4

In the myth of Osiris, Seth, a **god of storms**, came to personify evil. The **Greeks** linked him with **Typhon**, the monster who fought with **Zeus** and rampaged through heaven. Seth is usually depicted with the head of an animal which may be a pig or a donkey. The struggle between Osiris and Seth symbolises the oscillating balance of order and chaos, but it may also represent the clash of two historically separate cults.

Horus
5

The son of Osiris and Isis, Horus was seen as the god of the sky, and it was said that the Sun and the Moon were his eyes. Because of his connection with the Sun, the **ancient Greeks** identified him with **Apollo**. Horus is usually depicted as a **falcon**, or with the head of a falcon. He is seen as the first ruler of both Upper and Lower Egypt, and for this reason the falcon sometimes wears **the double crown** of a united Egyptian kingdom.

Ra
6

Ra is the **Sun god** and **creator of the world**. It was said the first men were made from his tears, possibly because the words 'men' and 'tears' sounded similar in Egyptian. Ra was believed to travel in his boat across the sky during daylight, visiting each of his 12 provinces. At night he descended into the Underworld, where he struggled with his enemy, the cosmic serpent.

SUN GOD Ra carries the Sun disc on his head.

Thoth
7

The **god of the Moon**, Thoth is also the **divine scribe** who records the weighing of the hearts of the dead. His association with the written word meant that he was seen as the god of learning and the inventor of **hieroglyphs**. He is depicted either as an ibis or as a baboon, sometimes with a crescent moon on his head.

SELF-MADE Thoth created himself at the beginning of time.

515 ★

Hathor

The goddess of joy, love and motherhood, Hathor looked after **all women**. One of the earliest Egyptian deities, she was patron of the sky, the Sun, the queen, music, dancing and the arts. Hathor was usually depicted either as a cow bearing the Sun disc between her horns or as a horned woman in queenly garb.

Other gods of Egypt
8

The ancient Egyptians had numerous gods. Some of the most important of them are listed below.

God	Description
Taweret	Goddess of childbirth and maternity, depicted as a hippopotamus
Bes	An ugly dwarf god whose role was to protect women and children
Ptah	A god of creation and so the patron of craftsmen
Sebek	A crocodile god
Sekhmet	Goddess of war, depicted with the head of a lioness
Amon	Called the 'king of the gods', and so identified by the Greeks with Zeus

Anubis
9

With the head of a jackal, Anubis is the god who attends to **funeral rites**. He had this role because it was he who prepared Osiris for burial after he was murdered by Seth, before Isis restored her husband's body. Anubis was said to be the guide who leads the newly dead to the hall of judgment, and weighs their heart in the scales against the Feather of Truth.

ANUBIS AND OSIRIS Anubis was referred to as the 'conductor of souls' by ancient Egyptians.

QUESTION NUMBER

The numbers or star following the answers refer to information boxes on the right.

ANSWERS

★ 96 Four

127 The Book of the Dead (or of Coming Forth by Day) 8

132 B: A crook and a flail 3

156 Papyrus 8

229 Nefertiti 3

295 The lotus 2

349 A bull 6

442 Bast, or Bastet 6

452 Scarab 6

484 The Nile 1 2

540 Through the nose 5

645 Great Sphinx 4

689 The Great Pyramid at Giza ★

728 A cat 6

833 The crocodile 6

856 White ★

Egyptian rites and symbols

Core facts 1

◆ The world of the ancient Egyptians was filled with sacred objects and symbols: the **Sun**, the **River Nile** which sustained life, and the **animals** which were the images of their many gods.

◆ The Egyptians were deeply concerned with death and with the life to come. Many of their rites were designed to supply the dead with all that they would need in the **afterlife**.

◆ The **pyramids** themselves were first and foremost the tombs of kings, though everything about them – from their shape to their alignment with the Sun – is imbued with deep **symbolic significance**.

The Nile 2

The annual flooding of the Nile brought the rich plains of Egypt into bloom and so for the Egyptians represented the crucial idea of **death and rebirth**. The Nile itself was symbolised by the **lotus flower** which, with its triangular head and long stalk, seemed to resemble the river's V-shaped delta and long winding reaches. The ancient Egyptians believed that the Nile ran through the centre of the Universe, and was surrounded by a great circular ocean.

The pharaohs 3

The word pharaoh derives from the Egyptian words for 'great house'. The pharaohs were **dynastic monarchs** who took their authority from the gods themselves. The Egyptians believed that the pharaohs were **gods incarnate**, and that the gods had been the first pharaohs. After the Fifth Dynasty they all bore the title **'sons of Ra'**, identifying themselves with the Sun god. Pharaohs are often depicted bearing the two tokens of royal office: a **flail** (a short whip) and a **crook** (a hooked sceptre).

SUN WORSHIPPERS The pharaoh Akhenaten, shown here with his wife Nefertiti, banned the worship of all gods but Aten, the Sun disc. After his death he was branded a heretic and the pantheon was restored.

IMMORTALISED IN STONE The face of the Great Sphinx at Giza is thought by many scholars to be a portrait of the pharaoh Khafre.

The Sphinx ❹

For the Egyptians, the sphinx was an **image of Ra**. The Great Sphinx at **Giza** faces the Sun and is there to protect the pyramids and oppose Ra's enemies. Its lion's body may simply be due to the shape of the limestone block from which it was carved, but this image of a lion-human was recreated in paintings and carvings. It then passed to the **Greeks**, who wove their own quite separate legends around the mythical beast.

★ 96 ★

The pyramids

The shape of the pyramids probably symbolises the **rays of the Sun** as they fall from heaven. They were originally faced with white limestone, so they would have shone brilliantly. The four sides of each of the pyramids at Giza are aligned exactly to the four points of the compass.

Tie-breaker ❼

Q What are the 'Granaries of Joseph'?
A The pyramids. The Great Pyramid of Khufu is 137 m (450 ft) high, and was, until 1889, the tallest building in the world. The name 'Granaries of Joseph' arose because the pyramids were mistakenly identified with vast granaries built as a precaution against famine, as recounted in the Bible.

Mummification ❺

The Egyptians preserved corpses because they believed that the soul roamed free after death and needed to recognise its own body in order to return to its tomb at night. The word '**mummy**' comes from an Arabic term meaning 'preserved in bitumen'. Bitumen in fact had no part in the process, which was refined and perfected over the centuries. The brain was removed through the nose, and the internal organs apart from the heart were taken out. The body was then dried and embalmed over a period of **70 days**, during which various ceremonies and funeral preparations were performed.

Holy animals ❻

Many animals were sacred to the ancient Egyptians, usually because of associations with certain gods.

The bull Called Apis, he was sacred to the god Ptah.
The cat Sacred to Bast, the cat-headed goddess of pleasure.
The cow Sacred to Hathor, the protectress of women.
The ram Sacred to the god Amun.
The crocodile Called Petesuchos and worshipped in the temple at Crocodilopolis.
The scarab This beetle rolls up balls of dung. The ancient Egyptians imagined a giant scarab rolling the Sun across the sky and associated the beetle with Ra.

CAT STATUE Real cats were often mummified as offerings to the gods.

The Book of the Dead ❽

When someone died, a collection of spells, charms and incantations was traditionally written on papyrus and buried with the body. The Egyptians called these formulae **The Book of Coming Forth By Day**. Knowledge of the spells was considered essential for the soul to achieve peace in the afterlife, so they were **placed in coffins** as a kind of handy reference for the deceased person to consult. The Egyptian Book of the Dead is not to be confused with the Buddhist text of the same name, which is a description of the largely unpleasant experiences that a soul must pass through between death and rebirth.

DAY OF JUDGMENT This extract from the papyrus of Anhai shows the deceased being led by Horus into the Hall of Judgment where her heart will be weighed against the Feather of Truth.

QUESTION NUMBER

The numbers or star following the answers refer to information boxes on the right.

ANSWERS

52	**Vishnu** ❶ ❸
69	**D: 8 640 000 years** ❷
120	**Shiva** ❶ ❹
★ 130	**The *Mahabharata***
369	**Calcutta** ❺
380	**Diwali** – celebrates Lakshmi, goddess of light
445	**Hanuman** ❽
448	**Nandi** (Shiva's guardian and symbol of fertility) ❹
449	**Ganesha** ❼
637	**B: An incarnation of Vishnu** ❸
674	**A snake** ❾
677	**Cowherds** ❻
722	**An elephant** ❼
727	**A monkey** ❽
752	**Vishnu** ❸
816	**Krishna** ❻
866	**Kali** ❺
992	**Brahma, Vishnu and Shiva** ❶ ❷ ❸ ❹

Hindu deities

Core facts ❶

◆ Hinduism encompasses a vast and tangled family tree of deities. Some of these date back to the ancient cultures that flourished on the Indian sub-continent 4000 years ago.

◆ Classical Hinduism's divine triad – called the **Trimurti** – consists of the overarching god **Brahma**, along with **Vishnu** and **Shiva**.

◆ There are many other gods who represent aspects or incarnations of the unknowable and supreme reality, which is called **Brahman**.

Brahma ❷

This shadowy god **created the world** and keeps it on its cosmic cycle. According to one story, Brahma was hatched from a golden egg, which floated upon the primeval waters. Brahma is usually depicted with **four heads**, which he grew so that he could always see his beautiful **wife Saraswati**. A day and night of Brahma's life is called a **kalpa** and is said to last 8 640 000 years. At the end of each kalpa the world dissolves and Brahma remakes it.

Hindu mythology holds that Brahma **created mankind.** In order to do so, he first created a goddess out of himself. One half of that goddess was Saraswati. The other half was the human race.

ONE OF THREE Brahma is considered the senior member of the Hindu trinity, which also includes Vishnu and Shiva. Traditionally, Brahma is depicted with four faces, four arms and red skin.

Vishnu the preserver ❸

Ensuring the triumph of good over evil is Vishnu's main purpose. To achieve this aim he is said to have taken on various forms or **avatars** at moments of great crisis. There are said to have been ten avatars of Vishnu, which include the turtle **Kurma** and the prince and demon-slayer **Rama**. The hero **Krishna** was the eighth incarnation; the **Buddha** has been identified as the ninth, and the tenth is yet to come.

MATSYA This avatar of Vishnu appeared as a fish. Vishnu is usually shown with dark blue skin and kingly garb.

★ 130 Mahabharata

Hinduism's greatest epic, the *Mahabharata* has existed in various forms for at least 2000 years. Between 300 BC and AD 300, it was collected into a unified **Sanskrit text** of 100 000 stanzas and distributed throughout India. The *Mahabharata* lays claim to being the **world's second-longest book**, after the *Gesar Epic of Tibet*. The **Bhagavad Gita** is contained in the text of the *Mahabharata*.

Shiva 4

Shiva is the **personification of destruction** and is often shown wearing a necklace of skulls. But Shiva **also contains a creative principle** – in fact all kinds of opposites are reconciled within his complex nature, and he is sometimes depicted as half-male, half-female. At root he is the soul of asceticism, a divine yogi whose meditation keeps the world in existence.

LORD OF THE DANCE Shiva can take the form of Nataraja, who has four arms and performs his dance steps to relieve the suffering of his followers.

Kali 5

The **personification of death**, Kali is depicted with mournful eyes, a protruding tongue and four arms. One of the arms holds a sword, another holds the severed head of a giant, and the other two – paradoxically – are raised in blessing. Kali wears a skirt of dismembered arms and (like Shiva) a necklace of skulls.

CITY GODDESS Calcutta is named after Kali – the name is a corruption of Kali Ghat, which means 'the steps of Kali'.

Krishna 6

Krishna is the **eighth avatar of Vishnu**, but he is so important that he has the status of a god in his own right. Krishna was hidden at birth from his uncle **King Kamsa**, who had been told that one of his nephews would depose him. When he reached manhood he killed his uncle. On a separate occasion he took part in the battle of Kurukshetra, in which two armies were annihilated. On the eve of battle, disguised as a charioteer, he recounted the **Bhagavad Gita**.

Ganesha 7

The son of Shiva and Parvati, Ganesha guards his mother's house, and according to one myth this was how he came by his **elephant head**. Parvati went to have a bath and told Ganesha not to let anyone in. When his father arrived, Ganesha barred the way. This so incensed Shiva that he decapitated his son. Parvati was distraught when she saw what had happened, and so Shiva replaced the severed head with the first one he laid hands on – an elephant's.

HOLY COUPLE Krishna was brought up by cowherds, and fell in love with the milkmaid Radha.

Hanuman 8

The **monkey god**, Hanuman is the epitome of wisdom and the **patron of learning**. He was also the general of a monkey army which came to the aid of the hero Rama in his battle with the demon Ravana. The figure of the monkey god was absorbed into Buddhism and adopted enthusiastically in China, where a great many tales were told of his exploits.

Sesha 9

A **cobra god**, Sesha rules over the **Nagas**, a race of serpents with human heads. Sesha is also known as **Ananta**, which means 'infinite'. He has a thousand heads, and when he yawns earthquakes occur. When Vishnu rests on the snake's coiled body, Sesha's hood acts as his sunshade.

QUESTION NUMBER

The numbers or star following the answers refer to information boxes on the right.

ANSWERS

49	***Seven Years in Tibet*** – Brad Pitt as Heinrich Harrer
66	**A: Spiritual truth** 5
146	**Buddha** 3
★ 365	**Bodh Gaya**
395	**C: A buddha-to-be** 5
428	**Buddha** 1 3 4
467	**Nirvana** (formed in 1987) 5
477	**Queen Maya** 2
514	**C: A sacred word** 5
690	**Nara** – temple is world's largest wooden building
756	**Avalokitesvara** 7
809	**Samsara** 5
917	**Tibet** 7
986	**The Dalai Lama** 7

Buddhist myths

Core facts 1

◆ Buddhism was founded in around 560 BC by the man known to history as **Siddhartha Gautama**. It has grown into a world religion with many traditions and denominations.

◆ The great division in Buddhism is between **Hinayana** (Lesser Vehicle) and **Mahayana** (Greater Vehicle). Hinayana stresses meditation and spiritual growth, and aspires to a minimum of ritual. Mahayana is more colourful – its teachings are full of imagery, stories, cosmic **bodhisattvas** and devotional cults.

◆ Most of the legends about the life of Buddha and his followers derive from the Mahayana tradition.

Maya 2

The Buddha's mother was a queen called Maya, wife of Raja Shuddhodana, a north Indian ruler. Before the Buddha was born, Maya had a **dream** in which she saw a white elephant enter her womb. As the moment came for the child's birth, the whole Universe rejoiced – trees blossomed spontaneously, rivers stopped flowing and musical instruments played themselves.

QUEEN MAYA According to legend, the Buddha's mother was the wife of a monarch of a small kingdom in northern India.

Siddhartha the prince 3

The infant Buddha was named Siddhartha. During his childhood, he was kept in the palace and shielded from the harsh realities of life. But as a young man he became curious and asked to see the outside world. During his visit to a nearby town, Siddhartha saw an ill person, an old man and a corpse. He realised, apparently for the first time in his life, that everybody must **suffer illness, grow old and die**.

FIRST OUTING The young Prince Siddhartha leaves the cocoon of the royal palace.

THOUSAND BUDDHAS
Although Hinduism now prevails, Buddhism was India's most important religion for several centuries. The rich paintings in the Ajanta caves of Maharashtra state are among the relics that have survived from that time.

Enlightenment

4

The knowledge of suffering plagued Siddhartha. Abandoning his family, he went to live the life of a wandering ascetic. He changed his name to **Gautama** and for six years lived a life of austerity, but it brought him no nearer to an understanding of the world. So he went to **Bodh Gaya**, sat beneath a fig tree, and resolved not to move until he had found enlightenment. At the end of five weeks he saw that desire is the root of all suffering, and in that instant he became the **Buddha**, or 'enlightened one'.

Some Buddhist terms

5

Some words in Buddhist texts describe particular concepts or states of being.

Term	Meaning
Bodhisattva	'Buddha-to-be', who delays entry into nirvana in order to help others towards enlightenment.
Dharma	A truth, or insight into the nature of the Universe.
Karma	The idea that a person's deeds are rewarded or punished by the circumstances of the next reincarnation.
Mantra	A sacred word or sound such as 'Om' used as an aid to meditation.
Nirvana	The blessed state of release from the cycle of reincarnation.
Samsara	The endless cycle of birth, death and reincarnation.

365

Bodhi Tree

A descendant of the tree under which the Buddha achieved enlightenment still grows at **Bodh Gaya** in India. A cutting of the original tree was planted in **Anuradhapura**, Sri Lanka, in the 3rd century BC. A cutting was later taken from that tree and returned to Bodh Gaya, where it grew into the Bodhi Tree alive today.

Legends of the Buddha

6

After the Buddha's death, many legends accrued to the bare bones of his biography. It was said, for example, that he was tempted under the Bodhi Tree by the demon **Mara**, who sent his daughters to seduce him, unleashed devils to terrify him and finally attacked him with a fiery discus. Later in the Buddha's life, there came a child who wanted to make an offering to him. The child collected some dust and brought it in cupped hands. The Buddha accepted this innocent gift and the child was subsequently reborn as the great emperor **Ashoka**.

NAGA HOOD Ancient India's cobra deity was adopted into Buddhism as the Lord Buddha's protector.

GIANT BUDDHA A 26 m (83 ft) statue at Tibet's Tashi Lhunpo monastery.

Tibetan gods

7

Influenced by Hinduism, Tibet developed a form of Buddhism, sometimes called **Lamaism**, in which many buddhas and bodhisattvas are venerated as deities. Chief among them is the bodhisattva **Avalokiteshvara**, who has become a kind of national god of Tibet. It is believed that the **Dalai Lama** is Avalokiteshvara incarnate.

QUESTION NUMBER

The numbers or star following the answers refer to information boxes on the right.

ANSWERS

40 ***Crouching Tiger, Hidden Dragon*** – released 2000

★ 114 **Confucius** ❻

133 **B: Way** ❶ ❸

168 **The dragon** ❺

298 **Japan's** ❽

375 **Japan** – the flag is called *Hi-no-maru*, 'The sun disc'

458 **Carp** – in a dream it also symbolises good luck

502 **Taoism** ❸

623 **Shinto** ❶ ❽

659 **China** ❷

675 **Buddha** ❶

679 **Old Master** ❸

691 **The Book of Changes** ❼

753 **Amaterasu** ❽

758 **Shou Lao** – Taoist god of long life and luck

807 **Butsudo** ❶

946 **The Sun** ❽

991 **100** (Tai Shan is the abode of the August Personage of Jade) ❷

Myths of China and Japan

Core facts ❶

◆ Chinese mythology is rooted in **ancestor worship**. During the time of the Shang kings, the first Chinese dynasty, ancestors were consulted as oracles, and the kings were seen as the direct descendants of divine rulers.

◆ The veneration of the ancestors grew and developed under the influence of three great philosophies: **Taoism**, **Confucianism** and **Buddhism**. The founders of these three all lived in the 6th century BC.

◆ Many Chinese ideas were passed to Japan, where they were absorbed into the faith called **Shinto**. In the 12th century Japan developed its own meditative variant of Buddhism called **Zen**.

GOD OF WAR The Taoist deity Guan-di is said to protect China from its enemies. He is also the patron of rulers and literature.

The Chinese pantheon ❷

China's gods are a mixture of Taoist deities and Buddhist divinities imported from India and adapted to the Chinese religious outlook. The most striking thing about the Chinese pantheon is that it is arranged like a well-ordered **civil service**. The gods preside over **ministries**. Their responsibilities include abstract concepts such as longevity, happiness and wealth, and more concrete things such as literature, examinations, ditches and doors. All of the gods have rank, and report to superior gods. At the top of this bureaucratic pyramid is the **August Personage of Jade**, a divine emperor who corresponds exactly to the emperor on earth.

Taoist myths ❸

Taoism is **China's oldest belief system**. It was founded in the 6th century BC by the semi-legendary figure **Lao Tzu** ('old master'). His poetical work, the ***Tao Te Ching***, advocates submissiveness, frugality and a joyful attitude to life. Over the centuries, this simple philosophy took on all kinds of mythical accoutrements. Central to Taoist mythology are the '**Eight Immortals**'. These jolly saints or demigods share an ability to fly and an unashamed love of wine.

WATCHED OVER A girl dreams of love as one of the Eight Immortals gazes down.

WEIRD AND WONDERFUL

4

Hanuman the Monkey is a deity in both Hindu and Chinese Buddhist mythology. The TV series ***Monkey*** was an adaptation of the myth in which the monkey accompanies the monk Tripitaka on a trek to India.

Chinese dragons

5

In China, dragons were seen as **benevolent spirits**, not as the aggressive and demonic beasts of western mythology. Only the emperor was allowed to have dragons with five claws embroidered on his clothes and possessions; dragons with four claws signified a prince, and three-clawed dragons stood for court officials.

COMPLEX BEAST Chinese dragons were said to have deer's antlers, a camel's head, eagle's claws, tiger's feet and the ears of an ox.

Confucius

6

Confucius lived in China in the 6th century BC and spent his life as a civil servant and teacher of wisdom. His philosophy promoted conservative moral values: people should be respectful, rulers should be benevolent and sincere, violence and extremism should be avoided. His thoughts on right behaviour were gathered by his followers after his death. Confucianism became the **state religion of China** in around 200 BC.

The *I Ching*

7

The *I Ching*, or **Book of Changes**, is a Chinese method of divining the future. The book contains 64 vague and oracular sayings such as 'A cautious halt halfway brings favour'. Each of these corresponds to a particular '**hexagram**' – a sign which is a combination of **yin and yang** lines. The user, with a specific question in mind, throws coins to arrive at a hexagram and its corresponding prophecy, which can then be applied to his or her situation.

114

Reluctant deity

According to legend, when Confucius was born a unicorn appeared and spat out a piece of jade on which was written that he would become an 'uncrowned emperor'. From his writings, Confucius appears not to have believed in the gods. But in 1907, 2500 years after his birth, he was himself declared **a god** – a honour which would have horrified him.

Shinto myths

8

The national religion of Japan, Shinto recognises thousands of **kami** – gods or spirits who inhabit objects, places and natural phenomena. Until recently **the emperor** was regarded as a living kami. The chief divinity in Shinto is **Amaterasu**, the sun goddess. She is seen as the ancestor of all the emperors who have sat on Japan's **'Chrysanthemum Throne'**. Amaterasu is the daughter of **Izanagi** and **Izanami**, Shinto's creator gods.

RELIGIOUS SYMBOL Shinto's holiest sites are marked with gates known as torii. This torii guards the island of Miya Jima near Hiroshima.

QUESTION NUMBER

The numbers or star following the answers refer to information boxes on the right.

ANSWERS

QUESTION NUMBER	ANSWERS
19	**The dragon** 6
★ 62	**C: Princess Margaret**
97	**12** 6
159	**Astrology** 1 2 3
196	**Aquarius** 5
255	**D: It does not say** 4
381	**'Circle of animals'** 7
390	**The cockerel** 6
398	**B: Polish** (1473-1543) 1
401	**12** 5
573	**Virgo** 5
634	**B: The Chaldeans** 2
660	**Leo** (the zodiac is held to begin with Aries) 5
699	**Ptolemy** 2
776	**Sagittarius** (the archer) 5
802	**Cusp** 5
808	**Wanderer** 3
822	**B: The snake** 6
835	**Aries** 5
883	**Capricorn** 5
922	**Signs of the Chinese zodiac** 6
945	**Cancer** 5
950	**Babylon** 2

The zodiac and astrology

Core facts 1

◆ Astrology is based on the idea that the position of the planets at the time of people's birth influences their personality and future life.

◆ Astrology died out as a serious scholarly pursuit after **Copernicus** demonstrated that the Earth is not the centre of the universe: it followed that the ascent and descent of the constellations, and the vagabond movement of the planets, is no more than an optical illusion.

◆ However, superstitions surrounding astrology persist: newspaper astrologers are among the highest paid journalists in Britain, while New Age writers have reinterpreted the old astrological ideas as a form of ancient wisdom.

History of astrology 2

EUCLID AND DALMATIN The 12th-century scholar Herman Dalmatin translated both Euclid's *Geometrical Elements* and Ptolemy's *Planisphaerium*.

The **Babylonians** first systematically mapped the positions and movements of the stars. A special caste of priests, called **Chaldeans**, used this astronomical data for divination. Their knowledge passed to the **Egyptians**, and then to the **Greeks**. **Ptolemy**, the greatest astronomer of Greek times, was also a keen astrologer. He wrote a treatise on star signs called **Tetrabiblios** (Four Books). Astrology remained a serious and popular concern throughout the Middle Ages. The German astronomer **Johann Kepler** developed a quasi-astronomical theory of the 'harmony of the spheres', and was for a time a court astrologer.

Planets in astrology 3

The word planet comes from the Greek for 'wanderer'. This is because, viewed from Earth, they appear to move through a narrow belt of sky – the **zodiac**. Each of the planets was believed to have attributes which corresponded to the characters of the gods for whom they were named: **Mars** stood for strife, **Venus** for love, and so on. When a planet was in any given sign it was thought to exert its influence – one might say, impose its personality – on everything symbolically associated with it. This system was lent greater complexity by the belief that the relative positions of the planets were also significant.

PLANETARY MOTION A late medieval table from Provence showing the movement of the planets.

Biblical astrologers

It is generally agreed that the **wise men** who came to find the infant Jesus were professional astrologers. The Bible speaks of their seeing 'a star in the east' which told them of the birth of a Jewish king. This appears to be a reference to an astrological event. Many scholars have tried to establish what this event may have been. Chinese records speak of a **comet** which appeared at a time close to when Christ would have been born. There is also evidence that **Jupiter**, signifying kingship, was in rare conjunction in the sign of **Aries**, symbolising Judea, around the time of Christ's birth.

IMPLICIT NUMBER The Bible says only that there were three gifts, not three kings.

5

Signs of the zodiac

The signs of the zodiac are named after the constellations each contained in the time of ancient Greece. The point when one sign passes into the next, around the 21st of the month, is called the **cusp**.

Sign	Symbol	Dates
Aries	Ram	21 Mar-20 April
Taurus	Bull	21 April-21 May
Gemini	Twins	22 May-22 June
Cancer	Crab	23 June-23 July
Leo	Lion	24 July-23 Aug
Virgo	Virgin	24 Aug-23 Sept
Libra	Scales	24 Sept-23 Oct
Scorpio	Scorpion	24 Oct-22 Nov
Sagittarius	Archer	23 Nov-21 Dec
Capricorn	Goat	22 Dec-20 Jan
Aquarius	Water Carrier	21 Jan-19 Feb
Pisces	Fish	20 Feb-20 Mar

62

Daily stars

The first astrological prediction in a newspaper was a horoscope for the new-born **Princess Margaret** in 1930. The article, in the ***Sunday Express***, contained a few forecasts for people with birthdays in the subsequent week. These provoked such a response from readers that the paper began a weekly horoscope column.

6

China's zodiac

As in the West, the zodiac in China is made up of 12 different signs. However, each sign in the Chinese zodiac is symbolised by **an animal** and represents a year rather than just a month. The **Chinese New Year** falls on the new moon between January 21 and February 20. As a result, every third year in the Chinese calendar contains 13 lunar months: all other years are shorter, comprising just 12 lunar months.

ANIMAL MAGIC In China, people born in particular years are thought to inherit characteristics associated with that year's animal.

Monkey	1968	1980	1992	2004
Cockerel	1969	1981	1993	2005
Dog	1970	1982	1994	2006
Pig	1971	1983	1995	2007
Rat	1972	1984	1996	2008
Ox	1973	1985	1997	2009
Tiger	1974	1986	1998	2010
Hare	1975	1987	1999	2011
Dragon	1976	1988	2000	2012
Snake	1977	1989	2001	2013
Horse	1978	1990	2002	2014
Goat	1979	1991	2003	2015

WEIRD AND WONDERFUL

7

The word 'zodiac' comes from Ancient Greek and means a **circle of animals**. However, the names of the 12 constellations or signs of the zodiac that we use today are in Latin.

QUESTION NUMBER

The numbers or star following the answers refer to information boxes on the right.

ANSWERS

6 Friday (2)

70 D: Winter (4)

91 October (7)

113 **'November Rain'** – a hit in 1992

177 Eos (4) (5)

211 Woe (3)

220 **Flora** – a festival, the Ludi Florales, held each spring

233 **March** (after Mars) (7)

251 **B: French hens** – 12 Days of Christmas 25/12 to 6/1

344 Works hard (3)

★ 557 False

574 Thursday (2)

614 Tuesday (3)

718 Monday (2)

867 Zephyrus (5)

885 Wednesday (2)

923 Greek wind gods (5)

988 Selene (5)

Time and the seasons

Core facts (1)

◆ The calendar that we use today is filled with mythological meaning. Most of the days of the week and some of the months of the year are named in honour of the **old pagan gods**.

◆ There is significance in the numbers in the calendar too. The **12 months** correspond to the houses of the zodiac, and the **seven days** of the week reflect the wandering planets (including the Sun and Moon) that were visible to the Babylonians.

◆ Divisions of time are an attempt to impose order on the march of the seasons. Myths about the origins of the weather are another way of making sense of **natural phenomena**.

The days of the week (2)

In imitation of the Babylonians, the **Romans** from the time of Emperor Constantine in the 4th century AD named the days of the weeks for the planets: the first day belonged to the Sun, the second to the Moon, then Mars, Mercury, Jove, Venus and Saturn in that order. When the **Saxons** adopted the Roman calendar they changed the names of the Roman gods to Teutonic ones in four cases. So the Romans' day of Mars, for example, became the Germanic Tiw's day – both are gods of war. In Romanised countries, the Latin names for the days were retained, so in French, for example, the days of the week derive from the Roman names for the gods.

Roman god (planet)	Germanic equivalent	Modern French	Modern German	Modern English
Sun (Solis)	Sun	Dimanche*	Sonntag	Sunday
Moon (Luna)	Moon	Lundi	Montag	Monday
Mars	Tiw	Mardi	Dienstag	Tuesday
Mercury	Woden	Mercredi	Mittwoch	Wednesday
Jove	Thor	Jeudi	Donnerstag	Thursday
Venus	Frigg	Vendredi	Freitag	Friday
Saturn	Saturn**	Samedi***	Samstag	Saturday

* From Latin '*dominicus dies*' – Lord's Day
** The Norse people had no equivalent god to Saturn
*** From Latin '*sambati dies*' – Sabbath Day

Monday's child (3)

There is an English folk rhyme which ascribes different attributes to children according to the day on which they were born. It reads as follows:

Monday's child is fair of face,
Tuesday's child is full of grace,
Wednesday's child is full
of woe,
Thursday's child has far to go,
Friday's child is loving and giving,
Saturday's child works hard for
a living,
But the child that is born
on the Sabbath Day,
is blithe and bonny, good
and gay.

MERCURY AND SATURN The Roman god of seed-sowing time and the harvest, Saturn (above) gave his name to the last day of the week. Mercury (left) gave his name to the fourth day, retained in the French word Mercredi. In Saxon countries, Mercury was replaced by Woden, making Wednesday (Woden's day).

Gods of weather

In most mythologies, the weather is created by the actions of the gods. In **Greece**, Zeus caused storms to rage, often as an incidental consequence of his anger. Eos, the goddess of dawn, sprinkled dew from a vase ahead of the sun chariot of Phoebus Apollo. The **Chinese** wind god carries the cold wind in a sack and sits astride a tiger, while the **Norse** poets speak of hail falling from the manes of the steeds ridden by the Valkyries as they thunder across the sky. In ancient societies, weather gods were among the most important gods of all. Tlaloc, the **Aztec** god of rain and agriculture, was directly responsible for the success or failure of the crops, and so the survival of the Aztec people. Similarly, the goddess Satet controlled the flooding of the Nile, which was essential to the agricultural system of ancient **Egypt**.

SAVIOUR OF A NATION The Japanese wind god Fujin carried the winds in a bag over his shoulders. According to legend, he sent the Divine Wind Kamikaze (a typhoon) to save Japan from Kublai Khan in 1282.

557

Different weeks

The ancient Greek calendar had lunar months but no concept of the week. For many centuries, the Romans had an eight-day week, beginning with **the Nundinae** (market day). Other days were referred to in terms of the Nundinae – the day after Nundinae, two days after Nundinae and so on. Emperor Constantine instituted the seven-day week in AD 321.

WEIRD AND WONDERFUL

Unlike the year, month and day, **the week** is not determined by the movements of the Earth and Moon. So it need not be fixed at seven days. From 1793 to 1803, revolutionary France had 'decades' of ten days.

The months

The **names** of the months in English, unlike the days of the week, are **all of Roman origin**. January is named for **Janus**, the god of beginnings. February derives its name from the festival of purification called **Februa**. March is so called in honour of the god of war, **Mars**, and the word April comes from the Latin ***aperire***, to open, because this is the time when buds and flowers unfold. The last four months of the year – September, October, November and December – are derived from the Latin words for seventh, eighth, ninth and tenth, because the Roman year began in March. The months of July and August were called 'fifth' and 'sixth' until they were renamed in honour of **Julius Caesar** and his grand-nephew, the first Roman emperor, **Augustus**.

Greek weather gods

The Greeks explained the march of the seasons through the story of **Persephone**, goddess of spring and summer. She was abducted by **Hades** and taken by him to the Underworld. After this, **Zeus** declared that she may return to Earth – but for just eight months of the year. Other Greek weather gods and goddesses included:

- **Selene** The Moon and sister of Helios.
- **Eos** The dawn and mother of the winds.
- **Astraeus** The starry sky, father of the winds.
- **Boreas** The north wind.
- **Zephyrus** The west wind.
- **Eurus** The east wind.
- **Notus** The south wind.

HELIOS The Sun god, Helios, rode across the sky in a chariot towed by winged horses.

Underworld of the ancients

QUESTION NUMBER

The numbers or star following the answers refer to information boxes on the right.

ANSWERS

- **61** — A: Hypnos ❹
- **68** — A: A kind of heaven ❶
- **215** — Valhalla ❼
- **216** — **Styx** – first appeared on the *Cornerstone* album
- **253** — C: Demeter ❻
- **399** — B: 21 ★
- **425** — Persephone ❻
- **438** — From a snake bite ❺
- **479** — Hades ❸
- **506** — Osiris ❷
- **652** — The Styx ❹
- **673** — A silver coin ❹
- **676** — Thanatos ❹
- **826** — B: Charon ❹
- ★ **862** — Yama
- **869** — **John Keats** (1795-1821) ❹
- **954** — **Lethe** ('Oblivion': drinking its water made souls forget their life on Earth) ❹

Core facts ❶

◆ The idea of an **afterlife for the soul** is one of the common threads of mythology.

◆ The Greeks divided their underworld, **Hades**, into the prison-like **Tartarus** and the sunny **Elysian Fields**. In other ancient cultures, however, all the dead went to the same rather shadowy and dreary Underworld.

◆ Mythology has many tales of characters who **descend into the Underworld** and return. Often they are connected with the death of nature in winter and its rebirth in spring.

◆ Stories of return trips to the kingdom of the dead are connected with the concept of the **dying and rising god**.

The afterlife in Egypt ❷

The Egyptians believed that death was a continuation of life on Earth, a place where one could retain one's social status, family connections and possessions. The lord of the Egyptian Underworld is **Osiris**, who was originally a god of vegetation and agriculture. He is usually depicted with the crook and flail, which are the tokens of kingship, and he is wrapped in mummy bandages to show that his kingdom is death. The Egyptians saw Osiris as a means to eternal life, and this was achieved by following the exact rituals of his **embalming**.

WEIRD AND WONDERFUL ❸

Hades is both the **abode of the dead** and the name of the god who rules over it. In Greek the name means '**that which is unseen**' – the Greeks averted their eyes when sacrificing to Hades.

Crossing the Styx ❹

In **Greek mythology**, the Styx was a river that looped nine times round **Hades**. To pass into the realm of the dead, a soul had to pay the ferryman **Charon** to take him across the Styx and the **River Acheron**. The fee was a silver coin, an *obolus*, which the Greeks put into a corpse's mouth for this purpose. Hades' other helpers included **Cerberus**, the three-headed dog that guards the gates of the Underworld; **Thanatos** (Death), who brings Hades his subjects; and Death's more gentle brother **Hypnos** – Sleep.

THE FERRYMAN Cupid's lover Psyche pays Charon in a painting by Sir Edward Burne-Jones. Right: A sculpture of Hypnos from the 1st or 2nd century AD.

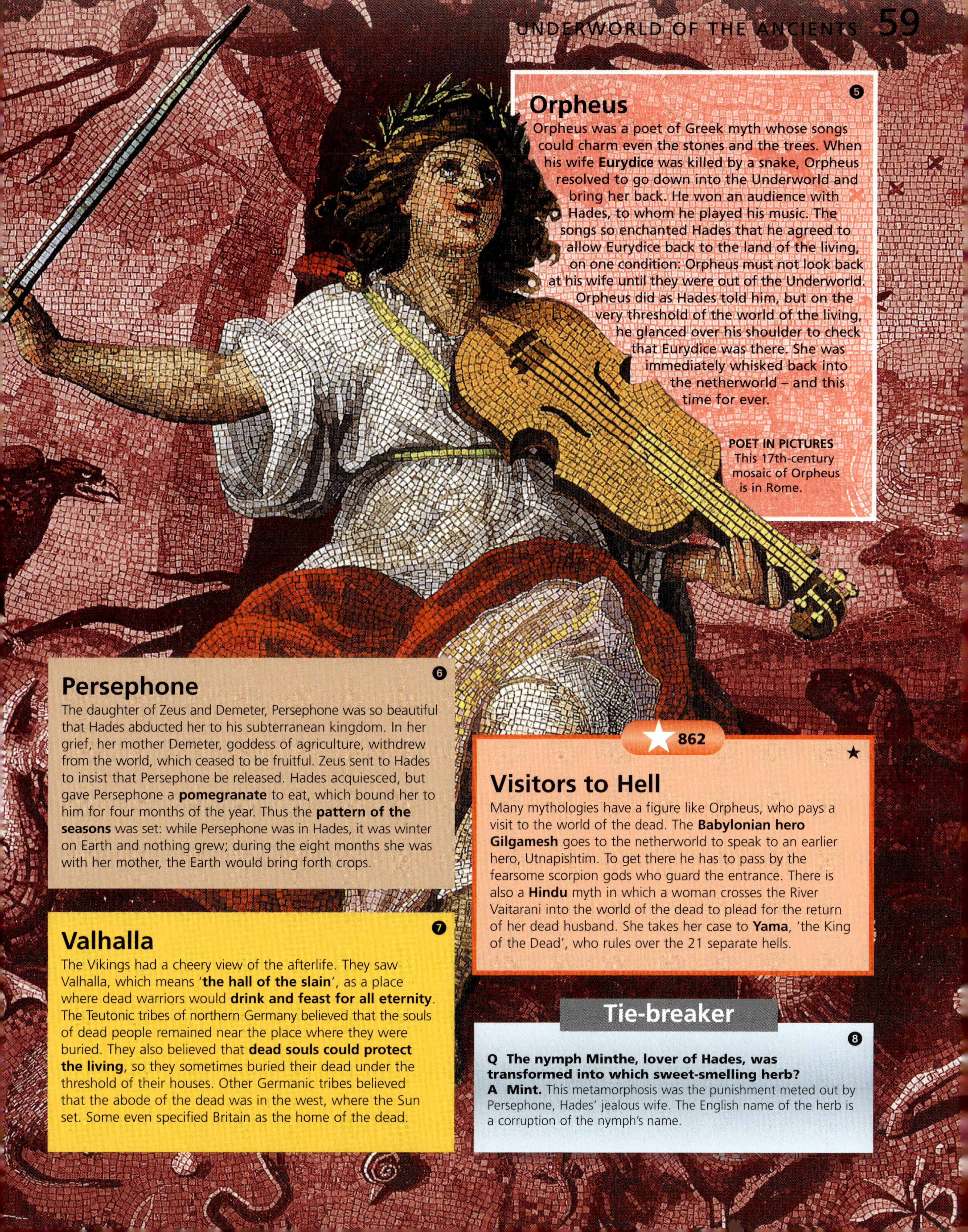

Orpheus

5

Orpheus was a poet of Greek myth whose songs could charm even the stones and the trees. When his wife **Eurydice** was killed by a snake, Orpheus resolved to go down into the Underworld and bring her back. He won an audience with Hades, to whom he played his music. The songs so enchanted Hades that he agreed to allow Eurydice back to the land of the living, on one condition: Orpheus must not look back at his wife until they were out of the Underworld. Orpheus did as Hades told him, but on the very threshold of the world of the living, he glanced over his shoulder to check that Eurydice was there. She was immediately whisked back into the netherworld – and this time for ever.

POET IN PICTURES This 17th-century mosaic of Orpheus is in Rome.

Persephone

6

The daughter of Zeus and Demeter, Persephone was so beautiful that Hades abducted her to his subterranean kingdom. In her grief, her mother Demeter, goddess of agriculture, withdrew from the world, which ceased to be fruitful. Zeus sent to Hades to insist that Persephone be released. Hades acquiesced, but gave Persephone a **pomegranate** to eat, which bound her to him for four months of the year. Thus the **pattern of the seasons** was set: while Persephone was in Hades, it was winter on Earth and nothing grew; during the eight months she was with her mother, the Earth would bring forth crops.

Valhalla

7

The Vikings had a cheery view of the afterlife. They saw Valhalla, which means '**the hall of the slain**', as a place where dead warriors would **drink and feast for all eternity**. The Teutonic tribes of northern Germany believed that the souls of dead people remained near the place where they were buried. They also believed that **dead souls could protect the living**, so they sometimes buried their dead under the threshold of their houses. Other Germanic tribes believed that the abode of the dead was in the west, where the Sun set. Some even specified Britain as the home of the dead.

★ 862

★

Visitors to Hell

Many mythologies have a figure like Orpheus, who pays a visit to the world of the dead. The **Babylonian hero Gilgamesh** goes to the netherworld to speak to an earlier hero, Utnapishtim. To get there he has to pass by the fearsome scorpion gods who guard the entrance. There is also a **Hindu** myth in which a woman crosses the River Vaitarani into the world of the dead to plead for the return of her dead husband. She takes her case to **Yama**, 'the King of the Dead', who rules over the 21 separate hells.

Tie-breaker

8

Q The nymph Minthe, lover of Hades, was transformed into which sweet-smelling herb?

A Mint. This metamorphosis was the punishment meted out by Persephone, Hades' jealous wife. The English name of the herb is a corruption of the nymph's name.

QUESTION NUMBER

The numbers or star following the answers refer to information boxes on the right.

ANSWERS

175 Hestia (1) (11)

236 Ares (1) (9) (11)

285 Aphrodite (1) (9)

384 A stag (10)

427 Paris (9)

473 Uranus ★

490 Poseidon (1) (4)

493 Caligula (AD 12-41) (1) (2)

533 His head (1) (8)

544 Zeus (1) (2)

592 The owl (1) (8)

669 Pluto (he controlled the riches in the Earth) (5)

684 Phidias (c.490-430 BC)

696 Hesiod (1)

704 D: Ambrosia – they also drank nectar

755 Apollo (1) (6)

773 The trident (4)

779 A bolt of lightning (2)

907 Hermaphroditos (7)

910 Apollo (1) (6) (10)

916 Greece (1)

★ 927 Titans

The gods of Olympus

Core facts (1)

◆ The gods of Greece are derived from primitive **cults** that flourished in the Aegean and in Asia Minor before the Hellenistic (**Classical Greek**) Age.

◆ The first attempt to establish a hierarchy and **family tree of the gods** belongs to Hesiod, who wrote his *Theogony* in the 6th century BC.

◆ Twelve of the **main gods** – Zeus, Hera, Poseidon, Hermes, Aphrodite, Athena, Ares, Apollo, Artemis, Hephaestus, Demeter and Hestia – dwelt on **Mount Olympus**.

◆ The passions, jealousies and ambitions of these **divine beings** were seen as the driving force behind human events.

Zeus (2)

According to legend, Zeus was the third son of the Titans **Cronus** and **Rhea**. Cronus believed that one of his offspring would dethrone him, so he devoured his children at birth. The infant Zeus was spirited away by his mother and raised in Crete. When he was old enough Zeus challenged Cronus, forced him to regurgitate his children and, with the help of two of his brothers, struck him dead with a bolt of lightning.

FATHER OF THE GODS Zeus ruled like a dictator, crushing dissent and punishing gods and humans alike.

Hera (3)

The queen of Olympus, Hera was the jealous wife of Zeus. Her cult is very ancient: she was originally an earth goddess, Zeus a sky god. The stories of their stormy marriage are in part an account of the fusion of these two cults. Hera was the daughter of Cronus and Rhea, and so Zeus's sister. She jealously pursued his lovers and illegitimate children, especially his son **Heracles** (see page 64).

Poseidon (4)

The **god of the sea**, Poseidon was allotted this fiefdom after he helped his younger brother Zeus overthrow their father Cronus. Like an unquiet sea, he is capable of great wrath; and like the abundant sea, he can show great generosity. He once plotted with Hera against Zeus, and for this was punished by being made to work for a year to build the walls of Troy.

SEA GOD Poseidon had a palace of coral and gems on the ocean floor and drove a chariot pulled by horses.

Hades (5)

Brother of Zeus and Poseidon, Hades took the **Underworld** as his kingdom. He is a grim god, but not demonic; and the Underworld, though shadowy, is not a place of punishment like the Christian Hell. Nevertheless, Hades was feared to the extent that his name was not spoken out loud. His wife **Persephone** spent a third of the year in the Underworld with him.

Apollo 6

The son of Zeus and twin brother of **Artemis**, Apollo is one of the most complex and intriguing of the Greek gods. He is associated with **music** (he played the lyre), **prophecy** and **archery**. He is also a **healer**, and it is possible that his worship is rooted in the fear of plague. One of his many sons is **Asclepius**, who was so skilled a doctor that Zeus punished him for interfering with divine control over life and death.

TEMPLE OF APOLLO The two remaining columns of Apollo's temple at Didymus, in Turkey, tower 18 m (60 ft) high and have stood intact for 2400 years.

LOVE GODS A Greek relief dating from 470 BC shows Aphrodite and Hermes being pulled along in a chariot by Eros and Psyche.

Aphrodite 9

The goddess of **love and desire**, Aphrodite is said to have been born of the *aphros* (surf), and to have stepped ashore in Cyprus. She was married to **Hephaestus**, the smithy god, but had an affair with **Ares**, the god of war. She also played a part in initiating the **Trojan wars**: she promised the mortal **Paris** that she would make **Helen** fall in love with him if he judged that she, Aphrodite, was the most beautiful of the gods.

927

The Titans

The children of **Uranus** (the sky) and **Gaia** (the earth), the Titans ruled before the Olympians. Their leader Cronus came to power after he emasculated his father with a sickle. When in turn Cronus was deposed by his son Zeus, the Titans were imprisoned in **Tartarus** – the land beneath the Underworld.

Artemis 10

The twin sister of Apollo, Artemis was the goddess of the **Moon**, the **wilderness and wild animals**. She is usually depicted as a huntress, and her main attribute – in contrast to all the other gods – is **chastity**. When **Actaeon** accidentally saw Artemis and her nymphs bathing naked, she turned him into a stag and had her dogs tear him to pieces. She demanded virginity of her female companions. When one of them, the nymph **Callisto**, was seduced by Zeus, Artemis turned her into a bear. Zeus set Callisto among the stars – the constellation **Ursa Major**. Artemis was tricked by Apollo into killing **Orion**, her chaste lover. He too was immortalised in the heavens.

Hermes 7

Son of Zeus and the jocular **messenger** of the gods, Hermes is usually depicted with winged sandals and a messenger's staff. **Hermaphroditos** (his son by Aphrodite) became a kind of female boy after merging physically with the nymph **Salmacis**.

Athena 8

With an owl as her symbol, Athena is the goddess of **wisdom, war** and **crafts**. She also decides the fate of warriors in battle. She is said to have sprung fully armed from the head of Zeus after he devoured her pregnant mother, **Metis**. She rescued **Orestes** from the Furies, and helped **Odysseus** on his journey home from the Trojan war.

WARLIKE FIGURE The Parthenon in Athens is dedicated to Athena, who protected the city.

Other Greek gods 11

- **Ares** The god of war.
- **Demeter** The goddess of the harvest, she was sister of Zeus and mother of Persephone.
- **Dionysus** Son of Zeus, said to have invented wine.
- **Hephaestus** Craftsman and armourer of the gods.
- **Hestia** Goddess of the hearth and hospitality.
- **Pan** The god of pastures, usually depicted with horns and the legs of a goat.

QUESTION NUMBER

The numbers or star following the answers refer to information boxes on the right.

ANSWERS

Question	Answer
4	Pan (1)
22	Dionysus (9)
92	Nine (8)
139	D: In a tree (1) (5)
173	The Fates (1) (3)
179	The Graces (1) (2)
246	*Primavera* (painted for the Medicis in 1478) (2)
248	Canova (1757-1822) (2)
388	Satyrs (9)
407	Three (7)
440	John Keats – first published in 1818
★ 494	Odysseus
498	Erato (8)
499	The Harpies (6)
519	A: Comedy (8)
627	The Furies (1) (4)
700	Clio (8)
702	C: In water (1) (5)
749	Dionysus (9)
751	Dionysus (9)
908	Orestes (4)

Greek supernatural beings

Core facts (1)

◆ Greek mythology abounds in spirits and supernatural beings, many of whom seem to stand for some aspect of the **natural world**: trees, woods, mountains, winds, seasons, lakes, rivers.

◆ Other spirits represented **abstract features** of the moral universe: destiny, correct behaviour, conscience, retribution.

◆ Many Greek spirits were **part human**, or looked human. Perhaps this was intended to convey the complex, intertwined relationship between man, society and the environment.

The Graces (2)

Daughters of Zeus and Hera, the Graces are usually held to be part of the retinue of Aphrodite. There were three: **Aglaia**, 'the brilliant'; **Thalia**, 'she who brings flowers'; and **Euphrosyne**, 'she who cheers the heart'. They were good-natured divinities who delighted in dancing with nymphs and spread joy in the world. They are usually depicted holding hands.

SOURCE OF INSPIRATION This Renaissance depiction of the Three Graces comes from Botticelli's painting of Spring, *Primavera*.

The Fates (3)

Called the Moerae by the Greeks and the Parcae by the Romans, the three Fates represented the **destiny** of individual men and women. **Clotho**, the spinner, teased out the thread of each human life. **Lachesis** measured the thread and, by twisting it, oversaw the element of chance that accrued to each life. **Atropos**, armed with a pair of shears, snipped off the thread of life at the allotted time.

The Furies (4)

Called in Greek the **Erinyes**, 'the angry ones', the Furies were the **avengers** of the Greek world. Their function was to pursue and punish wrongdoers, and to a modern mind they seem to represent the torments of remorse and regret. They vented their terror on Orestes, who killed his mother, Clytemnestra, in revenge for the murder of his father. When Orestes was acquitted of this crime by Athena, the Furies' name was changed to the **Eumenides**, 'the soothed ones'.

★ 494

Siren call

The Sirens were **sea nymphs** who tempted sailors onto the rocks with their irresistible song. When **Odysseus** sailed near the Sirens, he ordered his crew to stop their ears with wax, and had himself tied to the mast so that he could hear the song without being lured away by it. The **Argonauts** were protected by the singing of Orpheus.

WATER NYMPH ⑤ Naiads are always represented as beautiful and beneficent.

Nature spirits

Naiads and **dryads** were female spirits of nature, or nymphs. Dryads looked after groves and forests and inhabited trees. Naiads were nymphs of freshwater places such as lakes, fountains, streams, rivers and wells. Other kinds of water nymphs included **nereids**, who inhabited the Mediterranean, and **oceanids**, who dwelt in the open sea. The life of dryads and naiads was deeply connected with their habitat: if a dryad's tree was cut down or a naiad's water source dried up, they would die.

Harpies ⑥

The Harpies were monsters with the head and breasts of a **woman**, and the body and sharp talons of a **bird of prey**. Originally wind spirits, they carried off babies and those wounded in battle to the Underworld. Their name means 'robbers' or 'snatchers'.

SCAVENGERS Gustave Doré's illustration of *The Harpies Wood* from Dante's *Inferno*.

The Muses ⑧

The Muses were the companions of Apollo. Traditionally there were nine of them, each one presiding over a different aspect of the arts. In modern times, they have come to be seen as the embodiment of the **creative impulse**.

Name	Role
Calliope	Muse of epic poetry and eloquence
Clio	Muse of history
Euterpe	Muse of flute-playing
Thalia	Muse of comedy
Melpomene	Muse of tragedy
Terpsichore	Muse of lyric poetry and dance
Erato	Muse of love poetry
Polyhymnia	Muse of mimic art
Urania	Muse of astronomy

The Horae ⑦

The Greeks had only three seasons, spring, summer and winter, and the Horae were the goddesses of the **seasons**. They were called **Thallo**, **Auxo** and **Carpo**, names which mean 'budding', 'growth' and 'ripening'. Later the Horae came to be seen as the goddesses who regulated society as well as nature. In this role they had other names: **Eunomia**, 'good order'; **Dike**, 'justice'; and **Irene**, 'peace'.

Satyrs ⑨

Part human and part beast, satyrs were the gods of **woods and mountains**. They had a man's body, but the legs and tail of a goat, and a set of budding horns. They were the companions of the wine god **Dionysus**, and they amused themselves by drinking, playing tricks on men, and pursuing the nubile nymphs of the forest.

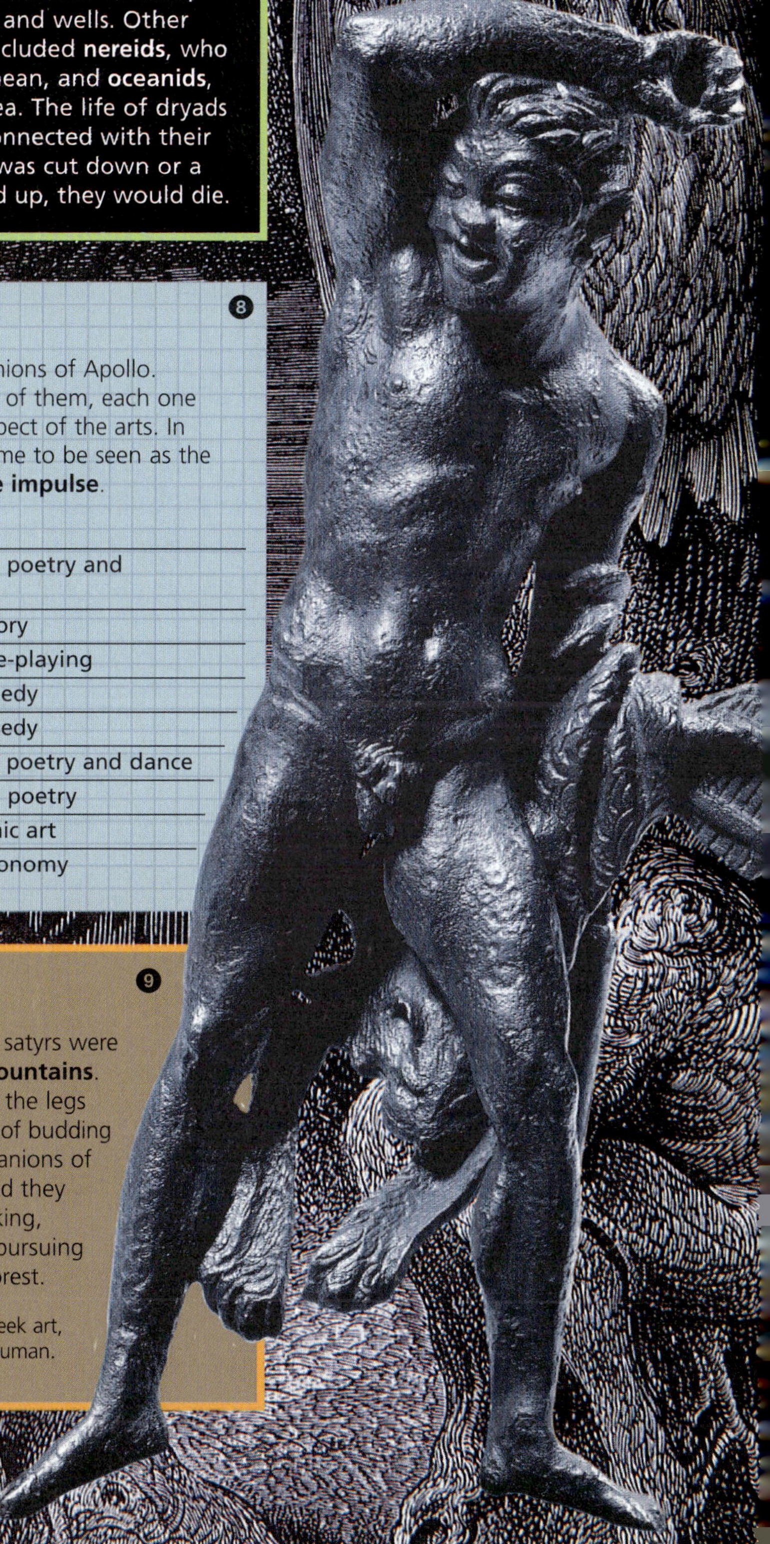

FORCE OF NATURE In later Greek art, satyrs were depicted as mainly human.

Between gods and men

QUESTION NUMBER

The numbers or star following the answers refer to information boxes on the right.

ANSWERS

QUESTION NUMBER	ANSWERS
100	12 ❷ ❸
135	**B: As a cuckoo** ❻
171	**Achilles** ❾
174	**To bring Cerberus up from the Underworld** ❷
180	**Sisyphus** ❽
205	**Mount Caucasus** ❹
258	**B: The concept of destiny** ❶
374	**Prometheus** ❹
391	**D: Hercules** ❷
491	**Heracles** ❷ ❸ ❻
492	**Helios** ❺
★ 500	**Tartarus**
549	**Europa** ❻ ❼
555	**Phaethon** ❺
563	**Hercules** ❷
591	**A swan** ❻
626	**A shower of gold** (their child was Perseus) ❻
865	**Castor** (they were children of Zeus and Leda) ❻

Core facts ❶

◆ The gods of **Greek mythology** were not distant, unknowable deities. Though they lived on Olympus, they moved in the same world as mortals, and frequently fell in love with them, feuded with them or did favours for them.

◆ In the Greek mind both gods and men were subject to **Moros**, a dark and overarching **Destiny**. None of the gods, not even Zeus, was all-powerful.

◆ Greek mythology is about the interaction between gods and humans. The tales are gripping – full of love, murder, deception, revenge, desire, sorrow and comedy. This is why they are still recounted today.

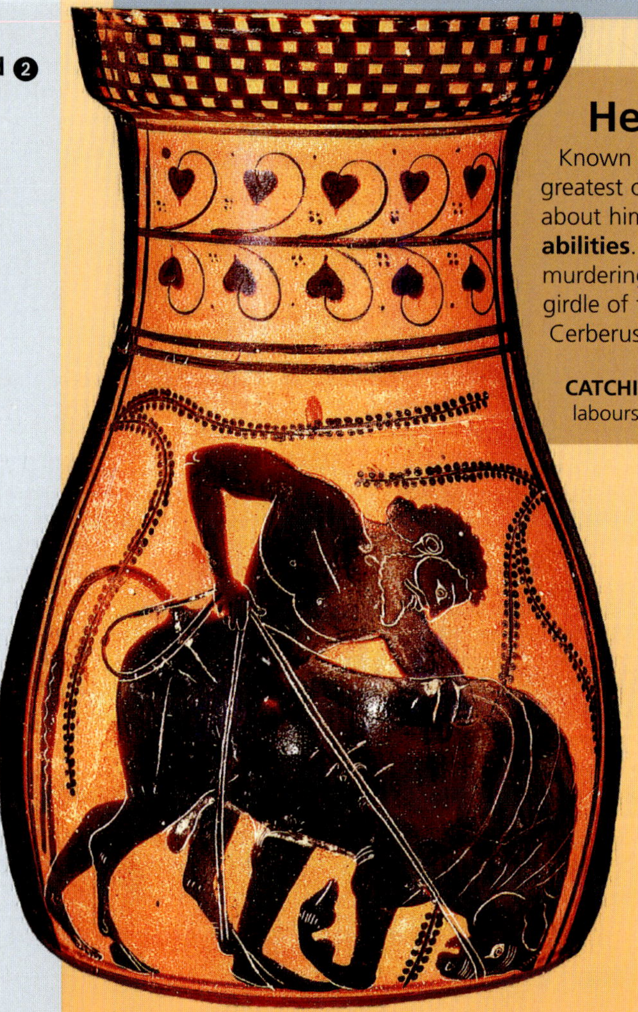

Heracles ❷

Known to the Romans as **Hercules**, Heracles is the greatest of the Greek heroes. Hundreds of tales were told about him, mostly concerning his **superhuman physical abilities**. His **'12 labours'** were in repentance for murdering his own family. They included stealing the girdle of the Amazon queen Hippolyte and subduing Cerberus, the dog at the gates of the Underworld.

CATCHING THE CRETAN BULL In the seventh of his '12 labours' Heracles used a lasso to capture a savage bull.

Tie-breaker ❸

Q Heracles is often depicted wearing the skin of which animal?

A A lion. He slew the Nemean lion as the first of his '12 labours'. It could not be harmed with arrows, so he killed it with his bare hands and wore its pelt as a trophy.

Prometheus ❹

The **creation of mankind** is credited to Prometheus. He fashioned clay models of the gods, which so charmed Athena that she breathed life into them. Prometheus wanted to give his creations all knowledge, but Zeus forbade it. Prometheus defied Zeus: he stole a spark of fire from the smithy of Hephaestus and brought it to humanity. Zeus was so enraged that he had Prometheus **pegged to a rock** on Mount Caucasus, where every day a vulture would come to peck out his liver.

ETERNAL TORTURE A vulture eats the liver of Prometheus.

★ 500 Tartarus

Zeus imprisoned most of the Titans in a a dark, sunless place called Tartarus. This was the **lowest region of the world**, far beneath even the Underworld. According to the poet Hesiod, a bronze anvil falling from Earth would take nine days and nights to reach Tartarus.

Phaethon

5

Over-ambition summarises the story of Phaethon. He was the son of **Helios**, the divine charioteer whose horses drew the Sun across the heavens each day. Phaethon begged his father to be allowed to drive the chariot. Helios relented, but Phaethon could not control the horses and the chariot ran amok. It came so close to the Earth that it dried up the rivers and scorched the land. To avert disaster Zeus struck Phaethon dead with a **thunderbolt**.

HIGH FLYER Phaethon wanted to drive his father's chariot of the Sun but his dreams were beyond his capabilities.

Zeus

6

Zeus assumed many different forms to seduce the women he desired.

Woman	Zeus's form
Leda	Swan
Europa	Bull
Hera	Cuckoo
Aegina	Eagle
Niobe	Cloud
Alcmena	Her husband Amphitryon
Dia	Horse
Danaë	Shower of gold

Europa

7

Zeus took a liking to this **Phoenician princess**. He disguised himself as a **bull** and came to the place where Europa and her handmaidens were picking flowers. The bull seemed so tame that the young women garlanded it with flowers, and Europa even dared climb on its back. At this, Zeus plunged into the sea, taking Europa with him. He carried her to the island of **Crete**, where he ravished her. She later married the king of Crete and bore him a son who became **King Minos**.

Sisyphus

8

This **cruel and devious** king of Thessaly won his kingdom by cheating his brother. Once Sisyphus tried to dupe Zeus himself and was sentenced to death by the god – but the wily Sisyphus managed to fool Hades into releasing him from the Underworld. Eventually Hermes, the god of trickery, dragged him off to the Underworld where he was forced to toil at **rolling a boulder up a hill** for all eternity.

WEIRD AND WONDERFUL

9

The nymph **Thetis** was told that her son would be greater than his father. This made the gods afraid to woo her, and they married her off to a mortal, Peleus. She did indeed bear a great son: the warrior **Achilles**.

SWEPT OFF HER FEET Pierre Gobert's depiction of Europa being carried off by Jupiter (the Roman name for Zeus) in the guise of a bull.

QUESTION NUMBER

The numbers or star following the answers refer to information boxes on the right.

ANSWERS

- **101** Jason 2
- **107** Hector 8
- **239** Paris ★ 8
- **474** Odysseus 6
- **482** The *Argo* 2
- **497** Heinrich Schliemann (1822-90) ★
- **531** Heel 8
- **541** Helen ★
- **561** Jason 2
- **565** Achilles 8
- **599** Icarus 7
- **663** The Golden Fleece 2
- **668** Midas – legendary king of Phrygia, in modern Turkey
- **863** Medea 2
- **868** Adonis 9
- **903** Jocasta 3
- ★ **909** Menelaus
- **919** Georgia 2
- **934** Oedipus 3
- **966** Troy ★
- **995** Ariadne 4
- **1000** Ilium ★

Mortal Greek heroes

Core facts 1

◆ The Greeks honoured a whole range of mythical heroes. Some of them were related to the gods, but most were **ordinary men**, albeit of aristocratic or royal lineage.

◆ Often the stories are **tragic**. Despite their admirable qualities, the heroes succumb to an unhappy, preordained fate.

◆ Both the Greeks and the Romans liked to claim descent from the heroes. **Aeneas**, a hero of the **Trojan war**, was said to have led a band of men to Italy where they founded the state that later became Rome. This claim of kinship suggests that the cult of the hero is connected to the **veneration of ancestors**.

Jason and the Argonauts 2

As the nephew of Pelias, king of Thessaly, Jason was due to receive part of the kingdom when he reached manhood. However, Jason's uncle refused to grant him his share unless he acquired the **Golden Fleece** from the kingdom of Colchis. Jason built a boat, the *Argo*, and gathered a crew of 50 heroes including Heracles. They sailed to Colchis where the sorceress **Medea** (daughter of the king of Colchis) helped them to steal the fleece from the dragon who was guarding it.

Oedipus 3

Laius, king of Thebes, had been warned by an **oracle** that his son would kill him. So when his son Oedipus was born Laius abandoned him in a wood. But the child was adopted by Polybus, king of Corinth, and brought up as his own. Years later, on hearing a **prophecy** that he would **kill his father and marry his mother**, Oedipus left Corinth. On the road he killed a stranger who turned out to be his true father, Laius. Later in Thebes Oedipus wed the queen Jocasta (his mother). When he realised what he had done, Oedipus **put out his eyes**.

INESCAPABLE FATE When Oedipus killed the Sphinx he won the hand of the queen of Thebes – his mother.

Theseus 4

Every year Athens had to send seven women and seven men to King Minos of Crete. There they were thrown to the **Minotaur** in the **Labyrinth**. Theseus, prince of Athens, resolved to join the hostages and kill the Minotaur. He was helped by **Ariadne**, daughter of Minos, who fell in love with him. She gave him a ball of string so that he could find his way out after slaying the monster.

BULL FIGHT Theseus struggles with the Minotaur – a half-man, half-bull monster that lived in the Labyrinth at Knossos in Crete.

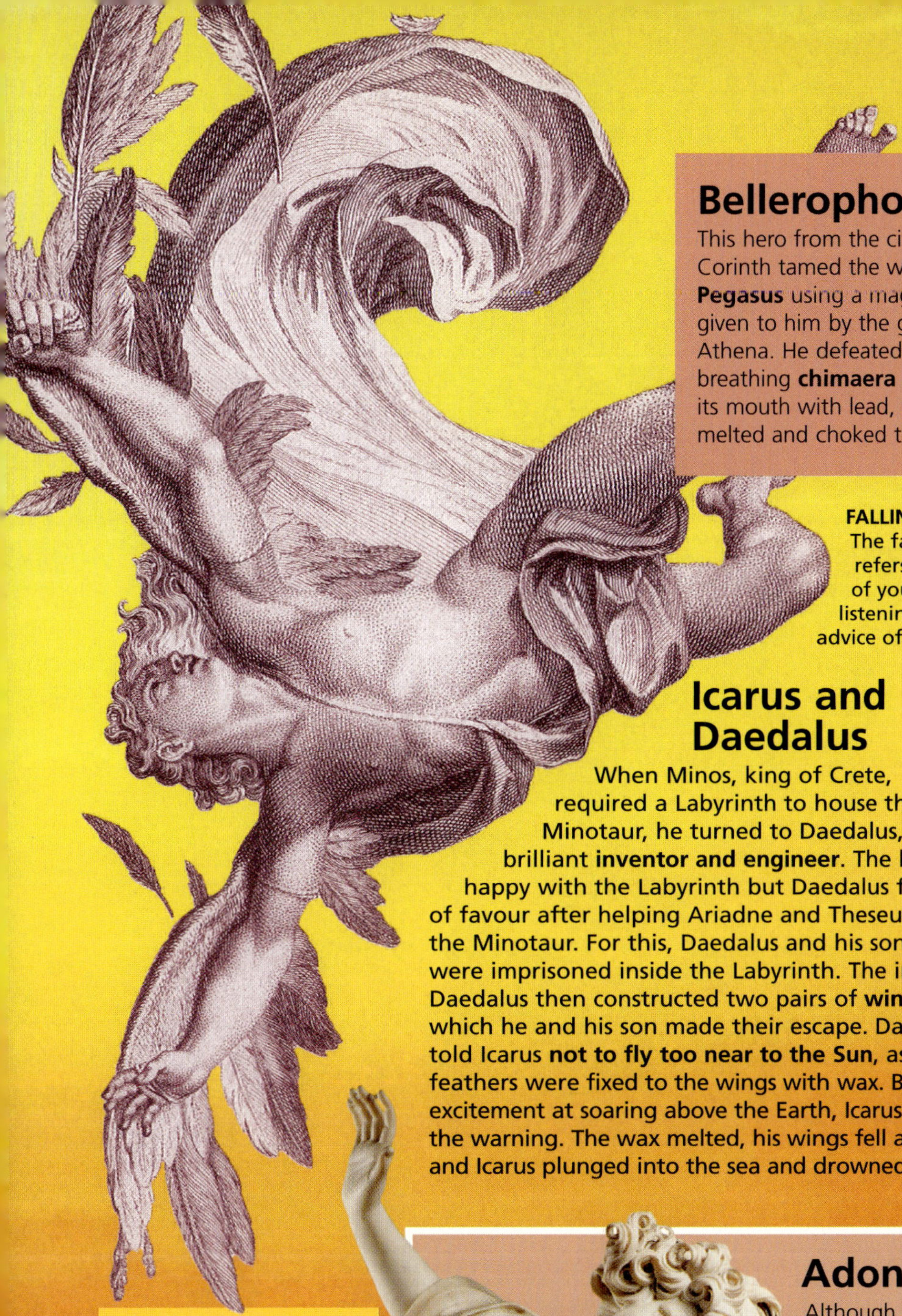

Bellerophon 5

This hero from the city of Corinth tamed the winged horse **Pegasus** using a magic bridle given to him by the goddess Athena. He defeated the fire-breathing **chimaera** by stuffing its mouth with lead, which melted and choked the monster.

FALLING TO EARTH The fall of Icarus refers to the folly of youth and of not listening to the advice of one's elders.

Icarus and Daedalus 7

When Minos, king of Crete, required a Labyrinth to house the Minotaur, he turned to Daedalus, a brilliant **inventor and engineer**. The king was happy with the Labyrinth but Daedalus fell out of favour after helping Ariadne and Theseus to kill the Minotaur. For this, Daedalus and his son Icarus were imprisoned inside the Labyrinth. The ingenious Daedalus then constructed two pairs of **wings** with which he and his son made their escape. Daedalus told Icarus **not to fly too near to the Sun**, as the feathers were fixed to the wings with wax. But in his excitement at soaring above the Earth, Icarus forgot the warning. The wax melted, his wings fell apart, and Icarus plunged into the sea and drowned.

Odysseus 6

Famous for his cunning, Odysseus was a leader in the Greek expedition against Troy. The **wooden horse** was his idea, but the gods blamed him for the slaughter of the Trojans and for the rape of **Cassandra**, a soothsayer. The gods decreed that he should wander for ten years. When he came home, he found a competition in progress for the hand of his wife **Penelope**: whoever could bend and string Odysseus' bow would marry her. Disguised as a beggar, Odysseus won the competition himself.

A CUNNING PLAN Many stories tell of Odysseus using his brains to get out of trouble. On one occasion he escapes a Cyclops by riding underneath a ram.

Achilles 8

As a baby Achilles was dipped in the river Styx by his mother, which made him impervious to harm – except for the **heel** by which she held him. He grew into a formidable warrior and when his friend **Patroclus** was killed by the Trojan **Hector**, Achilles sought revenge. He killed Hector in battle, but his own days were numbered. He was killed when **Paris** shot a poisoned arrow into his one weak spot – his heel.

Adonis 9

Although **Aphrodite** had many lovers, the **beautiful** Adonis was her favourite. The goddess adored him but was alarmed by his dangerous passion for hunting. Sure enough Adonis was one day killed by a **wild boar**. The grieving Aphrodite managed to secure his release from Hades for half the year. The story of Adonis symbolises the annual cycle of agriculture. He is said to have been born of a **myrtle tree**, and his cult derives from the Phoenicians.

BEAUTIFUL BOY Giuseppe Mazzuoli's marble statue shows Adonis about to be gored by a wild boar.

909 ★

Trojan War

In legend, the long, bitter war between the Greeks and the Trojans began when **Paris**, a Trojan prince, wooed the Greek queen **Helen** away from her husband **Menelaus**. The Greeks gathered a great force and set out to win her back. This is why Helen is called 'the face that launched a thousand ships'. The Greeks won the war after gaining access to the city of Troy via the **wooden horse**.

Greek monsters

QUESTION NUMBER

The numbers or star following the answers refer to information boxes on the right.

ANSWERS

- **2** A dog 3
- **9** ★ A bull
- **93** 100 5
- **103** The Hydra 8
- **106** They turned to stone 6
- **110** Daedalus ★
- **163** The peacock 5
- **176** Polyphemus 2
- **208** Mount Etna 8
- **252** D: Snakes 6
- **352** Invisibility 2
- **404** One 2
- **464** Orpheus 3
- **483** Scylla and Charybdis 7
- **496** Three 6
- **567** Perseus 6
- **703** B: Medusa 6
- **707** C: Metalworkers 2
- **723** The Sphinx 8
- **836** A snake 8
- **947** Andromeda 6

Core facts 1

◆ The monsters of Greek mythology are numerous and varied. Some are the **offspring of strange unions**; others are **accursed humans or nymphs**; others still are **avenging emissaries** of the gods.

◆ Monsters often figure in the stories of heroes, who set out to subdue or slay them.

◆ Some monsters may be **allegorical representations** of aspects of human nature. The Minotaur in its Labyrinth, for example, could appear to the modern mind to be an image of the subconscious with its violent urges.

◆ Others may be personifications of **natural phenomena** that people could not explain.

Cyclopes 2

This race of **one-eyed giants** had two distinct generations.

The older Cyclopes were **metalworkers**; they forged Zeus's thunderbolts, Poseidon's trident and Hades' helmet of invisibility. They were the allies of Zeus in the battle of the Titans

The second generation were a lawless **band of shepherds** living in Sicily. The best known was the man-eating Polyphemus, who captured Odysseus and his crew and held them in his cave. Odysseus escaped by getting the giant drunk and putting out his single eye with a sharpened stake.

MAN-EATER Polyphemus was blinded by Odysseus after eating some of his crew. This head, found in Italy, dates from c.150 BC.

Cerberus 3

The ancient Greeks believed that after a person died, his or her spirit went to the Underworld, the Kingdom of Hades. Cerberus was a **three-headed dog** that guarded the gates of Hades, allowing souls to enter, but none to leave. **Orpheus** passed Cerberus by lulling him to sleep with his lyre. **Heracles** mastered the monster by strangling it half to death, and then dragging it by the scruff of its neck to the upper world.

The chimera 4

A fire-breathing she-monster, the chimera had the head of a **lion**, the body of a **goat** and the tail of a **dragon**. She wreaked havoc in Lycia (in modern Turkey), destroying people and animals until killed by **Bellerophon** mounted on the winged horse **Pegasus**. The chimera may have been a personification of a **storm cloud** or a geological feature such as a **natural-gas fissure**.

COMPOSITE MONSTER The chimera had the strength of three beasts. This Etruscan bronze dates from the 5th century BC.

Argus Panoptes

Argus was a giant who served Hera. He was called Panoptes, 'all-seeing', because he had **100 eyes**, and only some closed when he slept, making him a fine watchman. He was asked by Hera to watch Io, a mortal woman whom Zeus had seduced and then turned into a heifer in order to hide his affair from Hera. She had guessed and taken the heifer into her care. Zeus would not be turned from his plan, however, and sent the trickster **Hermes** to rescue Io. Hermes lulled Argus to sleep with his flute and then beheaded him.

LIVING MEMORIAL In honour of her faithful servant Argus, Hera scattered his 100 eyes on the tail of her favourite bird, the peacock, as depicted in this 17th-century painting by Peter Paul Rubens.

Turning all to stone

Medusa was one of the three **Gorgons**, female monsters who had heads of living snakes instead of hair. Anyone who looked directly at Medusa would be instantly turned to stone. **Perseus** made it his task to kill her. In Medusa's lair, Perseus struck at Medusa while looking at her reflection in the polished surface of his shield. He severed her head with one blow and stowed it inside a sack. On arriving home, Perseus found his mother plagued by the unwanted attentions of Polydectes, king of Seriphos. Perseus disposed of him by holding up the head of Medusa; Polydectes looked at it, and was turned to stone.

The Minotaur

In his struggles for the throne of Crete, **King Minos** asked the god Poseidon to send him a **white bull**, which he would sacrifice in the god's honour. Poseidon complied, but the animal was so beautiful that Minos kept it. This angered Poseidon, who made Minos's wife Pasipha fall in love with the bull.

Pasipha's passion was such that she had Daedalus construct a wooden cow that she could climb inside and so make love to the white bull. This bizarre plan worked, but the offspring of the union was the Minotaur. This bull-headed creature wrought such havoc on Crete that Daedalus was asked to make a **Labyrinth** in which it could be imprisoned.

Scylla and Charybdis

These two monsters guarded the Strait of Messina between Sicily and the Italian mainland. Charybdis was a sea nymph who angered Zeus and was condemned to live in a cave, **sucking water in and out**. This is the mythic explanation of the rushing tides in the narrow strait. Charybdis was also described as a **whirlpool**. Scylla was a nymph who inhabited a rock in the strait. She was transformed into a **sea monster** by the sorceress Circe, who was her love-rival. Scylla and Charybdis were mortal dangers to sailors: if sailors avoided one, they were almost bound to fall into the clutches of the other.

Some other monsters

◆ **Echidna** Half woman and half serpent, she was the wife of Typhon, and mother of Cerberus and the Hydra. She was slain by the giant Argus.
◆ **Geryon** A man with three heads, three bodies, six arms and six legs. He was defeated by Heracles.
◆ **Hydra** A many-headed dragon. If one head was lopped off, two grew in its place. Heracles fought the monster.
◆ **Python** A huge serpent that was slain by Apollo.
◆ **Sphinx** A creature with a woman's head, a lion's body, and wings. The Sphinx chanted a riddle and killed anyone who tried and failed to give the answer. Only Oedipus solved the riddle.
◆ **Typhon** A 100-headed monster who fought Zeus and was imprisoned inside Mount Etna.

QUESTION NUMBER

The numbers or star following the answers refer to information boxes on the right.

ANSWERS

99	30 ❺
102	Janus ❹
104	Mercury (from Latin mercator, a merchant) ❽
108	Romulus and Remus ❸
155	Romulus ❸
162	A wolf ❸
217	Geniuses ❻
364	The Tiber ❸
412	Mars ❶ ❽
423	Mercury ❽
429	Vesta ❺
437	The Roman state ❷
★ 542	Augustus
616	Vespasian ★
638	B: Dido ❷
648	Jupiter ❶ ❽
754	Venus ❽
757	Diana – goddess of hunting, chastity, the Moon
821	A: Neptune ❽
892	Juno (goddess of women, marriage and childbirth) ❽
960	Minerva (goddess of wisdom and war) ❽
981	Venus (goddess of love and beauty) ❽

Roman mythology

Core facts ❶

◆ Much of the mythology of Rome came from Greece. The **Greek gods** merged with **local gods**, which often kept their Roman names.

◆ There are also some native Roman myths and gods that owe nothing to the Greeks. Some of these are genuine homegrown tales. Others, such as the story of **Aeneas**, seem to have been manufactured in order to lend legitimacy to the state of Rome.

◆ The Romans' warlike preoccupations led them to regard certain gods more highly than the Greeks did. For example, **Mars**, the god of war, was second only to **Jupiter** (Zeus) in the Roman pantheon.

The story of Aeneas ❷

The Romans were aware that they lacked a national epic to compare with the stories of the Greek heroes. At the request of **Emperor Augustus**, the poet **Virgil** wrote a long poem, the ***Aeneid***, which endowed the new Roman empire with a venerable past. Virgil made use of a longstanding tradition that the Romans were descended from Aeneas, a Trojan veteran of the war with the Greeks. The story goes that Aeneas was told in a vision to found a **new Troy**. After many adventures he came to the River Tiber and settled there.

FATAL FAREWELL On his travels Aeneas had a love affair with Dido, queen of Carthage. When Jupiter prompted Aeneas to sail on, the lovelorn Dido killed herself.

Romulus and Remus ❸

Twin offspring of a **Vestal Virgin** who was raped by the god **Mars**, Romulus and Remus did not have a great start in life. Their uncle, king of Alba Longa, wanted them killed so there would be no pretenders to the throne. But the king's servants merely cast the twins on the River Tiber in a cradle, which came to rest on a mudbank. Mars sent a **she-wolf** to suckle them, and so they survived. As adults, they set about founding **Rome**, but they quarrelled over the plans and Romulus ended up killing his brother.

RAISED BY A SHE-WOLF It is appropriate that Mars sent a she-wolf to suckle Romulus and Remus since the wolf is the god's sacred animal.

Janus

4

This purely Roman god has no equivalent in the Greek pantheon. The Romans associated him with **new beginnings** and **thresholds** of all kinds. Janus was invoked at New Year – January is named after him – and his image is found on city gates, doorways and bridges. He was regarded as the **guardian** of Rome during times of war, when the doors to his temple were kept open; in times of peace they were closed.

VIGILANT JANUS Depicted looking fore and aft, Janus was a watchful guardian of Rome.

Vestal Virgins

5

The Vestal Virgins were the priestesses of **Vesta**, the goddess of hearth and home, and special protectress of Rome. Her priestesses took a vow of absolute **chastity**, which they broke on pain of death. The Vestals were selected at the age of six from Rome's most powerful families, and they served the cult of Vesta for 30 years, after which they were allowed to marry. They enjoyed high prestige in Rome, granting pardons and favours. However, unchaste Vestals were buried alive.

SAFE HOUSE The Vestal Virgins lived in the House of the Vestals in the Forum in Rome. Wills were deposited with them for safekeeping.

WEIRD AND WONDERFUL

6

In Roman mythology the **Genius** was the god of groups or locations. Every town, district and street had its separate genius. Emperors set up cults of their own personal genius – which led to the modern sense of the word.

★ 542 ★

Deification of Caesars

The Romans were always happy to accommodate new gods. They welcomed the gods of defeated peoples into their pantheon, and came to see deification of the emperors as a natural extension of the honours afforded them in life. The Roman senate declared **Julius Caesar** a god posthumously. **Augustus**, the first Roman emperor, was deified less than a month after his death.

One god, two names

8

Greek	Roman
Zeus	Jupiter
Hera	Juno
Poseidon	Neptune
Ares	Mars
Aphrodite	Venus
Hermes	Mercury
Dionysus	Bacchus
Athena	Minerva

Vulcan

7

The powers of this ancient Italian god waned over the years. He was a god of thunderbolts until that role was taken over by Jupiter; he was associated with the Sun until usurped by Apollo; and he played the role of a war god until this function was assumed by Mars. Vulcan eventually became a **smithy god**, like the Greek Hephaestus. His fiery forges were believed to be underground – and so he gave his name to the natural phenomenon of **volcanoes**.

Tie-breaker

9

Q In Roman mythology, what are Lemures and Larvae?

A The mischievous ghosts of the dead, which were thought to return to the Earth and torment the living. They were regularly exorcised by the head of the household in a ceremony known as Lemuria.

Norse and German myths

QUESTION NUMBER

The numbers or star following the answers refer to information boxes on the right.

ANSWERS

17	Thor ❶ ❸
63	A: A Norse epic ❹
86	False ❶ ❽
137	A: A rainbow ❻
232	The Valkyries ❼
234	Odin, or Woden ❶ ❷ ❼
250	Iceland ❹
392	B: A berserker (specially dedicated to Odin) ❷
478	Odin, or Woden ❷ ❽
480	Frigg ❽
568	Thor ❶ ❸
609	Hel ❽
630	Winged horses ❼
631	B: Asgard ★ ❶ ❻
★ 708	C: An ash ❷
759	Odin ❷ ❽
772	Mistletoe ❽
778	A hammer ❸
928	Wagner's *Ring* cycle ❺
982	Loki ❽

Core facts ❶

◆ The Norse gods dwelt in **Asgard**, a kind of fortified Olympus, where they fought and loved and tricked each other.

◆ Norse gods were warlike, inquisitive and strangely mortal: all were destined to die at **Ragnarok**, the battle at the end of the world.

◆ The Vikings of Scandinavia and the Germanic tribes of northern Europe shared many myths. However, the names of gods differed slightly: **Odin** in Scandinavia was **Woden** to the Germanic peoples; **Thor** was **Donnar**; and **Tyr** was **Tiuz**.

Odin ❷

Chief deity of the **Norse pantheon,** Odin is the god of wind, war, magic and poetry. Also known as Woden or Wotan, he is the father of all who are slain in battle. It was believed that he gathered fallen warriors to fight for him at Ragnarok, the great celestial conflict at the end of the world. Odin is also a magician god, always hungry for mystical knowledge. He has only one eye, because he traded the other for a drink from a well that conferred wisdom. He is also said to have hung for nine days and nights from **Yggdrasil,** the world tree, in return for hidden knowledge. He is said to have discovered **runes** – an early alphabet and method of divination.

GODS OF THE LAND The Nordic gods fought many battles with frost giants – perhaps a reflection of the frozen northern landscape (background).

Thor ❸

Son of Odin, and the second god in the Norse pantheon, Thor is the god of **thunder**. He carries a magic hammer called **Mjollnir**, representing lightning, and wears a belt, **Meginjardir**, to double his strength. Storms were said to occur when Thor rode his chariot through the heavens. At Ragnarok, Thor will be drowned in a sea of venom produced by the world serpent **Jormungand**.

SUPERHERO As depicted in a Superman comic, Thor carries a magic hammer, which returns to him after being thrown.

4

The *Edda*

Most of what we know about the legends of the **Norse** peoples is contained in two collections of Icelandic writings called the *Edda*. The ***Poetic Edda*** contains poems that were handed down by oral tradition. The ***Prose Edda***, written by **Snorri Sturluson**, consists of poetry and prose.

POETIC LICENCE As well as mythological tales, Snorri Sturluson's *Edda* contains a genealogy and a guide to writing poetry.

5

Ragnarok

The great **apocalypse** of Norse mythology is said to happen at the Battle of Ragnarok. In this future time all the gods are destroyed in a **final clash of arms** and a new green world emerges from the wreckage. The term literally means 'destruction of the powers', but is usually translated as **'twilight of the Gods'** – a term popularised by **Wagner**'s operas on themes from Germanic mythology.

FREYA A goddess of love, wealth, fertility, battle and death. Friday takes its name from her.

6

WEIRD AND WONDERFUL

To the Norse people, the rainbow was a bridge called **Bifrost** between Asgard and the world of men. The different colours of the rainbow are reflections of precious stones in the bridge. **Heimdall** is the keeper of the bridge.

8

Other Norse gods

- **Tyr** The son of Odin and Frigg, and a god of war.
- **Frey** The gentlest of the Norse gods, Frey is the lord of summer sunshine and of Alfheim, the elf realm.
- **Freya** Twin sister of Frey and goddess of love. She is partly merged with the figure of Frigg.
- **Frigg** The wife of Odin and the goddess of motherhood, love and fertility.
- **Balder** Son of Odin, Balder represents joy, goodness and wisdom. He was killed by a spear made of mistletoe, the only thing that could harm him.
- **Loki** A trickster god, Loki was a one-time companion of Thor who turned increasingly to evil and engineered the accidental death of Balder.
- **Hel** The goddess of the Underworld. Her subjects were those who had the misfortune to die in old age rather than in battle.

7

The Valkyries

The Valkyries are **beautiful maidens**, servants of **Odin**, who are sent into battle to select who will be killed and so recruited into Odin's celestial army. Their name means **'choosers of the slain'**. In **Valhalla**, the great heavenly feasting hall that is the Norse paradise, the Valkyries' job is to wait on the warriors with ale and mead served up in the skulls of the vanquished.

RIDE OF THE VALKYRIES The light reflected from the Valkyries' shields as they traversed the sky was said to produce the Aurora Borealis.

★ 708

Yggdrasil – the world tree

The cosmic **ash tree** supports the nine worlds of Norse mythology in its branches. Its three great roots descend into **Jotunheim**, the land of the giants; the foggy world of **Niflheim**; and **Asgard**, stronghold of the gods. After the Battle of Ragnarok, Yggdrasil will be the source of new life.

QUESTION NUMBER

The numbers or star following the answers refer to information boxes on the right.

ANSWERS

- **43** **St Brendan the Navigator** ❺
- **54** **One** ❺
- **76** **The Salmon of Knowledge** ❷
- **85** **False** (he is the Hound of Cullan) ❸
- **116** **Finn MacCool** ❷
- ★ **125** **Geraint** ❹
- **206** **Ireland** (in legend, made by Finn MacCool) ❷
- **235** **Mebd of Connacht** (or Maeve) ❸ ❺
- **256** **B: A royal bodyguard** ❷
- **303** **Wales** ❹
- **439** **Oisin** ❷ ❺
- **444** **Cernunnos** – Celtic deity, the lord of wild things
- **601** **A banshee** ❺
- **741** **'Isle of Apples'** ❺
- **801** **The Blarney Stone** – at Blarney Castle, Co. Cork
- **820** **Morrigan** ❺
- **880** **Celtic cross** – with a circle round the centre
- **938** **Prince of Dyfed** ❹
- **965** **The Tower of London** (features in the *Mabinogion*) ❹

Celtic myths

Core facts ❶

◆ The Celts once occupied a territory that covered Britain, most of France and Spain, and even parts of Greece and Turkey. They were forced out of England by the Saxons, but their culture lived on in **Wales** and **Ireland**.
◆ The myths of Ireland were recorded by early **Christian monks**. They were not seen as pagan stories but as entertainments, and as such were not suppressed by the Church.
◆ Welsh myths, on the other hand, were not written down until well into the Middle Ages, so are overlaid with Christian morality and imagery – beneath which the original **pagan meanings** are faintly discernible.

Finn MacCool ❷

The high king of Ireland had an elite bodyguard called the **Fianna**, led by Finn MacCool (in Gaelic, **Fionn MacCumhaill**). As a boy, Finn went to learn poetry from **Finegas**, a bard and a seer. One day Finegas caught the fabled **Salmon of Knowledge** which, if eaten, conferred wisdom on the eater. Finegas asked Finn to cook the fish on a spit. Finn did so, but he burnt his thumb on the hot flesh of the salmon. He instinctively put his thumb in his mouth and became the first person to taste the fish, so gaining an insight into all things. Some stories claim that Finn did not die, but sleeps until Ireland needs him – like **King Arthur** in Britain.

Cuchullain ❸

Pronounced *koo-koo-lin*, the name of this Irish hero means **'the Hound of Cullan'**. He earned his name when he accidentally killed the dog of Cullan the smith and offered to take the dog's place as penance. Cuchullain single-handedly defended **Ulster** against **Medb**, the queen of Connacht. He was a ferocious fighter, his hair standing on end and emitting sparks. To stop his battle frenzy he had to be plunged in three vats of cold water.

TO THE DEATH Fatally wounded, Cuchullain fought to his very last breath, depicted here by 20th-century artist John Yunge-Bateman.

The Mabinogion ❹

A 19th-century translation of the 14th-century ***Red Book of Hergest***, the *Mabinogion* consists of four epics from Welsh mythology. The stories have pagan undertones. The first, for example, tells of **Pwyll**, prince of Dyfed, who changes places with **Arawn**, king of the underworld. In this guise he kills Arawn's enemies and Arawn thanks him. On his way home Pwyll meets **Rhiannon**, who is betrothed to **Gwawl**. Pwyll tricks Gwawl into relinquishing Rhiannon. This story may symbolise the struggle between winter (Pwyll) and summer (Gwawl) for the possession of spring (Rhiannon).

Celtic legendary characters

- **Balor** A one-eyed giant, the Cyclops of Irish mythology. His glance was deadly. He was killed by Lugh, the Sun god, who put out his eye with a slingshot.
- **Leprechaun** A mischievous Irish fairy, often believed to be in possession of a treasure horde.
- **Banshees** Fairies of the Irish countryside. It was believed that their wailing foretold a death.
- **Brendan the Navigator** A Christian saint who founded the monastery of Clonfert in County Galway in AD 561. A 10th-century text, *Brendan's Voyage*, tells how he set sail on a wondrous journey in search of the 'Land of Promise'.
- **Medb (Maeve)** A fierce warrior goddess and queen of Connacht, who led her people against Cuchullain and the forces of Ulster.
- **Morgan le Fay** Celtic sorceress, half-sister of King Arthur and queen of Avalon (the Isle of Apples) where Arthur rests.
- **Morrigan** The Irish goddess of death in battle. She often assumed the shape of a crow or raven.
- **Oisin** The son of Finn MacCool and the greatest poet in all Ireland.

BRENDAN THE NAVIGATOR This illustration from a 13th-century manuscript shows St Brendan and his monks as they come across a whale.

ISLAND SCRIBES A stone cross on the island of Skellig Michael off County Kerry marks the site of an early Christian settlement. In remote outposts such as this monks wrote down and preserved their country's myths and legends.

125

After King Arthur

The *Red Book of Hergest* contains stories that read like spin-offs from the Arthurian legends. One of these concerns **Kulwych** (pronounced *Keelhook*), a cousin of King Arthur who cannot marry his beloved **Olwen** until he procures 13 treasures. Each treasure involves him in a perilous quest – not unlike the labours of Heracles. In another tale **Geraint**, a round table knight, suspects his wife **Enid** of infidelity, and takes her on a gruelling journey to test her love.

WEIRD AND WONDERFUL

A potent symbol in Celtic mythology was the **cauldron of plenty**. It was owned by **Dagda**, the Irish father god who was associated with magic and abundance. His massive cauldron was inexhaustible and from it he fed the entire Earth.

QUESTION NUMBER

The numbers or star following the answers refer to information boxes on the right.

ANSWERS

Question	Answer
31	*Monty Python and the Holy Grail* – 1975
160	Merlin (10)
★ 199	The Holy Grail
277	Arthur – published in 1958
297	Lancelot (1) (7)
326	C: Chrétien de Troyes (1) (7)
343	Roxy Music – lead singer Bryan Ferry
362	Tintagel (1) (5)
424	*Camelot* – with Vanessa Redgrave as Guinevere
434	Geoffrey of Monmouth (1)
454	Camelot (1)
566	Lancelot (1) (7)
575	Merlin (2) (6) (10)
605	Mordred (9)
685	Winchester (4)
771	Excalibur (2) (6) (9)
789	Harrison Birtwistle – first performed 1991
824	D: Mark Twain – published 1889
858	Sir Gawain (8)
921	Knights of the Round Table ★ (4) (7) (8)
932	Uther Pendragon (2)
952	Galahad ★

King Arthur

Core facts (1)

◆ The legends of Arthur as we know them are the result of centuries of retelling. They have their roots in ancient Celtic stories.

◆ In the 12th century, **Geoffrey of Monmouth** depicted Arthur as a British leader in the battles against the Saxons, and gave an account of his youth, reign, marriage and death.

◆ A few years later the French writer **Chrétien de Troyes** introduced Lancelot and his love for Guinevere to the legend. In 1485 **Sir Thomas Malory** wrote *Le Morte d'Arthur* with its tales of Christian knights and chivalric values.

◆ All agree that Arthur was born at **Tintagel**, ruled at **Camelot**, and is buried at **Avalon**.

The sword in the stone (2)

Arthur was the illegitimate son of **King Uther Pendragon**. He was raised away from the court and ignorant of his parentage. After Uther's death, **Merlin** told the knights of the round table that the next king would be the man who could draw the sword from a stone in London. Many tried, but none could move it. One day the young Arthur, working as a page for an older knight, was sent to fetch a new sword for his master. He saw the sword embedded in the stone, and drew it out, revealing his birthright.

WEIRD AND WONDERFUL (3)

The Arthurian myths were treated with deadly seriousness in the **Middle Ages**. In 1113 there was a riot in the town of Bodmin, in Cornwall, because some French visitors denied that Arthur lived on in Avalon.

The round table (4)

Merlin made the table for Uther Pendragon who gave it to the king of Scotland. The king then presented it to Arthur when Arthur married his daughter **Guinevere**. Its circular shape **prevented jealousy** among the knights because no one sat at the head. It was said to accommodate 150 knights. The round table that resides in Winchester Great Hall, which is 5.4 m (18 ft) in diameter, claims to be the original, but was in fact made in the 13th century.

TINTAGEL CASTLE The ruins of Tintagel, said to be the birthplace of King Arthur, stand on the rocky Cornish coast. (5)

Excalibur and the Lady of the Lake (6)

Excalibur is sometimes said to be the sword that Arthur drew from the stone, but usually it is a different weapon. Merlin leads Arthur to a lake, where they meet a lady – Vivien, Merlin's mistress – who gives Arthur the magical Excalibur. Arthur is told that he cannot lose blood so long as he carries its **scabbard**. Armed with this new sword, Arthur goes on to be a great general and a much-loved king. But he eventually loses the scabbard to his treacherous sister, **Morgan le Fay**.

LADY'S FAVOUR The sword as depicted in the poster for the film *Excalibur* (1981).

Lancelot and Guinevere ⑦

There are several versions of the love affair between Guinevere, Arthur's wife, and Lancelot, 'the flower of the knights'. Guinevere is either forced into or engineers the affair, and Lancelot becomes torn between his love for her and for his king. In one version, Lancelot rescues the queen from execution for treason. The battle that then ensues between Arthur's knights heralds the end of the fellowship of the round table.

TRAGIC LOVE
Lancelot's adultery prevents him from finding the Grail because he is not chaste. In the most popular version of the legend today, the affair sparks the end of Camelot.

Gawain ⑧

A mysterious **Green Knight** challenges Gawain to strike a blow at his neck on condition that Gawain let the Green Knight reciprocate a year later. Gawain beheads the knight and thinks the contest is over but the knight picks up his severed head – and tells Gawain where to come for the return blow. On the way to the duel, Gawain lodges with **Sir Bercilak** and his wife. The wife tries to seduce Gawain but he refuses her. At the duel, the Green Knight turns out to be Bercilak himself. He swings his axe at Gawain, but cannot cut off his head because of Gawain's **purity**.

★ 199

The Holy Grail ★

The Grail is supposed to be the cup from which **Jesus** drank at the **Last Supper**. It was brought by **Joseph of Arimathea** to Britain, where it was lost or hidden. Many of Arthur's knights searched for the Grail, but only **Galahad** was virtuous enough to see it in its entirety. The covered Grail was brought to Camelot, where it filled the air with delicious smells. This detail betrays the Grail's connection to the Celtic **cauldron of plenty**.

The passing of Arthur ⑨

In the final act of Arthur's story, he is mortally wounded in battle by his nephew **Mordred**. Two of his knights bear him to a place near the lake where he received Excalibur, and he asks one of them to cast the sword into the water. Reluctant to throw away the magnificent sword, the knight twice disobeys. At the third time of asking, the knight hurls the sword, and a woman's arm reaches from the water to catch it. When Arthur is told this, he knows the knight has done his bidding. After this, Arthur is borne away on a magic ship to Avalon, where he rests – **not dead, but sleeping**.

ARTHUR IN AVALON A detail from a 19th-century Burne-Jones painting shows Arthur sleeping peacefully. Legend says that Arthur will return at the time of his country's most dire need.

Merlin ⑩

In the romances of Arthur, Merlin is an aged **wizard**, a wise counsellor to the young king. His name is a Latinised version of the Welsh **Myrddin**, which may have been a term describing ecstatic visionaries. Merlin is a powerful enchanter, but he is not infallible: in some versions of the story he is placed under an enchantment by the **Lady of the Lake**, who steals his knowledge and imprisons him inside a crystal; in others he is enclosed within a tree by his lover **Nimue**.

OLD WIZARD A pre-Christian Merlin existed before the one in Arthurian legend. One story claims that he built Stonehenge.

QUESTION NUMBER

The numbers or star following the answers refer to information boxes on the right.

ANSWERS

- **44** Baba Yaga ❻
- **64** B: AD 988 ❶ ❺
- **112** Finland ❶ ❷
- **136** C: The bathhouse ❼
- **305** Finland ❷
- **330** D: Folk tales ❹
- **394** C: Farming ❼
- **461** **Igor Stravinsky** – based on a Russian folktale
- **505** **Jean Sibelius** (1865-1957)
- **624** **A self-playing harp** – Koshchei 'the Deathless'
- **651** **Jean Sibelius** – written 1892 and 1899
- **678** **The Slavonic god of thunder** ❹ ❺
- **705** B: A water nymph ❸
- **785** **Dvořák** (Antonín, 1841-1904) ❸
- **860** **Chernobog** ❶
- ★ **896** **A forest spirit**
- **897** **In a field** ❼

Slavic and Finnish myths

Core facts ❶

◆ The cosmology of the Slavic peoples (Russians, Ukrainians, Poles and Serbs) was simple and rustic. At first their religion was dualistic, with two gods: **Byelobog**, the good 'white god'; and **Chernobog**, the evil 'black god'.

◆ The gods grew in number but when Christianity arrived they were downgraded to spirits and demons, or added to stories of the saints.

◆ Finland's mythology goes back to the time when Finns and Hungarians were the same people. The pantheon included a Zeus-like god of thunder, **Ukko** – also called Jumala.

A SCENE FROM THE *KALEVALA* The Finnish epic is packed full of fantastic tales. Here Seppo Llmarinen is shown ploughing the field of snakes.

The Finnish *Kalevala* ❷

Practically everything that is known about Finnish mythology is the result of the work of 19th-century folklorist **Elias Lonnrot**, author of the *Kalevala* (or 'Land of the Heroes'). He collected thousands of Finnish ballads, folk tales, fairy tales and proverbs, then wove them together – adding material of his own – to make a coherent story in long poetic form. The story centres on **Väinämöinen** and his companions in their attempts to defeat the frost giants of the North.

UNDERWATER WORLD Both Alexandr Dargomyzhsky and Antonín Dvořák wrote operas called *Rusalka*. ❸

Rusalka

A rusalka is a **water nymph**. They were thought to be the spirits of drowned girls and their aim was to drown other people. In southern lands, the nymphs were beautiful and lured people into the water; in the north they were harridans who dragged their victims from the river banks.

★ 896

The leshy: forest spirits

In Slavonic folk tradition every wood or forest has a spirit called a leshy. These spirits look human but are **blue-tinged** because of the colour of their blood. They can change size; in the forest they are as tall as trees, but at the forest's edge they shrink to the size of the undergrowth. They are **mischievous** but not malevolent, and delight in leading mushroom-hunters in circles.

Bylini: the Russian sagas 4

The bylini are Russian folk tales about heroes of the past. Like the Arthurian legends, they are Christian in character but draw on pre-Christian images and stories. One of these, *The Lay of Igor's Host*, is like a Russian *Beowulf*: it recounts the adventures of a martial prince and his battles. The most popular stories concern the cheerful superhero **Ilya-Muromets**, who builds a cathedral at Kiev and flies through the air on his magical horse. Ilya-Muromets seems to be a pious reworking of the thunder god Perun.

RUSSIAN TALE This illustration from the story of the 'Wonderful Self-playing Harp' shows Prince Astrach on his horse.

Perun 5

The **thunder** god of the Slavs, equivalent to Thor, is known as Perun. He was worshipped at Kiev until the conversion of the Russians to Christianity in AD 988. There he was depicted with a **silver head** and a **gold moustache**. Perun was invoked to bring **rain**. A surviving account of the rain-making ceremony says that it involved a naked young woman draped in flowers dancing ecstatically.

Baba Yaga 6

In Russian folk tradition there is a hideous **witch-demon** called Baba Yaga. She lives in a house that stands on huge chicken legs and runs around. She eats humans and once used their bones to build a grisly fence around her house.

WILD WITCH Baba Yaga moves around in a flying mortar propelled by a pestle (in her right hand).

Gods and spirits of pagan Russia 7

- **Bannik** Spirit of the bathhouse.
- **Dazhbog** God of the Sun, and son of Svarog.
- **Domovoi** Little hairy household spirit, protector of the home.
- **Dvorovoi** Bad-tempered spirit of the farmyard.
- **Mati Syra Zemlya** The Earth goddess – literally 'Moist Mother Earth'.
- **Mesyats** The Moon – sometimes a beautiful maiden, sometimes the bald uncle of the Sun.
- **Ovinnik** Spirit of the barn.
- **Polevik** Spirit of the field.
- **Svantovit** God of war, worshipped by the Baltic Slavs.
- **Svarog** God of the sky.
- **Volos** God of farming and of domesticated animals.

QUESTION NUMBER

The numbers or star following the answers refer to information boxes on the right.

ANSWERS

46	**Walkabout** 2 8
117	**Maui** 3
129	**Bruce Chatwin** 2
165	**Africa** 7
209	**Mount Kilimanjaro** – 5900m (19 364ft) high
240	**The Zulus** 5
315	**Dreamtime** 2
385	**Human beings** 4
588	**False** (they face inland) 6
★ 775	**The boomerang**
847	**Toto** – name of US band and Dorothy's dog
929	**Polynesian gods** 4

Africa and Oceania

Core facts 1

◆ We know relatively little about the myths of **Africa** and of the **Pacific** region. This is because the beliefs of these peoples were either ignored by European colonists or actively suppressed by missionaries.

◆ Many of the concepts are very different from European mythologies: the African idea of spirit, for example, bears little relation to that known in the 'old world' of Europe.

◆ At a deeper level, however, the themes are the same: how the **world** came into being; **mankind's role** in the universe; and the concept of an **afterlife**.

Dreamtime and songlines 2

The Australian Aboriginal dreamtime, or ***alchera***, is the remote era when the ancestral spirits walked the Earth, **singing** the landscape and all living things into existence as they went. After this 'time before time' the ancestors retreated underground and went back to sleep. As a result of their creative activity, the land is crisscrossed with **songlines**, paths that were formed by the ancestors as they left musical notes and magical words in their wake.

WARNAMPI, THE QUIET SNAKE Aboriginal art tells stories from the dreamtime using concentric shapes and dots.

Maui the cunning hero 3

The myths of **Polynesia** and **New Zealand** often refer to Maui, a cunning hero who uses his **wits** to get the better of his adversaries. But he is also **strong** like Heracles – he raised the heavens with a poker because he did not have room to work. And he is a **friend to mankind** – he is even said to have stolen fire and made a gift of it to humanity. Maui once **snared the Sun** because it was racing too fast across the sky and so making the days too short; after a beating from Maui it could only move at a crawl. The best-loved legend of Maui tells how he fished up the islands from the depths of the ocean using a **magic fish-hook**. The South Island of New Zealand is known to the Maoris as 'Maui's canoe'.

The gods of Polynesia 4

Among the most significant of the Polynesian gods is **Ta'aroa** the creator who, like the Chinese Pangu, emerged from a **cosmic egg** before making the world. In Tahiti he was once offered human sacrifices, which were euphemistically termed 'long-legged fish'. There is also **Tangaroa**, the sea god; **Rangi**, the sky god; **Papa**, god of the Earth; and **Tane**, god of forests and wood.

TANGAROA As the sea god, Tangaroa was said to separate Rangi (sky) from Papa (Earth).

Africa's universe 5

African mythology is extremely diverse and the details of the beliefs of many of the ancient peoples have been lost. But there are some common ideas, among them a belief in a **supreme being**. The creator god of the warlike Zulus, for example, is called Unkulunkulu. He is responsible for death being in the world because he sent the wrong messenger – a chameleon – with the message of immortality. The chameleon stopped to eat, and was overtaken by a lizard carrying the message of death. Another common thread is the animistic idea that everything is invested with a **spirit** that can be manipulated. So sorcery can be used to invoke rain or cure sickness.

ASKING THE GODS Masks like this one from West Africa were used in rain-making rituals.

Easter Island 6

The inhabitants of Easter Island have bequeathed us one of the wonders of mythological art. All along the coast stand huge **statues** in human form, some up to 10 m (30 ft) high. All have the same expressionless, elongated face, all are carved from a single piece of rock, and all face inland. The exact significance of the statues is unknown but they may represent gods or deified ancestors intended to protect the island. A local legend says that the statues once walked at night, which may be a clue that they were transported upright.

SENTRY DUTY The statues that are said to guard Easter Island are carved out of volcanic rock.

Mr Spider 7

The **trickster** god of West Africa has the ability to outwit other creatures, including mankind. Tales of his exploits have spread to the West Indies, where he is called **Anansi**. The spider only once lost out, when he met the **Wax Girl**. Not realising she was a dummy, the spider became incensed at the girl's refusal to talk and struck at her. One after another, all his limbs became stuck in the wax.

WEIRD AND WONDERFUL 8

The Aboriginal **songlines** are akin to **leylines** in that they are invisible routes of **power**. They also serve as paths of communication and bonds of kinship between tribes.

775

Boomerang

According to legend, the boomerang was invented by the ancestral snake named **Bobbi-Bobbi**, who made the first boomerang out of one of his own ribs.

QUESTION NUMBER

The numbers or star following the answers refer to information boxes on the right.

ANSWERS

QUESTION NUMBER	ANSWERS
29	**Pontiac** (3)
59	**The Toltecs** (1)
65	**C: The bald eagle** – bald meaning white, not hairless
118	**North America** (3)
169	**The Aztecs** (5)
221	**Shaman** (2)
257	**A: An hallucinogenic drug** (2)
320	**The Alamo** – fortress in San Antonia, Texas
370	**The Incas** (4)
426	**D.H. Lawrence** (published in 1926) (5)
487	**The Inuit** – Sedna was goddess of the sea
★ 509	**The Maya**
578	**The pipe of peace** (3)
582	**True** – she lived on Spider Rock, Arizona
709	**C: Xoxotl** (5)
843	**The Milky Way** ★
895	**The Inca** (in celebration of Inti) (4)
958	**Quetzlcoatl** (5)

Myths of the Americas

Core facts (1)

◆ Many civilisations flourished in North and South America before the arrival of Europeans, and most of them had highly developed religious and mythological beliefs.
◆ As long as 3000 years ago the **Olmec** people of Mexico were carving giant stone warrior heads. They were succeeded by the **Toltecs**; and then came the **Aztecs** who practised ritual human sacrifice to their gods.
◆ To the south of the Aztecs there was the **Maya** civilisation, whose beliefs were bound up with the study of astronomy. In the land that is now Peru were the **Incas**. They worshipped a Sun god, Inti, above all others.

Medicine men (2)

More properly known as **shamans**, medicine men were intermediaries between men and gods. They would work themselves into a **trance**, sometimes using hallucinogens, during which they were believed to be able to control the spirits that cause disease. They could also invoke the spirits of the weather (hence the so-called **rain dance**), confer with animal spirits and seek advice from ancestors.

MEDICINE MASK DANCE Medicine men would be asked to commune with the spirits before a hunt or a battle to bring success.

★ 509

The Maya ★

Compared to the Aztecs and the Incas, the Maya were a peaceable people. The main god, **Itzamna**, is entirely benevolent. He is god of medicine, lord of the Moon, and usually depicted as a toothless but kindly old man. The **Milky Way** held a special place of veneration in the Mayan cosmology. Depending on the season, they called it the World Tree or the White-Boned Serpent.

Beliefs of the North Americans (3)

The many groups inhabited a vast and diverse geographical area, but there are common threads in their beliefs. The belief in a **Great Spirit** was widespread. This spirit, called Manitou by the Algonquin groups of the east, was an animistic deity that occupied everything in nature: trees, stones, animals. It was in honour of the Great Spirit that plains Indians such as **the Sioux** ritually smoked the **pipe of peace**. Many Indian peoples told stories of animal heroes. **Raven**, who flapped his wings to make the land rise from the ocean, created mankind from clamshells and stole fire from heaven for man. The more sinister **Coyote** rejoiced when death entered the world.

FIRST CONTACT Europeans recorded their encounters with New World peoples in books such as the *Brevis Narratio*.

The Incas

❹

Nowadays, the ruined city at **Machu Picchu** is the Incas' most famous monument, but their capital was at Cuzco. Legend says that the Sun god **Inti** sent his children, **Manco Capac** and **Mama Ocollo**, to Earth to bring civilisation to the people of the Andes. He gave them a gold nugget, saying that wherever it sank they were to build a city. Manco Capac and Mama Ocollo went on to become the first rulers of the Incas.

The bloodthirsty Aztecs

❺

The Aztecs dominated Mexico for two centuries. During that time they maintained a brutal cult of human sacrifice. The principal deity of the Aztecs was **Quetzalcoatl**, the 'plumed snake', who was previously a Toltec god. One myth about Quetzalcoatl said that he left the land on a raft of snakes, but would one day return in the form of a light-skinned bearded man. When the Spanish commander **Hernán Cortés** arrived in 1519, the Aztecs took him to be Quetzalcoatl incarnate.

Tie-breaker

❻

Q Which animal was most commonly sacrificed by the Incas?
A The llama. White or albino llamas were slaughtered to gain the gods' blessings for the people; black ones were sacrificed in order to bring rain.

GUNSLINGING HEROES The story of Butch Cassidy and the Sundance Kid resembles the legends of marksmen such as William Tell and Robin Hood.

Myths of the Wild West

❼

The romantic concept of the **cowboy** has become established through countless books and Hollywood films. But this relatively new American myth owes much to medieval tales of **knights** in armour. Both cowboy and knight ride horses; both are warriors with a special code of conduct (don't shoot unless your opponent has drawn first); and both have chosen a life of austerity and male companionship.

QUESTION NUMBER

The numbers or star following the answers refer to information boxes on the right.

ANSWERS

41	St Christopher ❹
67	C: St Olaf ❻
83	False ❺ ❻
204	St Bernard ❺
230	Hagiography ❷
243	St Luke ❺
264	St Catherine ❸
301	St Andrew ❻
310	St George ❻
316	Cistercian – established at Cîteaux in France
★ 504	Beatification and canonisation
524	Matthew, Mark, Luke and John ❺
598	St Francis of Assisi (c.1182-1226) ❷
604	St Lawrence ❸
621	St Thomas More ❺
629	St Matthew ❺
683	Woodworkers ❺
876	St Andrew's cross ❻
911	St Patrick ❻
915	St Nicholas ❻
920	St David ❻
983	St Joseph ❻
998	St Martin ❹

Medieval saints

Core facts ❶

◆ The roll of saints includes the **apostles**, **gospel writers** and **first martyrs**, plus a large number of pious individuals who have demonstrated **heroic Christian virtue**.

◆ In the 12th century **Pope Alexander III** established official procedures for canonising saints. The lives of candidates for sainthood are thoroughly examined by the Catholic Church as part of the process of canonisation.

◆ Saints can be **demoted**. In 1969 the Vatican downgraded feast days of St George, patron saint of England, St Catherine the martyr, and St Nicholas (Santa Claus) after investigations showed that they never existed.

Medieval hagiography ❷

Hagiography is a Greek term for the **life story of a saint**. In the Middle Ages, hagiographies were very popular. Though many of the saints were more or less fictional, their tales contained **moral truths** that the Church was keen to promote. An example is the *Golden Legend* – a calendar of saints' days and their stories. The best-known Protestant hagiography is Foxe's *Book of Martyrs* (1563).

ANIMAL LOVER St Francis of Assisi is the patron of ecologists. He has his own hagiography: *Little Flowers of Saint Francis*.

Martyred saints ❸

Some saints are remembered primarily for their steadfastness in the face of death. **Catherine of Alexandria** is said to have been strapped to a spiked wheel. When the wheel miraculously broke, she was beheaded and milk instead of blood flowed from her severed neck. She is patron of many occupations connected with wheels, including millers and spinners. **St Lawrence** was martyred by being roasted on a gridiron, and so became the patron saint of cooks and chefs. **St Sebastian**'s story (see below) is in equally poor taste.

PINNED Pierced with so many arrows that he resembled a pin cushion, St Sebastian became the patron saint of pin makers.

Divine stories ❹

Many of the stories of saints tell of them performing a miracle, or having a wondrous encounter with Jesus. **St Christopher** meets Christ in disguised form. He carries a child across a stream, but finds the burden increasingly heavy – until he is told that the child is Christ, carrying the sins of the world. **St Martin** has a similar encounter. He shares his cloak with a beggar who turns out to be Jesus.

Patron saints of occupations

Saints have always been associated with particular occupations and groups of people. Usually there is a link – sometimes a tenuous one – with the trade.

Occupation	Patron saint
Accountants	St Matthew, a moneychanger before he became a disciple.
Artillerymen	St Barbara, who was saved from martyrdom by a thunderbolt.
Artists	St Luke, who is said to have painted the first icon.
Bricklayers	St Stephen, who was killed with stones.
Comedians	St Vitus, possibly because of the nervous disorder St Vitus' Dance, which causes jerky movements and was once considered comical.
Fishermen	St Andrew, who was a fisherman in Galilee.
Lawyers	St Thomas More, a lawyer by trade.
Librarians	St Jerome, who compiled the first Latin translation of the books of the Bible.
Mountaineers	St Bernard of Menthon, 'the apostle of the Alps'. He founded hospices in the Alps and his monks trained the first rescue dogs now named after him.
Postal workers	St Gabriel, the angel who brought a message from God to Mary.
Paratroopers	St Michael, the archangel, usually depicted as a winged warrior.
Woodworkers	St Joseph, the carpenter who was the father of Jesus.
Writers	St John the Evangelist, author of the fourth gospel.

National saints

Curiously, national saints are not often citizens of the countries they represent. Some are patrons of more than one country.

Nation	Saint
Belgium	St Joseph
Czech Republic	St Wenceslas
England	St George
France	St Joan of Arc
Germany	St Boniface
Greece	St Nicholas
Ireland	St Patrick
Netherlands	St Willibrord
Norway	St Olaf
Russia	St Nicholas
Scotland	St Andrew
Spain	St James
Wales	St David

MONSTER SLAYER St George is usually held to be a Roman soldier. The story of him defeating a dragon owes much to Greek mythology.

504

Becoming a saint

There are two stages in becoming a saint. The first is **beatification**, when it is declared that a person has led a life of heroic virtue and is worthy of veneration. The second stage is called **canonisation**, when that person is formally admitted to the roll call of saints.

WEIRD AND WONDERFUL

The story of **St Nicholas** says that he was a **bishop** who gave away three bags of gold to three poor women. Although he is no longer recognised as a saint, he is still remembered as the giver of gifts – in the form of **Santa Claus.**

QUESTION NUMBER

The numbers or star following the answers refer to information boxes on the right.

ANSWERS

- **3** A gryphon ❸
- **7** The nightingale ❶
- **278** The Bible ❻
- **323** A: In the sea ❻
- **387** An ape ❼
- **584** True ❷
- **593** The ostrich ❼
- **595** The pelican ❼
- **596** The phoenix – a symbol of the Resurrection
- **600** The goldfinch – also known as the wild canary
- **710** A: Couchant – from French *coucher*, to lay down
- **724** A snake ❼
- **729** Centaur ❹
- **810** Leviathan ❻
- **834** True ❶
- ★ **837** The narwhal (*Monodon monoceras*)
- **840** The unicorn ★ ❷
- **845** A dragon ❺
- **972** Basilisk ❼
- **974** Salamander – the real amphibian belongs to the order Caudata

The medieval bestiary

Core facts ❶

◆ Bestiaries are **books of animals** that were extremely popular in the Middle Ages. They contained both real and familiar animals such as toads and beavers, alongside mythical animals such as dragons and unicorns.

◆ Some of the mythical animals were derived from Greek legends, and some of the real animals were credited with **magical powers** that made them seem extraordinary. For example, bestiaries state that lions never sleep, that a nightingale will sing itself to death and that bees are born of the dead carcass of an ox.

◆ Very often the descriptions of the beasts contain a **Christian moral**.

Unicorns ❷

In classical times the unicorn was described as a white deer with a horse's mane and a **spiral horn** growing out of its forehead. In **heraldry** this image was simplified: the unicorn became a horned horse. It is likely that the unicorn derived from garbled descriptions of the **rhinoceros**. The unicorn had **magical powers** – it could detect poison, for example, by dipping its fluted horn into a drink.

THE LADY AND THE UNICORN
It was believed that a unicorn would rest in a virgin's lap and that this was how to capture one.

Gryphons ❸

The gryphon has the **head of an eagle** and the **body of a lion**. **Pliny** believed that they came from Scythia, north of the Black Sea. The gryphon stood for **Christ's dual nature**: its eagle half, which belonged in the heavens, signified Christ's divinity; and the earthbound lion half represented his humanity.

★ 837

Tusk or horn ★

The myth of unicorns was perpetuated when early explorers came across **narwhal tusks** washed up on the shore. The narwhal is a whale that lives in the Arctic and North Atlantic. Males grow a twisted tusk that can be up to 3 m (10 ft) long. People thought the tusks were discarded unicorn horns.

Centaurs

4

With the body and legs of a **horse**, and the upper body of a **man**, centaurs probably have their origin in sightings of the aggressive horsemen of the Steppes. In keeping with this, centaurs are seen as savage and reckless. In Christian terms, centaurs stood for heresy and the conflict between man's animal and spiritual nature. But in Greek mythology the centaur **Chiron** was a renowned healer. He personified wisdom and was tutor to Achilles.

STAR HORSEMAN Jupiter placed the centaur Chiron in the heavens where he became the constellation Sagittarius.

Dragons

5

These creatures made their way into Christian mythology from the myths of the Greeks (the **hydra** is very like a dragon) and from the legends of West Asia (in Babylonian myth there is a she-dragon called **Tiamat)**. The dragon is a symbol of **Satan**. Dragons are sometimes shown swallowing their own tails. This image, called a **uroborus**, crops up in many cultures and is a symbol of eternity.

ST MICHAEL BEATS THE DEVIL Satan took the guise of a dragon when he fought with St Michael.

Behemoth and Leviathan

6

These two monstrous creatures are mentioned in the Bible, but are not described. Behemoth is a land monster that is sometimes identified with the relatively small and harmless **hippopotamus**. Leviathan is **a sea monster** – the name in Hebrew suggests something that writhes, like a **serpent**.

BEASTLY CREATURES An 18th-century illustration of the book of Job showing a leviathan and a behemoth.

Bestiary 'facts'

7

- **Ape** Gives birth to twins, one of which it loves and the other it hates.
- **Basilisk** A small but deadly snake. It kills men with a glance, but dies if it is spotted first.
- **Elephant** Gives birth in water to prevent dragons from seizing its offspring.
- **Hedgehog** Shakes grapes from the vine, which it then collects on its sharp spines.
- **Ostrich** Eats red-hot horseshoes from the forge.
- **Pelican** Feeds its young with its own blood (and so is a symbol of Christian self-sacrifice).
- **Toad** Can live for centuries if it is buried in sand.

Traditions and oral history

QUESTION NUMBER

The numbers or star following the answers refer to information boxes on the right.

ANSWERS

39	**Charlton Heston** ❼ ❽
119	**A race of dwarves** ❺
123	**Seamus Heaney** ❹
★ 154	**Urban myth**
219	**Passion play** ❻ ❾
224	**Miracle plays** ❻ ❾
237	**Valencia** ❼
241	**The *Odyssey*** ❷
307	**Denmark** ❶ ❹
367	**Oberammergau** ❾
522	**Homer** ❷
603	**The Black Death** ❾
786	**Richard Wagner** ❺
870	**Mary Magdalene** (in *The Passion of the Christ*) ❾
955	**El Cid** ❼
979	**Pageant** ❻

Core facts ❶

◆ Most European nations have tales of times of yore, which are **passed down** through the generations.

◆ Some stories are entirely fictional; others involve historical figures who have been mythologised beyond recognition. For example, we can be sure that **Beowulf**, if he ever existed at all, did not fight a fire-eating dragon.

◆ Many such **folk tales** envisage a more heroic age that is now gone. The **oral tradition** of storytelling bridges the gap, often centuries, between the events and their being written down.

Homer's tales ❷

It is now generally agreed that the stories told in the ***Iliad*** and the ***Odyssey*** are the culmination of an oral tradition, not the product of one man's imagination.

Almost nothing is known of the poet Homer. Tradition says that he was blind, and that he lived in Ionia. His works were written down in the 8th century BC, soon after the Greeks acquired the art of writing from the Phoenicians.

There is much evidence in the text that the epic poems were designed to be **performed**, not read. There is the use of stock-phrases (swift-footed Achilles, grey-eyed Athena), and the many repetitions of long passages. These are like musical themes and phrases, around which the rest of the story would have been **improvised**.

WEIRD AND WONDERFUL ❸

Many of our **nursery rhymes** have been around since the 17th century, some even earlier. They are still evolving and there are various theories as to their hidden meanings. Some may have been an early form of political comment.

Beowulf ❹

This long **poem** was written in the Anglo-Saxon language, probably during the 8th century AD.

Though it was **written in England**, the poem is **set in Denmark** and harks back to the 5th century. The noble warrior Beowulf helps the king of Denmark by killing two man-eating monsters who are terrorising the land.

After this heroic act, Beowulf goes home to his own people, where he becomes king and reigns for 50 years. But then his kingdom is threatened by a fire-breathing dragon. Beowulf slays the beast, but is mortally wounded. The poem ends with a description of Beowulf's funeral.

The poem, one of the founding texts of English literature, was recently translated into modern English by the Irish poet Seamus Heaney.

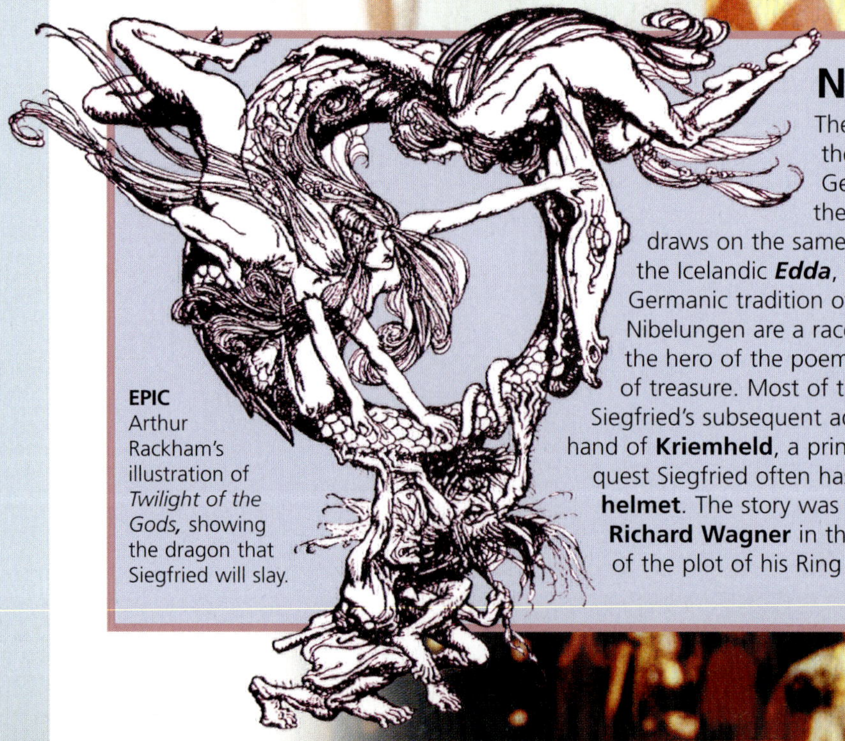

EPIC Arthur Rackham's illustration of *Twilight of the Gods*, showing the dragon that Siegfried will slay.

Nibelungen ❺

The Saga of the Nibelungen, or the ***Nibelungenlied***, is a German epic poem written at the end of the 12th century. It draws on the same ancient set of legends as the Icelandic ***Edda***, and so is part of the oldest Germanic tradition of storytelling. The Nibelungen are a race of dwarves from whom the hero of the poem, **Siegfried**, obtains a hoard of treasure. Most of the poem is concerned with Siegfried's subsequent adventures as he seeks the hand of **Kriemheld**, a princess of Burgundy. In this quest Siegfried often has recourse to a **magic helmet**. The story was revived by the composer **Richard Wagner** in the 19th century. It forms part of the plot of his Ring cycle of operas.

Mystery plays

Also called **miracle plays**, these were a form of drama popular in the Middle Ages. Clergy were forbidden to perform in them, so they were staged and watched by lay people. **Common themes** included the creation, the Second Coming of Christ and the lives of the saints. Sometimes each scene would be performed on a wagon or a wheeled stage – known as a **pageant**. Each pageant then moved on, and the scene was played again for a new audience. Eventually the name of the wagon came to mean the procession itself, hence the modern sense of the word.

154

Tall stories

A current form of the oral tradition is the **urban myth**. These stories of **dubious provenance** are recounted as though true. Many have a humorous or ironic element. They include the story of the Iranian woman said to have given birth to a frog, widely reported by normally reliable news organisations in 2004.

El Cid

The man known to history as El Cid was a real historical person. His name was **Rodrigo Díaz de Vivar**, and he was a military commander in 11th-century Spain. He served both the King of Castile and, after he fell from royal favour, the Moorish ruler of Saragosa (the title Cid is from the Arabic word for lord). He besieged and captured Valencia from the Moors in 1094 and became its ruler. His reputation as a soldier and adventurer grew after his death, and he became a Spanish folk hero – rather like William Wallace for the Scots. Two hundred years after his death, the exploits of El Cid were recounted in an epic poem called the ***Cantar de Mio Cid***. This series of ballads turned the historical general into a legend, and later authors have built on the myth.

LARGER THAN LIFE The 1961 blockbuster *El Cid*, starring Charlton Heston, is one of many fictional works inspired by the life of the legendary Spanish soldier.

Oberammergau

Passion plays are a particular kind of mystery play dealing with the suffering, death and resurrection of Christ. They were common in Germany in medieval towns. The best-known passion play is the one performed in the Bavarian village of Oberammergau. After an outbreak of the **Black Death** in 1633, the villagers undertook to stage the play **every ten years** if their lives were spared. The text has been revised several times, most notably to remove anti-Semitic statements. The current text was written by a local monk in 1810.

A PIOUS PLAY Christians travel to Oberammergau as a form of pilgrimage. More than 250 000 people visited the Bavarian village when the passion play was staged in 2000.

QUESTION NUMBER

The numbers or star following the answers refer to information boxes on the right.

ANSWERS

53	**Hope** 4
98	**Nine** 7
134	**C: March 25** (the Feast of the Annunciation) 6
145	**Dice** 5
152	**Pandora** 4
223	**Beelzebub** 5
269	**A snake, or serpent** 2
451	**Satan** 5
459	**Angel** 6 7
510	**Savannah, Georgia** – also a film with Kevin Spacey
552	**Playing cards** 5
640	**A: Cain** – he murdered his brother Abel
670	**Evil** – 1 Timothy chap 6, verse 10
777	**The Garden of Eden** 2
795	**Job** 3
★ 805	**Karma**
811	**Culture Club** ★
980	**Armageddon** – identified with Megiddo in Israel

Good and evil

Core facts 1

◆ Many of the world's religions and mythologies are **dualistic** in that they believe the events in the world are driven by a cosmic struggle between good and evil.

◆ Clashes of opposites include God and the Devil or Satan; angels and demons; George and the Dragon.

◆ Such stories help to explain why bad things happen: evil events are merely minor victories for evil in the greater struggle.

◆ It is reassuring that **good always wins** in the end, even when it appears to be the weaker party (as in the stories of David and Goliath, and Luke Skywalker and Darth Vader).

The fall from Grace 2

The story of **Adam and Eve** in the **Garden of Eden** attempts to explain how evil entered the world. In this garden the first man and woman were free from hunger and pain, and were apparently immortal. God had commanded that they should not eat the fruit of one tree, but Eve was persuaded by the **serpent** to taste it and to give some to Adam. In that moment, the pair became aware of their nakedness. They made clothes and hid from God among the trees. God knew what they had done, and dealt out swift punishment: the woman would now suffer pain in childbirth, and the man would have to earn food by the 'sweat of his brow'.

FORBIDDEN FRUIT By tradition, the fruit of the tree in the Garden of Eden was an apple, although the Bible does not specify.

Job 3

The biblical story of Job tackles the question of why **bad things happen to good people**. Job is a righteous man but Satan says to God one day that Job is good only because he is blessed. If God were to take away these blessings, Job would curse him. God accepts the challenge and allows Satan to deprive Job of his health, wealth and family. But Job is steadfast and will not curse God or question his actions. God rewards him after many trials by restoring his former prosperity.

Pandora's box

4

Greek myth, like the Old Testament, holds the first woman responsible for the evils of the world. This woman was Pandora, who was fashioned from clay by the god Hephaestus. Zeus sent her to live among mankind. She took with her a **sealed vase** (wrongly translated as 'box' in English) containing all the woes of the world, such as sickness, old age and vice. She was told not to open the jar, but her curiosity overcame her. All the woes flew out like insects to all corners of the world. Only hope remained in the jar.

THE VASE UNSEALED Louise Brooks as the nymphomaniac Lulu in G.W. Pabst's 1929 silent movie *Pandora's Box*.

TAKING A CHILD A 14th-century depiction of the Devil. In those days he was a very real entity with cloven hooves, horns and a tail.

The Devil

5

The Devil of myth and folklore has many names. **Satan** is a biblical word meaning 'adversary'; **Beelzebub** means 'lord of the flies'. In the 17th century he was known as **Old Nick**, which may be connected with the German Nickel, meaning 'goblin'. Legend says that he was created as an angel but fell from grace – an idea given great artistic expression in Milton's poem *Paradise Lost*. His job is to tempt mankind into sin. The medieval dread of the Devil has left a deep mark on our culture and language. Playing cards, for example, are called the 'Devil's picture book'; dice are the 'Devil's bones'.

Angels

6

The word 'angel' comes from the Greek for **messenger**. In Bible stories, angels are benevolent spiritual beings who convey special news to individuals, as in the Annunciation when **Gabriel** appeared to Mary before the birth of Jesus. In popular folklore, there is the idea that every person has a **guardian angel** who looks after them throughout their life.

★ 805

Karma

★

Hindu and **Buddhist** philosophies have an explanation for good and evil that does not depend on a benevolent god and a malicious devil. Karma is the idea that every moral act has an effect in this life or future incarnations. In simplest terms, a wicked act will rebound upon a person as a misfortune, and a noble act will be rewarded somewhere down the line.

USE THE FORCE Luke Skywalker takes on Darth Vader in an epic tale of good versus evil. Good wins, of course.

Ranks of angels

7

In medieval times a **hierarchy of angels** was identified from biblical references to them. In descending order, the nine are:

- Seraphim
- Cherubim
- Thrones
- Dominions
- Virtues
- Powers
- Principalities
- Archangels
- Angels

QUESTION NUMBER

The numbers or star following the answers refer to information boxes on the right.

ANSWERS

QUESTION NUMBER	ANSWERS
94	**Five** 7
126	**His burden of sin** 1 3
★ 143	**A sheep's**
147	**Jesus** 7
189	***Animal Farm*** 5
273	**Jonathan Swift** (1667-1745) 6
276	**John Bunyan** (1628-88) 1 3
325	**B: Herman Melville** (1819-91)
389	***The Insect Play*** 6
408	**40** 1 7
441	**Simorgh** – represents the goal of self-knowledge
512	**C: Samaritan** 2
606	**Lazarus** 7
639	**C: A pig** 5
667	**The Prodigal Son** 4
730	**George Orwell** 5
937	***The Faerie Queene*** (published 1590-96) 1
940	**Solomon** – c.974-937 BC, son of King David

Parable and allegory

Core facts 1

◆ An allegory is a story with a hidden or secondary meaning. The story of **the tortoise and the hare**, for example, is an allegory of human perseverance and human complacency.

◆ Parables are related to allegories in that they have a deeper meaning than appears on the surface. They also have a clear moral message. Christ's story about the shepherd who seeks a lost sheep explains the doctrine of salvation.

◆ Allegories and parables can be a simple metaphor, such as Jesus' **parable of the prodigal son**, or complex narratives such as ***Pilgrim's Progress*** or ***The Faerie Queene*** by the Elizabeth poet Edmund Spenser.

Helping hand 2

The story of the **Good Samaritan** is about compassion. In modern times, it has often been recast as an allegory of **racial tolerance**, since the Samaritans were a group despised by orthodox Jews. The story tells of a man who was robbed, beaten and left to die on the road from Jerusalem to Jericho. As he lay there a priest and a Levite, members of the religious elite, saw him but both passed on the other side. Then a Samaritan came by. He picked the man up, bound his wounds and took him to safety.

Bunyan 3

John Bunyan's ***Pilgrim's Progress***, written in 1678, is perhaps the best-known allegorical tale in English. It tells the story of **Christian**, whose pilgrimage from the **City of Destruction** to the **Celestial City** represents the journey through life towards Salvation. Along the way he encounters various symbolic moral perils, such as the **Slough of Despond** (the temptation to give in to despair) and **Vanity Fair** (the distractions of materialism).

★ 143

Simple truths

Aesop's fables are attributed to a Greek storyteller who lived in 600 BC, but they may have roots in much earlier times. The stories are often about **animals**. In 'The Wolf in Sheep's Clothing' a wolf diguises himself so that he can get close to and kill sheep. The story is simply saying that appearances can be deceptive.

The Prodigal Son 4

Jesus told this story about a man who had two sons. The **younger son** asked his father for his inheritance, which he **frittered** away on riotous living. When it was gone he returned home and begged his father to take him back into the home as a servant. But his father, who had thought he was dead, kisses him and holds a **feast** in his honour. The elder brother, who has worked for his father all his life, complains that it is unfair. But the father says it is right to celebrate the son who was **lost** and is now **found**.

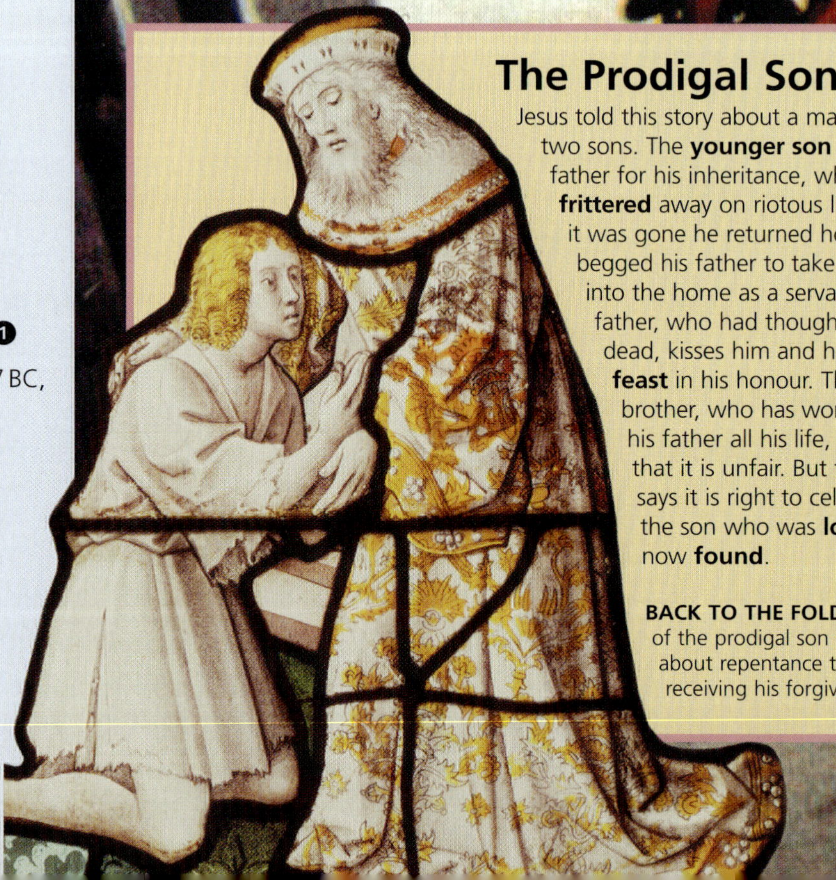

BACK TO THE FOLD The story of the prodigal son is ultimately about repentance to God and receiving his forgiveness.

Animal Farm ❺

George Orwell's novel *Animal Farm*, written in 1945, is **a political allegory** in the form of a children's fairy tale. It tells of the attempt of animals to take over the farmyard and run it for themselves. But it is also the story of the **Russian Revolution** and its descent into terror and despotism. The pigs represent the Bolshevik revolutionaries, the cart-horse is the long-suffering Russian people, and the ousted farmer is the old tsarist regime.

ANIMAL WRONGS The animals seek freedom from a cruel master but find tyrants amongst themselves.

❻

Some allegorical works

◆ ***Gulliver's Travels*** (Jonathan Swift) High politics is made to look ridiculous when conducted by tiny people.
◆ ***The Lion, the Witch and the Wardrobe*** (C.S. Lewis) The lion Aslan (Jesus) sacrifices himself to the White Witch (Satan) to redeem a 'son of Adam'.
◆ ***The Insect Play*** (Karel Čapek) Ants stand for industrial labour, dung beetles for capitalist acquisitiveness.
◆ ***The Divine Comedy*** (Dante) A poet is led through Heaven and Hell, where the rewards and punishments fit the merits and sins of those who receive them.

❼

Some of Jesus' parables

◆ **The pearl of great price** A man gives up all he owns in order to gain something more precious.
◆ **The rich man and Lazarus** Both men die, but the beggar Lazarus goes to 'Abraham's bosom', while the rich man languishes in Hell. Though he was poor in this world, Lazarus receives his rewards in Heaven. The rich man, who was not charitable in this world, receives no charity in the hereafter.
◆ **The wise and foolish virgins** Five virgins bring oil for their lamps, and so are ready to meet the bridegroom; five do not, and so miss the wedding feast. The story is saying that you should be ever vigilant for the coming of the Lord.
◆ **The sower** The seeds that the farmer scatters on good soil flourish and produce a good crop, while those that land on poor soil wither and die.
◆ **The house** A wise man built his house on the firm foundation of rock. When the floods came his house stood, while the houses without foundation fell down. The firm foundation can be taken to mean faith in God.

Rebel heroes

QUESTION NUMBER

The numbers or star following the answers refer to information boxes on the right.

ANSWERS

21	**Clyde Barrow** ❶ ❺
73	**William Tell** ❸
88	**False** ★ ❼
128	**Peter Carey** ❻
151	**Little John** ❷
282	**Maid Marion** ❷
336	**Kevin Costner** ❶ ❷
417	**Ned Kelly** ❻
435	**Blind Harry** ★ ❼
466	**Mick Jagger** ❻
564	**William Tell** ❸
★ 569	**William Wallace**
570	**Robin Hood** ❶ ❷
635	**C: Earl of Huntingdon** ❶ ❷
694	**Friedrich Schiller** (1759-1805) ❸
783	**Rossini** (Gioacchino, 1792-1868) ❸
844	**Rob Roy** (1671-1734)
855	**Lincoln green** ❷
886	**Friar Tuck** ❷
935	**Edward I** ('Hammer of the Scots') ★
936	**Robert the Bruce** (Robert I, 1274-1329) ❶
939	**Alfred the Great** (c.849-c.901) ❶
964	**Nottingham** ❷

Core facts ❶

◆ Folk tradition abounds with heroes whose role is to challenge injustice. Some are real people whose lives have been mythologised; others, such as **Robin Hood**, are invented.

◆ There are various categories of rebel heroes, including: **patriots** waging war against oppression; **nobles** deprived of their rightful inheritance; and **representatives** of the masses fighting the system.

◆ In many cases, the myths have been given a new lease of life by being turned into **films**. The legends of Bonnie and Clyde, William Wallace, and even Sinbad, would be far less well-known without the intervention of Hollywood.

Robin Hood ❷

There have been many attempts to identify an historical Robin Hood, but the fact is he is entirely fictional. His legend is probably connected with the old pagan idea of the **Green Man** (see page 96).

Robin Hood was a well-known English folk hero by the 14th century. The oldest tales have Robin in conflict with the Sheriff of Nottingham, but almost all the other elements of the myth are later additions. These newer elements include: the **Merry Men** – John Little (known as Little John), Will Scarlet and Friar Tuck – and the hideout in Sherwood Forest; the idea that Robin is the true Earl of Huntingdon; and the practice of robbing the rich to give to the poor.

The character of Robin Hood is a reflection of the solid yeomanly virtues of the Middle Ages: Robin is always courageous, light-hearted, chivalrous, fair and an incomparable archer.

MEN IN TIGHTS Robin Hood has been portrayed in several films over the years. In 1938 he was played by Errol Flynn, facing Basil Rathbone as the evil Sheriff of Nottingham.

William Tell ❸

The legend says that William Tell, **national hero of Switzerland**, refused to doff his cap to **Gessler**, the bailiff of the Austrian king. As a punishment he was ordered to shoot at an apple on the head of his own son. He passed this trial, but was jailed because he told Gessler he would have killed him if his son had been harmed. Tell escaped from prison, and killed Gessler, sparking a revolt that led to Swiss independence.

SWISS HERO Tell's story inspired Rossini to write an opera about his life.

Rebel leaders

Throughout history rebel leaders have emerged. Some were driven by oppression, others by ideology – and a few by both.

Name	Brief biography
Che Guevara	Helped Fidel Castro overthrow the Cuban dictator Fulgencio Batista and in the process became a popular hero.
Mahatma Ghandi	Pioneered peaceful disobedience in the successful fight to free India from colonial rule.
Spartacus	A Roman soldier who deserted the army, was sold into slavery and then trained as a gladiator. Spartacus raised an army of slaves in an ultimately unsuccessful revolt against Rome.

Outlaws

Bonnie Parker and **Clyde Barrow** are seen as inheritors of the long tradition of the American outlaw. There is something inspiring about their doomed love, their daring string of bank raids and their dying together in a hail of bullets. But their story shows that the most unpromising characters can be romanticised and mythologised. They were in fact a deeply unlikeable pair, who killed at least ten people in the course of their crime spree.

NO LOVERS Bonnie and Clyde's fabled romance never happened – Clyde Barrow was actually a homosexual.

569

William Wallace

The **Scottish general** William Wallace was one of the leaders of a rebellion against the English king **Edward I**. His status as a champion of Scottish nationalism rests on a poetic account of his life written by a minstrel known as Blind Harry. The 1995 film *Braveheart*, starring Mel Gibson, was based in part on this epic poem.

Ned Kelly

Ned Kelly was an Australian bushranger and leader of the Kelly gang. He became an outlaw after he shot a policeman who was trying to arrest his brother. Ned Kelly was famous for wearing homemade armour during his robberies. He was captured after a shoot-out in 1880 and hanged in Melbourne. Kelly's myth grew after his death, and he has become a hero of Australian folklore. His life has been celebrated by the Australian painter **Sidney Nolan**, he was played on film by the young **Mick Jagger**, and his story has recently been retold in a novel by the Australian writer, **Peter Carey**.

WEIRD AND WONDERFUL

The poem listing the supposed adventures of **William Wallace** was written at the same time as the tales about Robin Hood were gaining popularity in England. In the poem, the Scottish hero is even given a lover named Marion.

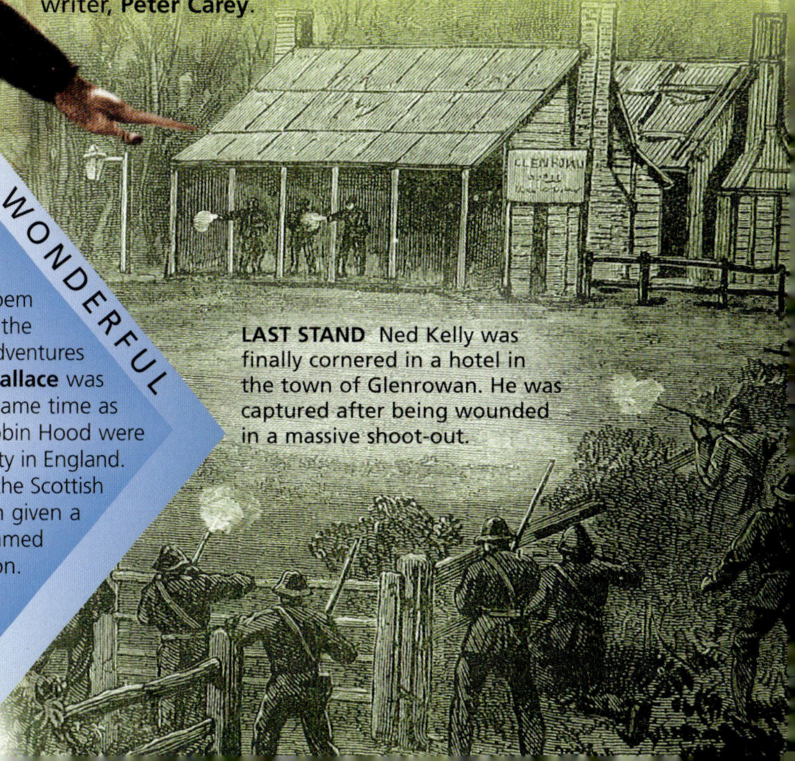

LAST STAND Ned Kelly was finally cornered in a hotel in the town of Glenrowan. He was captured after being wounded in a massive shoot-out.

QUESTION NUMBER

The numbers or star following the answers refer to information boxes on the right.

ANSWERS

QUESTION NUMBER	ANSWERS
8	**The mermaid** (7)
36	**A mermaid** (7)
115	**The Wandering Jew** (1) (5)
294	**The Green Man** (1) (3)
329	**B: Mermaids** (1) (7)
422	**Run away** (it is the bogeyman) (4)
463	**The Pied Piper** (2)
485	**Mermaid** (1) (7)
★ 525	**Santa's reindeer**
666	**St Nicholas** (8)
680	**A goblin** (4)
732	**Robert Browning** (1812-89) (2)
827	**C: Father Christmas** (8)
838	**Reindeer** ★
849	**Donner and Blitzen** ★
913	**Germany** (2)

Folk figures

Core facts (1)

◆ Some stock figures crop up in different folk traditions. **Mermaids**, for example, appear in several traditions, with various powers and attitudes ascribed to them.

◆ Sometimes folk figures are adopted from other cultures. The tale of the **wandering Jew**, for example, became known in France and England within ten years of its being published in a book in Germany.

◆ Often the universality of a folk figure springs from a deep-rooted human urge. For instance, the idea of the **Green Man** expresses the ancient fear that warm days and lush pastures will fail to return after winter.

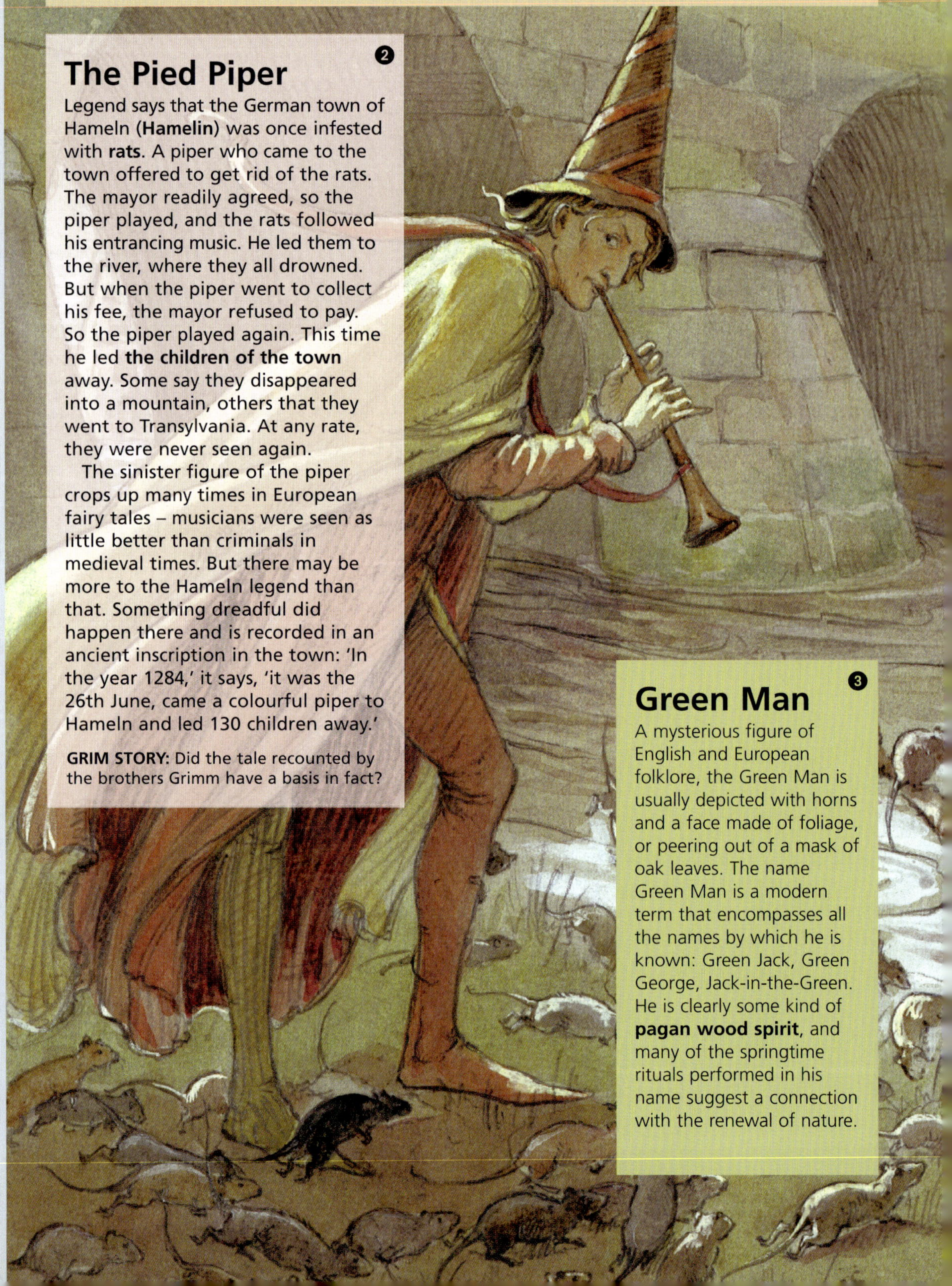

The Pied Piper (2)

Legend says that the German town of Hameln (**Hamelin**) was once infested with **rats**. A piper who came to the town offered to get rid of the rats. The mayor readily agreed, so the piper played, and the rats followed his entrancing music. He led them to the river, where they all drowned. But when the piper went to collect his fee, the mayor refused to pay. So the piper played again. This time he led **the children of the town** away. Some say they disappeared into a mountain, others that they went to Transylvania. At any rate, they were never seen again.

The sinister figure of the piper crops up many times in European fairy tales – musicians were seen as little better than criminals in medieval times. But there may be more to the Hameln legend than that. Something dreadful did happen there and is recorded in an ancient inscription in the town: 'In the year 1284,' it says, 'it was the 26th June, came a colourful piper to Hameln and led 130 children away.'

GRIM STORY: Did the tale recounted by the brothers Grimm have a basis in fact?

Green Man (3)

A mysterious figure of English and European folklore, the Green Man is usually depicted with horns and a face made of foliage, or peering out of a mask of oak leaves. The name Green Man is a modern term that encompasses all the names by which he is known: Green Jack, Green George, Jack-in-the-Green. He is clearly some kind of **pagan wood spirit**, and many of the springtime rituals performed in his name suggest a connection with the renewal of nature.

The bogeyman

4

An **evil hobgoblin** who enjoys frightening children, especially at night, the bogeyman probably derives from the spectre known in Northern England as the 'boggard' or 'boggart'. In Scotland the same figure is called the 'bog', and in the Isle of Man the 'buggane', where it is described as having a large head and long, sharp teeth. At some point the bogeyman seems to have emigrated to America, where he is now better known than in Europe. In the USA he is still occasionally invoked by parents to scare their children into good behaviour: 'Be good or the bogeyman will get you'.

SCARE TACTICS The bogeyman is usually more mischievous than evil.

525 ★

Reindeer

The names of Santa's eight reindeer came from the poem ''Twas the Night Before Christmas', attributed to the US poet Clement Clarke Moore:

Dasher	Comet
Dancer	Cupid
Prancer	Donner
Vixen	Blitzen

Rudolf the red-nosed reindeer came from a poem popularised in Gene Autry's 1949 hit single.

Mermen and mermaids

7

Merpeople are usually depicted as **half-human**, **half-fish**. They live in the sea, and are sometimes considered the subjects of the god **Neptune**. Many peoples have myths about a sea-dwelling race. Greek mythology speaks of the malevolent **Sirens**, and in Norse mythology there are the short-tempered **havfine**. Most of the fairy stories concentrate on attractive young mermaids. Often they leave their natural habitat for the love of a man.

Santa Claus

8

The original Father Christmas, if he existed at all, was the 4th-century bishop Nicholas from Myra in Turkey. Legend says that the bishop gave three bags of gold to three poor girls, and this is the origin of his role as a bestower of gifts. Saint Nicholas is the patron saint of Russia, where he is known to children as **Grandfather Frost** and has a helper named Snegurochka, the snow maiden.

MANY NAMES Santa Claus is a corruption of Sinte Klaas, the Dutch for Saint Nicholas. Santa's pseudonym Chris Cringle, which is common in America, may be a corruption of the German dialect word 'Christkindl', Christ child.

The Wandering Jew

5

The legend of the wandering Jew arose in the 16th century. It says that Christ was mocked by a Jewish shoemaker as he carried the cross to Calvary. The shoemaker, who is sometimes called **Ahasverus**, told Christ to go faster. 'I shall go, but you shall wait till my return,' replied Christ. Thus the shoemaker was condemned to immortality, and forced to walk the Earth until the Second Coming.

Tie-breaker

6

Q Which Christian festival features rabbits?

A Easter. The Easter Bunny has its origins in pagan Europe. Before the arrival of Christianity, Saxon peoples celebrated the spring festival of the goddess Eastre (or Ostara), whose symbol was a hare. This festival became Easter as it was absorbed into the Christian calendar.

QUESTION NUMBER

The numbers or star following the answers refer to information boxes on the right.

ANSWERS

131	**B: Snakes** – he fasted there for 40 days
157	**Glastonbury** ❼
201	**True** – inhabited only by Orthodox monks
202	**Mount Fuji** ❷
210	**Silbury Hill** – 40 m (130 ft) high
314	**Cape Finisterre** ❸
327	**C: St Cuthbert** (c.635-687)
★ 361	**Mecca**
363	**Lhasa** ❺
366	**Santiago de Compostela** ❸
368	**Medina** ★
382	**A dog** ❹
501	**Lindisfarne** – off the Northumberland coast
646	**Stonehenge** ❻
686	**Lhasa** ❺
687	**Abraham** ★ ❽
859	**The Slaughter Stone** ❻
882	**Merlin** ❻
962	**Tokyo** ❷

Sacred sites

Core facts ❶

◆ The world is studded with sites that are places of power for the people who believe in them. These sites can be man-made cities or edifices, such as **Stonehenge** or **Lhasa**, or they may be outstanding natural features such as **Uluru** or **Mount Fuji**.

◆ Some sacred sites are seen as dwelling-places of gods, or resting places of heroes. Just as often they conceal some secret – an entrance to another world, a holy relic or a hero's grave.

◆ Many sacred sites are places of **pilgrimage**. People come to them in order to pay homage and to tap into the spiritual power of the place, and to take a portion of it away with them.

Mount Fuji ❷

The extraordinarily regular form of Mount Fuji (or Fuji-Yama, the Never-Dying Mountain) has become famous around the world. To the **Buddhist** way of thinking it resembles an inverted lotus – the flower that is sacred to the Lord Buddha. The mountain has long been a place of pilgrimage. One legend says that it is inhabited by a goddess known as Radiant Blooming As The Flowers of the Trees, who throws down any pilgrims who are impure of heart. Another legend says that the mountain came into being in one night.

HOKUSAI'S INUME PASS Mount Fuji appears in countless Japanese works of art. The artist Hokusai produced 46 woodblock prints featuring the mountain in the 1830s, the most famous being *The Great Wave*.

Santiago ❸

This city in northern Spain has been a place of pilgrimage for over 1000 years, and some say the cult of the spiritual traveller existed in this region before the 9th century. The cult may be connected with a symbolic journey to **Cape Finisterre** on the Galician coast. The word Finisterre means 'end of the Earth'. Beyond this point lay the great unknown, and so to be here was to stand on the frontier between this life and the next.

HOLY CITY Santiago de Compostela is said to be the burial place of the Apostle St James (Sant Iago), the patron saint of Spain.

Uluru ❹

For Australian aborigines, Uluru has great mythic significance. It is said that in the **Dreamtime** two groups of snake people fought a great battle in this place, which was a sand hill by a water hole. The bodies of the defeated snake people formed rocks, and their hair made the shrubs. The sand hill itself erupted from the earth and solidified, making the great rock of Uluru. Its spectacular red colour is the result of another dreamtime conflict – between a lizard and a wild dog. The lizard killed the dog, and dragged it to the rock, where its blood ran all over. Hence its red glow in the evening sun.

Lhasa

5

Meaning 'land of the gods', Lhasa is the sacred city of **Lamaism**, the Tibetan form of Buddhism. The main temple of the city is said to have been set over the heart of a demoness. She was exerting a negative influence that was impeding the spread of Buddhism in Tibet. According to another legend, the first Buddhist king of Tibet threw a ring in the air, which turned into a temple at the point where it landed. A hidden gate leads from this temple to the Underworld, and Lhasa is the city that grew up around it.

ROOF WITH A VIEW High in the Himalayas, Lhasa's Johkang Temple is the spiritual centre of Tibet.

Stonehenge

6

Legends swirl like mist around the standing stones of Stonehenge. Many of the stories are linked to **King Arthur**. One very old tale says that the stones were erected by Merlin, another that Arthur's father, Uther Pendragon, is buried at the centre of the ring. Another legend claims that Salisbury Plain was once inhabited by a race of **giants**, who were one night dancing in a ring when they were suddenly turned to stone – so creating the circle.

Glastonbury

7

The town of Glastonbury in **Somerset** is said to be the place where **Joseph of Arimathea** began the conversion of the British people. He came there in AD 63, bringing with him the **Holy Grail**, the chalice from which Jesus drank at the Last Supper. The chalice is said to be buried inside Glastonbury Tor, the strange terraced hill outside the town. Glastonbury is also identified with **Avalon**, the Celtic 'Island of Blessed Souls' which is Arthur's resting place. The **Glastonbury Thorn**, a kind of hawthorn that flowers around Christmas time, is believed to be derived from the staff of Joseph of Arimathea, which took root after he planted it in the ground.

★ 361 ★

Mecca

The birthplace of the prophet Muhammad, Mecca is one of the two holiest cities of **Islam**. The other is Medina, where Muhammad took refuge. All Muslims are required to make the pilgrimage to Mecca once in their lives. The most sacred site in Mecca is the **Ka'aba**, a shrine that has the Black Stone built into its wall.

NAME CHANGE Previously known as Ayer's Rock, and now officially called by its aboriginal name, Uluru, this massive sandstone monolith lies almost at the geographical centre of Australia.

WEIRD AND WONDERFUL

8

Legend has it that the **Black Stone of Mecca** was given to the patriarch Abraham by the angel Gabriel. It passed to Muhammad, who built it into the wall of the Ka'aba.

QUESTION NUMBER

The numbers or star following the answers refer to information boxes on the right.

ANSWERS

QUESTION NUMBER	ANSWERS
48	**Walter Raleigh** 5
★ 124	**James Hilton** (also wrote *Goodbye Mr Chips*)
193	**Moses** 8
200	**Babylon** 6
242	**Brueghel the Elder** 1 4
311	**No place** – from Greek *ou* = not, no + *topos* = place
489	**Atlantis** 2
529	**Kubla Khan** 7
558	**Edward Elgar** (also called 'In London Town') 1 4
655	**The Shangri-Las** ★
665	**El Dorado** 5
743	**Cockaigne** 1 4
762	**Christian** 6
953	**Shangri-La** ★
970	**Zion** 6
985	**Lyonnesse** 3
989	**John Wayne** – also starred Robert Mitchum

Mythical places

Core facts 1

◆ Myths about fabulous cities and countries fall into two types: there are places like **El Dorado**, which are or were believed to exist somewhere in the real world, and there are lands such as **Cockaigne**, which are understood to belong to fairy tales.

◆ Both types of mythical place are wonderful: they are heavens on earth, lands of plenty, the hubs of glorious civilisations, or the abode of uncountable riches.

◆ In a sense, all mythical places represent the fulfilment of human desire. It seems the mind needs to believe in some kind of **promised land** – in this world or the next.

Atlantis 2

The first mention of Atlantis occurs in the work of the Greek philosopher **Plato**. In his time it was already a legend, an island civilisation submerged generations before. Many attempts have been made to locate the lost city of Atlantis. Various theories have placed it in locations as diverse as Antarctica, South America and Indonesia. Most likely, the legend is a folk memory of the destruction of the **Minoan civilisation**, and of the disappearance of a large chunk of the Greek island of **Santorini** in a catastrophic earthquake around 1300 BC.

Lyonnesse 3

Lyonnesse is the **English Atlantis**. It is the name given to a kingdom which, according to legend, once connected Cornwall to the Isles of Scilly. In the 18th century, sailors occasionally claimed to have fished up door handles and windows from the waters off Cornwall. It is said that the land of Lyonnesse was overwhelmed in one night by a great wave. There was only one survivor, a man named **Trevelian** who rode on a white horse to safety ahead of the wave.

The land of Cockaigne 4

An **imaginary world of medieval fantasy**, Cockaigne is a place where no one works, where men are paid to drink ale, and where food is available at every step. In Cockaigne, fences are made of sausages, tarts cook themselves, the streets are paved with pastry, and the rafters of the houses are grilled eels. There is a fountain that makes the old young and beautiful, and sex is as freely available as food.

BRUEGHEL'S DEPICTION Stories of Cockaigne circulated throughout Europe from the 13th century. With its unending leisure and constant supply of luxuries, it represented a peasant's idea of sensual paradise.

El Dorado

5

This is a legendary country awash with gold which Spanish explorers imagined they would find somewhere along the Amazon river in South America. The capital of El Dorado was said to be the city of **Manoa**, where the roofs of all the houses were golden.

The legend of El Dorado was treated very seriously by explorers of the 16th and 17th century. Sir Walter Raleigh twice went in search of it, but came back empty-handed.

GOLDEN BOY El Dorado means 'the gilded one'. It refers to the king of Manoa, who was said to have his body covered with gold dust every day, so that he looked like a living gilded statue.

The city of Zion

6

A real place, the hill of Zion can be seen in the Jewish quarter of **Jerusalem**. For centuries the idea of Zion has represented a spiritual as well as a physical homeland for Jews and Christians. The psalms speak of the Israelites in Babylonian exile: 'By the rivers of Babylon, where we sat down, there we wept when we remembered Zion.' This has been interpreted as a kind of homesickness for God. So, in *Pilgrim's Progress*, **John Bunyan** gives to the celestial city the name Mount Zion.

WEIRD AND WONDERFUL

7

In the poem *Kubla Khan* by Samuel Taylor Coleridge, **Xanadu** was a fabulous city with a great 'pleasure dome'. It had its origins in a real place in south-east Mongolia: Shang-tu, a summer residence of Kublai Khan.

The land of milk and honey

8

'A land flowing with milk and honey' is a biblical phrase. It was used by **Yahweh** to describe the country to which Moses would take the people of Israel once he lead them out of Egypt. The Hebrews identified this land with **Canaan**, where they eventually settled. But the phrase has since come to stand for any as-yet unattained place of contentment and plenty – essentially, the land of Cockaigne without the over-indulgence.

GIANT FRUIT According to the Bible, the grapes from the land of milk and honey were so large that they had to be carried on a pole between two men.

★ 124

Shangri-La

The name Shangri-La was coined by the English novelist **James Hilton**, who described a hidden Tibetan paradise in his novel *Lost Horizon* (1933). In 1937, the book was made into a film, directed by Frank Capra and starring Ronald Colman. US President Franklin D. Roosevelt took the name for his mountain retreat in Maryland.

Wizards and witches

QUESTION NUMBER

The numbers or star following the answers refer to information boxes on the right.

ANSWERS

- 191 **Halloween** – All Hallows Even, October 31
- 194 **Gandalf** 2
- 260 **B: Abracadabra** – first used by Gnostic heretics
- 270 **A broomstick** 5
- 296 **Druids** – possibly from Celtic *dru* = tree
- 358 **Ruby slippers** 2 4 5
- 376 **Serafina Pekkala** 2
- 409 **12** 5
- 476 **Morgan le Fay** 8
- 556 **Witchfinder General of England** 6
- 642 ***Fantasia*** 3
- 653 **Wicca** 5
- 742 **Circe** – daughter of the Sun god Helios
- 782 **Prospero** 2
- 787 ***Macbeth*** 5
- 846 **Witch** 1
- 888 **Professor Dumbledore** 2
- 898 **Samantha** – the series ran 1964-72
- 971 **Warlock** 2
- ★ 984 **Saul**

Core facts 1

◆ The words wizard and witch both derive from an old word meaning 'to know'. They are related to the word 'wise'.
◆ The first witches were actually people who possessed **special knowledge** of medicinal plants, or who practised pagan divination.
◆ After the coming of Christianity, this knowledge was deemed profane. Herbal remedies became magical potions, and divination was seen as the casting of evil spells.
◆ Witches were persecuted in trials and **witch-hunts** that lasted from 1300 to 1800. Most convicted witches were harmless old women, unfortunate victims of malice and superstition.

Fictional wizards and witches 2

In fiction, as in history, wizards are usually seen as benevolent and powerful, while witches are malevolent and flawed. There is even a separate word for a bad wizard – a warlock. Among the many portrayals of good wizards are **Prospero**, the spell-weaving sorcerer of Shakespeare's *The Tempest*; **Professor Dumbledore** in the Harry Potter stories; **Gandalf** in *The Lord of the Rings*; and L. Frank Baum's **Wizard of Oz** – who, though fraudulent, is ultimately kindly. Witches in fairy tales are invariably bad. One exception is the enigmatic **Serafina Pekkala** from Philip Pullman's *His Dark Materials* trilogy, which challenges Christian ideas about good and evil.

Magic trainee 3

The story of the **sorcerer's apprentice** comes from a poem by **Goethe**, in which a trainee wizard gets his broom to carry water. But he cannot make the broom stop, and soon the house is awash. The poem inspired French composer **Paul Dukas**'s orchestral piece, *L'Apprenti sorcier* (1897), and was animated for Walt Disney's ***Fantasia***, in which Mickey Mouse played the role of the apprentice.

★ 984

The witch of Endor

This strange story is told in the Bible (Samuel book 1, chapter 28). **Saul**, the king of Israel, had outlawed witchcraft. But on the eve of a crucial battle, having consulted God and received no answer, he decided to ask a witch in Endor to divine the outcome. The witch summoned the spirit of the prophet **Samuel** to help with the divination. Samuel rebuked Saul for disturbing his rest, and told him he must die the next day.

Witch movies 4

Cast a Deadly Spell	1991
Halloween 3: Season of the Witch	1982
I Married a Witch	1942
Practical Magic	1999
Teen Witch	1989
The Blair Witch Project	1999
The Craft	1996
The Witches of Eastwick	1987
The Wizard of Oz	1939
Warlock	1988

HOCUS POCUS Disney's 1993 film starred Bette Midler and Kathy Najimy.

The ways of witches

The common Christian view of witches is to be found in Shakespeare's ***Macbeth***, where in the opening scene three 'weird sisters' huddle round a cauldron. Later they concoct a potion with the words 'Double, double, toil and trouble...'

Folklore says that **a coven** consists of 12 witches, plus the Devil to make 13. A witch can fly on her **broomstick**, and is usually with her 'familiar' – a **black cat**.

In modern times there has been a revival in witchcraft. Proponents refer to it by the Old English word **'Wicca'**, and see it as a healing art.

WICKED WITCH OF THE WEST The witch in *The Wizard of Oz* craves ruby slippers. Both she and the magical shoes are common fairy-tale motifs.

WEIRD AND WONDERFUL

Matthew Hopkins, Witch-finder General, was active in East Anglia in 1645-7, during the turmoil of the English Civil War. He was paid by each town for advising how to obtain evidence against suspected witches.

Sink or swim

Accused witches were often '**swum**' to establish their guilt. If they floated it was deemed to be because water, the sacred means of baptism, would not hold them. Hence they were guilty. If they sank and drowned, then they could be posthumously declared innocent. Some victims were simply thrown into the water; others were strapped to a device called a **ducking stool**, then dipped into a river or lake.

Morgan le Fay

In Celtic legends, Morgan le Fay is a gifted sorceress, the half-sister and implacable **enemy of King Arthur**. She steals the sword Excalibur from the king and puts it into the hands of a knight named **Accolon**. She also gives a charmed shield to **Tristram**, who uses it in a joust against Arthur.

However, Morgan is also a healer. Sometimes called the Queen of the Isle of Avalon, she is said to be one of the three women who take Arthur's body away to its place of safekeeping.

ENCHANTING Most witches are portrayed as hags, but Morgan is an example of the beautiful enchantress.

Giants and dwarfs

QUESTION NUMBER

The numbers or star following the answers refer to information boxes on the right.

ANSWERS

- 84 True 5
- 238 The Philistines 3
- 306 Lilliput 5
- ★ 331 Doc
- 386 Taurus the Bull 4
- 402 Seven ★
- 421 Playful ★
- 488 Orion 4
- 613 Jack and the Beanstalk 6
- 644 **Golden eggs** (he also steals a golden harp) 6
- 711 Big Friendly Giant 1
- 796 Goliath 3
- 889 Tom Thumb 2
- 914 Brobdingnag 5
- 942 Orion 4
- 943 Atlas 4
- 951 Lemuel 5

Core facts 1

◆ Giants feature in the mythology of almost every culture. It has been suggested that this is because all of us inhabit a world of giants as children, with adults towering over us. This also explains the parallel fascination with being small.

◆ The giants of myth and fairy tale are usually the enemies of mankind, monstrous and brutish. The **Big Friendly Giant** of Roald Dahl's children's story is a deliberate reversal of this convention.

◆ In most tales, from **Goliath** to **Jack and the Beanstalk**, the bad giant is overcome by a weaker opponent who uses his wits rather than sheer strength.

Tom Thumb 2

An anonymous nursery tale named *The History of Tom Thumbe* was published in England in 1621. It is believed to be the work of **Richard Johnson**, but it may draw on a folk tale known throughout Europe. In the story, Tom Thumb is a tiny boy given to a farmer and his wife who are desperate for a child. Tom's diminutive size leads to all sorts of adventures – in one, he is swallowed by a fish, which then ends up on his mother's chopping board. Tom comes through all these adventures unscathed, and despite being no bigger than a thumb he lives happily ever after.

BIG DADDY Tom's tiny size made giants of his family and other people around him.

David and Goliath 3

In the Bible story, Goliath is the **champion of the Philistines**. His height is given as 'six cubits and a span' – about 3.2 m (11 ft). Goliath challenges the Israelites to decide the battle by single combat. The shepherd boy **David**, who is delivering food to his brothers, hears of the challenge and accepts it. David uses his slingshot to hurl a stone, which strikes Goliath in the forehead and kills him outright.

★ 331

The seven dwarfs ★

There is a long tradition of mystical groups of seven, which includes the Seven Churches of Asia, the Seven Sages of Greece, the Seven Seas, and the constellation Pleiades known as the Seven Sisters. The Seven Dwarfs of the Grimm fairy tale are in this tradition. In the **Disney** cartoon version of the story their names are: **Happy**, **Dopey**, **Sleepy**, **Sneezy**, **Doc**, **Grumpy** and **Bashful**.

LITTLE HELPERS In the fairy tale, the seven dwarves befriend Snow White.

Greek giants
4

Giants figure prominently in Greek myths. One of the best known is **Atlas**, who was condemned to carry the world on his shoulders in punishment for defying Zeus. **Orion**, a son of Poseidon, was so tall that he could walk on the seabed with his head above the waves as he hunted. He was killed by the goddess Artemis and raised to the stars, where he seems to be aiming an arrow at Taurus.

THE WORLD ON HIS SHOULDERS Depictions of Atlas holding the globe led to his name being adopted in the 16th century for books of maps.

HUGE PRESENCE
The giants in most fairy stories are male. But in the 1958 film *Attack of the 50 Foot Woman* the giant is female – and after a cheating husband. The giant, Nancy Archer, is played by Allison Hayes. In 1993, the film was remade, starring Daryl Hannah as Nancy.

NASTY SURPRISE
After arriving in Lilliput and falling asleep, Gulliver awoke to find himself tied to the ground.

Gulliver
5

In **Jonathan Swift's** book, the ship's surgeon **Lemuel Gulliver** spends time both as a giant (among the tiny Lilliputians) and as a doll-sized dwarf (among the giants of **Brobdingnag**). In **Lilliput** he uses his size to great effect. He tows away the fleet of the king's enemies, and puts out a fire at the palace by urinating on it.

Giants and Jack
6

The story of **Jack and the Beanstalk** has almost absorbed a similar tale named **Jack the Giant-Killer**, in which the boy overcomes a giant who has been terrorising Cornwall. In the tale as we now know it, Jack is duped into selling a cow for a handful of beans. In despair he plants the beans, which overnight grow into a stalk that reaches into the clouds. Jack climbs the stalk and comes to a country inhabited by a giant. The giant detects Jack, and recites the chilling rhyme: 'Fe, fi, fo fum, I smell the blood of an Englishman. Be he alive or be he dead, I'll grind his bones to make my bread.'

QUESTION NUMBER

The numbers or star following the answers refer to information boxes on the right.

ANSWERS

16 Midsummer's night ❶ ❸

47 A gremlin ❼

142 Elf ❼

183 *Goblin Market* ❻

222 Leprechaun ❷

291 Gnome ❼

342 Jinn, or genie ❼

431 Ariel ❸

508 *Goblin Market* ❻

546 Titania ❶ ❸

★ 641 Tooth

682 Trolls ❼

712 Pixie ❼

736 *The Water-Babies* ❻

770 Tinkerbell ❻

817 Brownie ❼

891 Puck ❸

930 Fairies in *A Midsummer Night's Dream* ❸

933 Oberon ❶ ❸

977 Goblin ❼

Fairy folk

Core facts ❶

◆ Fairies are happy, ethereal spirits of European folklore. They are usually kind to humans, but they are also timid and private creatures, rarely seen. The realm of the fairies is ruled over by **King Oberon** and **Queen Titania**.

◆ It is said that fairies are visible to human eyes during a full Moon on Midsummer's Eve, when they can be observed dancing. They can also be seen by someone using a stone that has a natural hole in its centre, like a telescope.

◆ Some fairies are said to be the same size as humans and pass incognito in human society. More usually they are thought to be small people, no more than a few inches in height.

Leprechauns ❷

The word leprechaun may be derived from the Irish Gaelic for 'maker of one shoe'. They are **fairy cobblers**, but they only ever make one shoe of a pair. Leprechauns will perform tasks for humans in payment for acts of kindness. They are said to get drunk in the evenings, and can then be seen riding on sheep.

Shakespeare ❸

A Midsummer Night's Dream draws on fairy lore known to the Elizabethans. The title is a reference to the one night when fairies can be seen by mortals. A sub-plot deals with a conflict between the fairy king and queen, **Oberon and Titania**, who are attended by Cobweb, Moth, Mustardseed and Peaseblossom. The other fairy character in the play is the mischievous **Puck**, also called by the traditional English fairy name Robin Goodfellow. A more serious fairy features in ***The Tempest***. This is **Ariel**, the servant of the sorcerer **Prospero**.

TITANIA AND BOTTOM
In Shakespeare's play *A Midsummer Night's Dream*, the weaver Bottom is given an ass's head by the mischievous fairy, Puck.

641

Tooth fairy

In European and American folklore, the tooth fairy leaves a coin in exchange for a milk tooth placed under a **child's pillow**. This well-known tradition is very new – the tooth fairy is not part of any established mythology and its origin is unknown.

Fairies in literature

6

Perhaps the best-known literary fairy is **Tinkerbell**, the jealous companion of Peter Pan in J.M. Barrie's play. When the play is staged, children in the audience are encouraged to declare their belief in fairies and so restore the dead Tinkerbell to life. In Charles Kingsley's ***The Water-Babies*** a child chimney sweep runs away from his cruel employer and falls into a river, where he is transformed into a kind of aquatic fairy. Christina Rossetti's poem ***Goblin Market*** tells the story of two sisters who are tempted by goblins to eat forbidden fruit, like young Eves in the Garden of Eden. One sister succumbs and is stricken ill, the other resists and saves her sister.

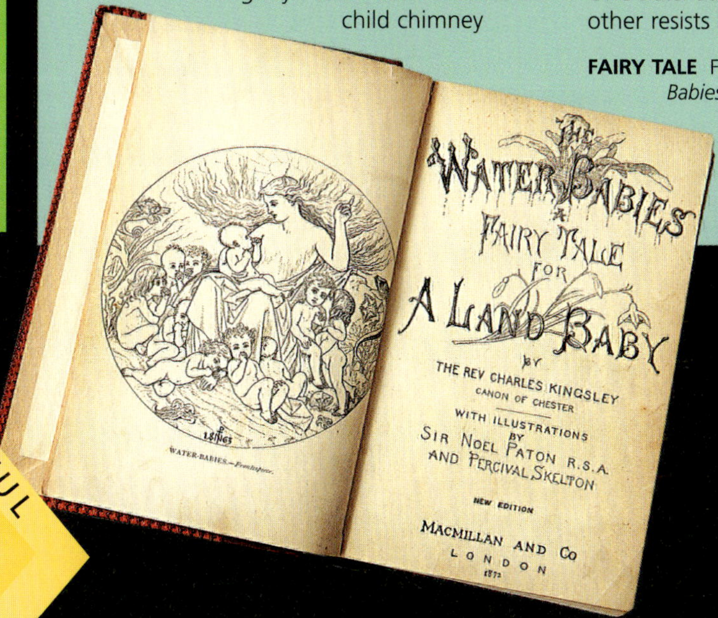

FAIRY TALE First published in 1863, *The Water-Babies* tells the story of Tom, who escapes his master, Grimes. Tom has many adventures beneath the water and meets the other water babies and their rulers, Mrs Doasyouwouldbe-doneby and Mrs Bedonebyasyoudid.

WEIRD AND WONDERFUL

4

The **banshee** is a rather scary figure in **Irish folklore**. She is a fairy spirit who foretells a death in the household by wailing. If she is caught she must reveal the name of the person who is soon to die.

Different kinds of fairy

7

- **Brownie** A Scottish spirit of the home, who does small domestic jobs while the household sleeps.
- **Pixie** A kind of fairy native to the counties of Devon and Cornwall.
- **Elf** In Teutonic mythology, a nasty and dangerous kind of fairy (in German, an elf-dream is a nightmare). Tolkien saw elves as brave and wise – a vision more in tune with the modern concept of them.
- **Goblin** A little house demon who plays practical jokes on humans and can curdle milk by smiling at it.
- **Gremlin** A modern fairy, rather like a goblin. Gremlins were blamed by wartime RAF pilots for everything that went wrong with their aircraft.
- **Troll** A Scandinavian fairy, skilled in metalwork and inclined to steal from humans.
- **Jinn** Often called a 'genie', the demon of Arab myth. Bad genies are ugly, and good ones superbly beautiful.
- **Gnome** A spirit that guards mines and quarries. The name comes from the Greek *geo-nomos*, meaning 'earth-dweller'.

JINN According to the Koran, God created jinns from 'a smokeless flame of fire'.

TROLL According to legend, trolls hate the Sun. If caught in its rays, they are turned to stone.

The fairy cult

5

The **Victorians** were obsessed with fairies. Our present-day image of fairies as lithe creatures, 20 cm (8 in) inches tall with butterfly wings, is a product of the Victorian imagination. **Fairy painting** became a genre in its own right, and many **books of fairy lore** were published. **Alleged photographs** of fairies were treated with complete seriousness as scientific proof of their existence. One of the most famous sets of fairy photos was endorsed by **Arthur Conan Doyle**, author of the Sherlock Holmes stories.

QUESTION NUMBER

The numbers or star following the answers refer to information boxes on the right.

ANSWERS

Question number	Answer
25	**Gary Oldman** ❶ ❷ ❽
35	**Dracula** ❶ ❽
78	**Garlic** ❸
81	**True** ❸
284	***The Hunger*** ❽
318	**Werewolf** ❹
332	***Thriller*** (released in 1983) ★
456	**Vlad** ❺
553	***Nosferatu*** ❽
581	**False** ❹
589	**False** ❷
★ 608	**Voodoo**
692	**Anne Rice** ❽
715	**Mr Hyde** ❻
739	**Bram Stoker** ❷
774	**A silver bullet, or silver arrow** ❹
842	**Van Helsing** ❷

Vampires and werewolves

Core facts ❶

◆ Modern myth is full of **shape-changers**, monsters who hide among us until they strike.
◆ Many of these monsters came to the forefront of the popular imagination at the end of the **Victorian era**, when it was realised that there are dark corners of the human mind where terrors may lurk. **Dracula** and **Dr Jekyll** both belong to this Gothic tradition. They tell us that evil may lurk below the most respectable façade.
◆ In the 20th century, and especially in **film**, it was the sexually predatory aspect of vampirism that interested us most. The male vampire's bite is seen as a dangerous kind of kiss.

Bram Stoker's Dracula ❷

Bram Stoker's novel *Dracula* endowed folklore with a new and terrifying monster, the undead vampire. The novel tells how the sinister count has his dormant body shipped to England from his castle in **Transylvania**. En route he makes victims of the entire crew, then escapes from the ship in the form of a wolf (not a bat). His bloodsucking activities come to the attention of **Professor Van Helsing**, who resolves to pursue the vampire back to Transylvania. Van Helsing neutralises all the vampire's boxes of earth (the only places he can rest) by sprinkling communion wafers on them. Finally, he corners Dracula in his castle, beheads him, and stabs him through the heart.

GOTHIC HORROR
Bram Stoker was born in Dublin, Ireland. His most famous novel, *Dracula*, was first published in 1897.

Vampires ❸

There is a body of vampire lore which is adhered to in most retellings of the story. Not all of it derives from Stoker's novel. It is generally agreed that **vampires dread the light** and must always be in their coffin by sunrise. They can be kept at bay by the **sign of the cross** and by **garlic**. Their **reflection** does not show up in mirrors. They can change themselves into **bats**, and use this ability to gain access to their sleeping victims. A vampire's bite usually turns the victim into a vampire, too.

Werewolves ❹

'Wer' is an Old English word for a man, so a werewolf is a man-wolf. They are also known by the Greek term **lycanthrope** (wolf-man). The idea of a man becoming a wolf is ancient – one tale in Ovid's *Metamorphoses* tells how **Lycaon**, king of Arcadia, is turned into a wolf by the god Jupiter. As the myth has come down to us, werewolves transform into their animal form during the night at full Moon. They can only be killed by silver arrows or bullets.

Tie-breaker ❺

Q By what name is Vlad Tepes better known to history?
A Vlad the Impaler. He ruled Wallachia, part of modern Romania, during the 15th century. His exceptionally cruel and bloodthirsty methods are said to have inspired the vampire myth.

Jekyll and Hyde

To the modern mind, Robert Louis Stevenson's novel *The Strange Case of Dr Jekyll and Mr Hyde* reads like an allegory of the subconscious. The uncontrollable Mr Hyde, the alter ego of the affable Dr Jekyll, looks like the Freudian id – the animal urges that we have to suppress. The book also seems to prefigure the crimes of **Jack the Ripper** – who has himself now become a bogeyman of the imagination. It is no surprise that many people are unsure whether Jack really existed.

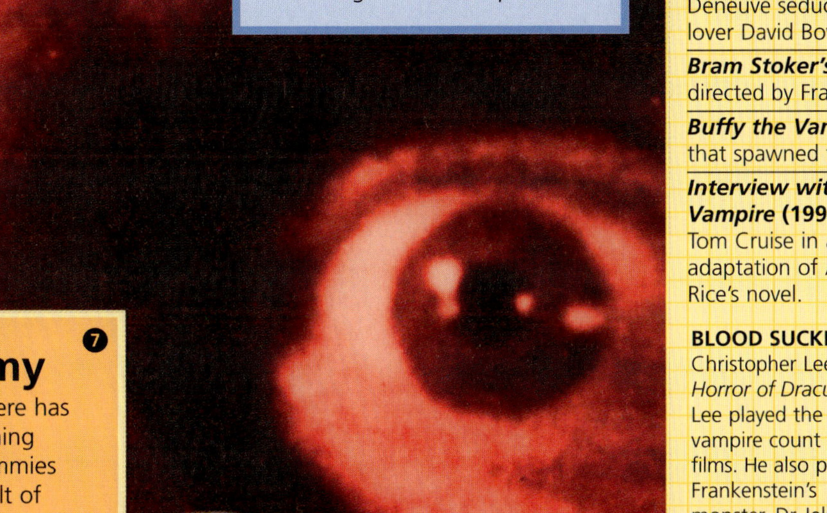

DUAL ROLE Shown here (background) as Mr Hyde, Spencer Tracy played Dr Jekyll and his crazed alter ego in a 1941 screen adaptation of Robert Louis Stevenson's novel.

Zombies

608 ★

A zombie is an apparently living person from whom the soul has been removed. In the **voodoo** cult, zombies act as servants to a sorcerer. The idea of a zombie is part of a larger religious cult that includes a god of the dead named **Ghede** or Baron Samedi. He guards the road to the afterlife and absorbs the knowledge of all who pass him.

Some vampire films

***Nosferatu* (1922)** Max Schreck plays the pallid and ghoulish Count Orlock.

***Dracula* (1931)** Bela Lugosi in the title role, which he played many more times in the 1930s and 1940s.

***Horror of Dracula* (1958)** A Hammer horror film.

***Nosferatu – The Vampire* (1979)** Klaus Kinski in a remake of the 1922 film.

***Love at First Bite* (1979)** A vampire spoof starring George Hamilton.

***The Hunger* (1983)** Vampire Catherine Deneuve seduces Susan Sarandon when her lover David Bowie grows old.

***Bram Stoker's Dracula* (1992)** Gary Oldman directed by Francis Ford Coppola.

***Buffy the Vampire Slayer* (1992)** The film that spawned the TV show.

***Interview with the Vampire* (1994)** Tom Cruise in an adaptation of Anne Rice's novel.

BLOOD SUCKER Christopher Lee in *Horror of Dracula*. Lee played the vampire count in nine films. He also played Frankenstein's monster, Dr Jekyll, and the Mummy.

The Mummy

To Western eyes, there has always been something demonic about mummies and the Egyptian cult of death. After the discovery of **Tutankhamun's tomb** there arose the myth of the **'mummy's curse'** after the expedition's sponsor, Lord Carnarvon, suffered an untimely death.

HAMMER HORROR Several films have been made based on mummies. *The Curse of the Mummy's Tomb* was a British take on the theme.

QUESTION NUMBER

The numbers or star following the answers refer to information boxes on the right.

ANSWERS

33 ***Westworld*** – directed by Michael Crichton, 1973

186 ***The Wizard of Oz*** ❹

187 ***Frankenstein*** ❶ ❷

271 **Mary Shelley** ❶ ❷

289 **Pygmalion** ❺

★ 312 **Karel Čapek**

333 **Arnold Schwarzenegger** ❽

337 **Data** ❻

345 **Man-like** ❻ ★

350 ***My Fair Lady*** – musical play by Alan Jay Lerner ❺

436 ***The Winter's Tale*** – wife of Leontes, king of Sicilia

470 **Kraftwerk** – first version 1978

526 ***Wonderful Wizard of Oz*** ❹

527 **Pinocchio** ❸

528 **Its maker** ❷

571 ***Terminator*** ❽

633 **B: A clay man** ❼

697 ***Frankenstein*** ❶ ❷

726 **Toto** ❹

905 **Gepetto** ❸

990 **R2-D2 (or Artoo-Detoo)** – from the planet Naboo

Man-made men

Core facts ❶

◆ Writers and myth-makers have long been fascinated by the idea of a person creating another human being by artificial means.

◆ Very often the initial success of the man-maker turns to disaster. **Frankenstein**, like **Prometheus** in the Greek myths, is punished for overstepping his authority. The moral is that the act of creation should be left to the gods.

◆ Some stories focus on the early struggles of the automaton. **Pinocchio**, for example, longs to be a real boy, but must suffer like a human to achieve his goal. The **tin man** wants to have a heart, but he must demonstrate a capacity for love first.

Frankenstein ❷

The story of the man created by Doctor Frankenstein was written by **Mary Shelley** in 1818. The doctor constructs his man from human body parts, and brings it to life with electricity harvested from lightning. But the created man rebels against his unnatural existence and turns into a murderous monster. Dr Frankenstein, it is suggested, transgresses the limits placed on man by usurping God's role as creator, and is punished for it.

SILENT ROLE The monster played by Boris Karloff was mute – in the novel he spoke.

CARVING A SON The kindly puppet-maker Gepetto at work on his creation.

Pinocchio ❸

The story of *Pinocchio* was written by the Italian journalist **Carlo Collodi** in 1881. It begins with the words: 'Once upon a time there was a piece of wood'. This wood is carved by **Gepetto** into a living puppet. The puppet longs to become a real boy, but first it must overcome its naughty ways. When Pinocchio tells lies, his nose grows longer.

Collodi's tale is much darker than the familiar cartoon version: in the original story Pinocchio loses his wooden feet in a fire, he is robbed, imprisoned and even hanged.

The tin man 4

The tin man is one of the companions of **Dorothy** and her dog **Toto** on their journey to find the **Wizard of Oz**. As the story unfolds, each of Dorothy's companions contributes the very thing they lack: the cowardly **lion** shows courage, the brainless **scarecrow** is intelligent and resourceful, and the heartless **tin man** is full of compassion.

PRINT FIRST
The 1939 film *The Wizard of Oz* was based on the novel by Lyman Frank Baum, published in 1900.

Pygmalion and Galatea 5

The story of a man creating a woman, some versions say that Pygmalion was the king of Cyprus, who commissioned a statue of a perfect woman. Others say that Pygmalion was the sculptor himself. Either way, Pygmalion fell in love with the ivory woman and wished he could find a real woman like her. Seeing his misery, **Aphrodite** brought the statue to life.

LOVE COMES TO LIFE
Pygmalion later married the woman he had made.

Data 6

In the ***Star Trek*** series, Data is the most advanced android ever built. He constantly points out his inability to feel love, grief, friendship, sorrow or any of the quintessential human emotions. But in fact he demonstrates these qualities all the time – he merely expresses them in terms of his own electronic physiology.

The golem 7

In **Jewish folklore** the golem is a clay man brought to life by magic. Some versions of the legend say the first golem was created by a rabbi in Prague in 1580 to protect Jews from pogroms. But the golem began to run amok, and so had to be 'deactivated'. There are different ways of breathing life into the golem. One is to write the secret name of God on a parchment and place it in his mouth. Another is to write the Hebrew word *emet* (truth) on his forehead. To stop the golem, one erases the first 'e', making the word *met*, meaning death.

The Terminator 8

The Terminator, as played by **Arnold Schwarzenegger**, is a cyborg, a man-made man who is simultaneously superhuman and sub-human. He has superhuman strength but is devoid of human emotion. His moral blankness means that he can be used for evil, as in *Terminator 1*, or for good, as in *Terminator 2*.

MAN-MACHINE The Terminator is in a long tradition of scary robot figures in film: one of the first was the woman created in the film *Metropolis*.

★ 312

Robots ★

The word robot was coined by the Czech writer **Karel Čapek**. The name comes from the word ***robota***, meaning labour. An **android**, from the Greek for man-like, is a robot that outwardly resembles a human being.

Archetypal fairy tales

QUESTION NUMBER

The numbers or star following the answers refer to information boxes on the right.

ANSWERS

QUESTION NUMBER	ANSWERS
12	**100 years** ❸
15	**Midnight** ❶❷❹
37	***The Company of Wolves*** (released in 1984) ❺
79	**Snow White** ❽
140	**B: Jean Cocteau** (1889-1963)
192	**Goldilocks** ❶❻
★ 197	**Beauty and the Beast**
212	**Esther and Abi Ofarim** – reached No.1 in 1968
261	**Once upon a time** ❶
266	**A pumpkin** ❶❷❹
353	**Glass** ❷
406	**Two** ❷❹
534	**Little Red Riding Hood** ❺
551	**Rossini** – Gioacchino Antonio (1792-1868)
580	***Snow White and the Seven Dwarves*** ❽
746	**Currants** – he was eventually eaten by a fox
828	**A: Sleeping Beauty** ❸
853	**Snow White** ❽
999	***Into the Woods*** – opened in New York in 1987

Core facts ❶

◆ Similar motifs run through many tales. The main protagonist is a girl. Her mother is dead or absent, her father is distant or ineffectual, and stepmothers are invariably wicked.

◆ The heroines never have a real name. **Goldilocks**, **Cinderella** – these are descriptions of appearance or circumstance.

◆ Many tales are set in medieval kingdoms with dark forests and high castles, populated by talking animals, witches and fairy godmothers.

◆ The stories are usually topped and tailed with the same formulaic phrases: '**Once upon a time...**' and '**they all lived happily ever after**'.

Cinderella ❷

A beautiful girl is treated as a slave by her stepmother and two stepsisters. When the king announces a ball, Cinderella is not invited. But her **fairy godmother** comes to her aid: she turns a pumpkin into a carriage, mice into horses, a rat into a coachman and lizards into footmen. Cinderella herself is given fine clothes to wear. But she is told that the magic will wear off **at midnight**. At the ball, she dances with the **prince**, who falls in love with her. She too is so entranced that she forgets the time, and has to rush from the palace as her clothes turn back to rags. In her haste, she loses one of her **glass slippers**. The prince takes the slipper, and declares that he will marry whomsoever it fits. In this way he finds Cinderella again.

BELLE OF THE BALL Unlike her ugly and selfish step-sisters, Cinderella was beautiful, good-natured and kind.

Sleeping Beauty ❸

Charles Perrault's Sleeping Beauty (called Briar Rose in the Grimm version) is a princess. Seven good fairies come to bestow blessings at her birth, but one bad fairy is forgotten. This snubbed fairy places a curse on the child, saying that one day she will **prick her finger** on a spindle and die. The last of the good fairies uses her blessing to mitigate the curse: now the princess will not die, but will **sleep for 100 years**. The king outlaws spindles, but the curse nevertheless comes to pass when the princess is 16 years old. The good fairy comes to the castle and sends all the servants to sleep too. She makes a forest grow around the castle so that it lies hidden for 100 years. At the end of that time a prince from another family spies the castle from afar, and makes his way to it through the forest, which parts magically for him. The princess awakes, they fall in love, and marry.

BEAUTY SLEEP The idea that the princess is awakened by a kiss from the prince is a later addition to the tale.

WEIRD AND WONDER ❹

In the Charles Perrault version of **Cinderella**, the step-sisters are forgiven and brought to live in the palace. In the Grimm account they have their eyes pecked out by birds when they try to attend her wedding.

Little Red Riding Hood

5

A young girl is told by her mother to take some food to her ailing grandmother, on the far side of the forest. In the Grimm version, her mother warns her 'not to stray from the path'. Along the way she encounters **a wolf**, to whom she innocently discloses her errand. The wolf runs on ahead, devours the grandmother, and climbs into her bed to await Little Red Riding Hood. When she arrives, she does not recognise the wolf, but remarks with growing suspicion on the wolf's appearance. At the moment when she realises the danger, the wolf devours her too. And that, in the Perrault version, is the end of the story. In the Grimm version, however, she and the grandmother are rescued by a huntsman who disembowels the wolf and sets them free.

STRANGE BEDFELLOWS
Many different versions of the Red Riding Hood story have been told. Perrault has her climbing into bed with the wolf before remarking on his vulpine body.

Snow White

8

The Grimm version of this tale contains some characteristically gory details. Snow White is a princess with hair as black as ebony, lips as red as blood and skin as white as snow. The queen, her stepmother, has a **magic mirror**, which tells her that she is the most beautiful woman in the kingdom. But one day, the mirror says that Snow White is now more beautiful. The queen, enraged, tells a huntsman to take Snow White into the forest and kill her. But the huntsman cannot bring himself to do it. Instead he kills a boar, and takes its heart back to the queen. (In the Grimm version, the queen eats the heart.) Meanwhile, Snow White finds safety with the **seven dwarves**. But the mirror tells the queen that Snow White is not dead. Three times she comes to the dwarves cottage disguised as a pedlar, and tries to kill Snow White.

Goldilocks

6

Out of sheer curiosity, Goldilocks breaks into the house of the **Three Bears**, tucks into their porridge, sits in their chairs and goes to sleep in their beds. At the end of the story she runs away – without even trying to apologise or make amends, as Snow White does in similar circumstances.

In the first version of the story, written in 1837 by **Robert Southey**, the intruder is not a little girl at all but an old hag. In an 1849 version by **Joseph Cundall**, the hag becomes a little girl (called **Silver Hair**) which allows the narrator to speak in upbraiding terms about the act of trespass.

The **name Goldilocks** was first used as recently as 1904. In the now familiar version, the bears are a family – not just three bears of differing size as in the first version. The main attraction of the story, despite its unsatisfactory conclusion, is the growing tension as the bears close in on Goldilocks: 'Someone's been sleeping in my bed – and she's still there!'

Tie-breaker

7

Q In the Disney version of *Sleeping Beauty*, what is the name of the princess?
A Aurora. This name is borrowed from the Charles Perrault version, where the name of the princess's daughter is Aurore. She also bears a son, named Day.

★ 197

Beauty and the Beast

The story of Beauty and the Beast is an allegory of the **transforming power of love.** When Beauty can genuinely love the Beast, despite his hideous appearance, he is restored to his handsome princely self.

FRENCH TALE The classic version of this story was written by Jeanne-Marie LePrince de Beaumont.

QUESTION NUMBER

The numbers or star following the answers refer to information boxes on the right.

ANSWERS

50	**Richard Burton** ❹
51	**Rumpelstiltskin** ❷ ❸
55	**Bluebeard** ❺
111	**Sleeping Beauty** ❺
161	**Puss in Boots** ❺
★ 185	***Uncle Remus*** ❻
188	**Puss in Boots** ❺
213	**Little Red Riding Hood** ❺
275	**Uncle Remus** ★ ❻
465	**Bremen** ❸
520	**C: Ali Baba** ❹
545	**Rapunzel** ❸
550	**Sheherezade** ❹
693	**The Grimm Brothers** ❷ ❸
713	**Cinderella** ❺
720	**Brother** ❻
735	***The 1001 Nights*** ❹
769	**Hansel and Gretel** ❸
997	***Tales of Mother Goose*** ❺

Collectors of fairy tales

Core facts ❶

◆ As the industrial revolution gathered pace in Europe at the end of the 19th century, scholars noticed that the old stories told in **peasant communities** were in danger of being lost.
◆ Some writers began to collect the old tales. They interviewed elderly people, recorded their stories and published the collections.

◆ This process went hand in hand with growing national awareness. Though many of the stories have ancient roots, it was felt that folk and fairy tales somehow expressed the national character. The **Grimm brothers** in particular wanted to encourage readers to appreciate the distinctive German-ness of the tales in their collection.

The Brothers Grimm ❷

Jakob Grimm was born in the German town of Hanau in 1785; his brother Wilhelm was born a year later. They lived together in the same house for most of their lives and they single-handedly established folklore as an academic field.
Their main achievement in this area was their two-volume ***Household Tales***, in which many familiar stories were recorded. Some of them are versions of tales noted earlier by Perrault, but all are transcribed without censorship or editorial additions or alterations (though all the stories are told in standard literary German rather than peasant dialect). The brothers' aim was to produce a faithful picture of the stories told by peasants in German-speaking territories.

FOILED The queen was told Rumpelstiltskin's name by a messenger who overheard him saying it.

Famous Grimm stories ❸

◆ **The Frog King** A frog helps a princess, who reluctantly agrees to make him her pet. But she grows tired of him and throws him against a wall (she does not kiss him). As she does this, he turns into a prince.
◆ **Rapunzel** A beautiful girl imprisoned in a tower lets down her long hair so that her prince can climb up it and visit her.
◆ **The Musicians of Bremen** Animals scare off robbers with their cacophonous music.
◆ **Rumpelstiltskin** The little dwarf has a claim on the Queen's child, and will release her only if the queen can guess his unusual name.
◆ **The Brave Little Tailor** The tailor kills seven flies with a single blow, and manages to convince the world he is a hero.
◆ **Hansel and Gretel** Abandoned children encounter a witch in a gingerbread house. They throw her in the furnace, and follow a trail of breadcrumbs they had left earlier to find their way out of the forest.
◆ **Snow White and Rose Red** Kind sisters aid a grateful bear and a thankless dwarf. It turns out the dwarf had laid a curse on a prince and turned him into the bear. The sisters marry the prince and his brother.

1001 Nights ❹

The 1001 Nights is a series of stories written anonymously in Arabic. They are also known as *The Arabian Nights*, though most are set in India. They tell the tales of such heroes as **Ali Baba**, **Aladdin** and **Sinbad**, and are replete with genies, magic carpets and fair maidens. The stories are said to have been told by **Sheherezade** to her husband the king, who had the custom of killing his wives after their wedding night. She kept him entertained with the tales night after night, until eventually she was reprieved. The stories, many of which are at least 1000 years old, were translated into English by the 19th-century adventurer and linguist **Richard Burton**, who also translated the *Kama Sutra*.

Perrault and Mother Goose

5

Charles Perrault was primarily a poet. In 1697 he published a small collection of eight fairy tales under the title *Contes de ma mère l'oye*, ***Tales of Mother Goose***. The stories were adapted from traditional European tales, and are recounted with great panache and wit. They are the first literary versions of such well-known stories as **Sleeping Beauty** (*La Belle au bois dormant*), **Little Red Riding Hood** (*Le Petit Chaperon rouge*), **Bluebeard** (*La Barbe-bleue*), **Puss in Boots** (*Le Chat botté*) and **Cinderella** (*Cendrillon*). **Robert Samber** translated them into English in 1729, and they have remained popular.

CREATED AND COLLECTED Perrault invented Mother Goose (right) for the title of his slim collection of fairy tales. Puss in Boots (left) was one of the eight tales he included in the book, which he published under his son's name, Pierre.

Joel Chandler Harris

6

From a young age, Joel Chandler Harris (1848-1908) spent most of his time with the black slaves working on the plantations of Georgia and absorbed their stories and their mode of speech. While still a boy, he worked as a printer's assistant, then went on to become a journalist. In 1879 he published a short story called *The Story of Mr Rabbit and Mr and Mrs Fox, As Told by Uncle Remus*. This was the first of many tales of **Brer (Brother) Rabbit** and other animals, recounted in the voice and manner of an elderly freed slave. Some of the Brer Rabbit stories, such as ***The Tar Baby***, hark back to tales told in Africa before slavery. Brer Rabbit himself is an archetypal African trickster character transposed to an American setting.

CHILDREN'S STORIES Brer Rabbit tells tales of his adventures to eager young ears.

185

Hard life

Joel Chandler Harris had a tough childhood – his labourer father had deserted his mother, Mary, just before he was born. Poor and illegitimate, he suffered from low self-esteem and developed a pronounced stutter. Harris became famous for his **Uncle Remus** stories but he later wrote other tales, such as ***Free Joe***, which showed the much darker side of slavery.

QUESTION NUMBER

The numbers or star following the answers refer to information boxes on the right.

ANSWERS

26	**Hans Christian Andersen** ❶
32	**Danny Kaye** (1913-87) – US actor, comedian, singer
182	***Thumbelina*** ❻
287	***The Steadfast Tin Soldier*** ❶
346	***The Princess and the Pea*** ❾
348	***The Little Mermaid*** ❸
360	***The Emperor's New Clothes*** ❹
★ 547	**A clockwork nightingale**
602	***The Little Match Girl*** ❷
628	**A tinderbox** ❽
765	**Thumbelina** ❻
832	**A swan** ❶ ❺
918	**Danish** ❶

Hans Christian Andersen

Core facts ❶

◆ Born in **Denmark**, Hans Christian Andersen was the son of a cobbler and a washerwoman. Yet in his own lifetime he was fêted as a storyteller of genius. He was as astonished as anybody by this transformation – which he explored in ***The Ugly Duckling***.

◆ Hans was never entirely happy, and a certain melancholy found its way into his stories. He was tortured by unrequited love, which he describes in ***The Steadfast Tin Soldier***.

◆ His stories have endured because they contain important truths, expressed in language for children. Andersen was the first writer ever to do this, and that is his great achievement.

Match Girl ❷

The story of the match girl is one of Andersen's most sentimental tales. It is a bitterly cold New Year's Eve. The match girl has sold nothing all day, and dare not go home. She huddles in a corner and strikes matches to warm herself, but sees **a picture of happiness** in each one: a warm room set for dinner, a beautiful Christmas tree. In the morning she is found frozen to death, and 'no one knew of the sweet visions she had beheld'.

Little Mermaid ❸

A little mermaid sacrifices her life in the oceans to be with a **prince** on land. She goes to a witch who changes her tail into legs. The witch also cuts out her tongue, so she cannot speak or sing. But the prince, though he loves her, plans to marry another. The mermaid is told she must kill the prince in order to revert to her former self, but instead she throws herself into the sea, and is borne away to heaven.

THE STORM The little mermaid swims to the prince's rescue.

Emperor's New Clothes ❹

The story of the emperor's new clothes is a **satire of vanity**. Two rogues claim they can make a suit of clothes that will be **invisible** to anyone who is unfit for his office. The emperor pays them, and then pretends that he can see the imaginary clothes. First his ministers, then the entire population join in the pretence because no one is prepared to admit their own apparent ignorance. This universal pomposity is punctured by one small boy who cries: **'The emperor has nothing on at all.'** The title of the story, like *The Ugly Duckling*, has become a proverb. It is used as a cipher for pretentiousness or empty pomposity.

ONE MAN'S WORK Andersen's fairy tales were all his own inventions, unlike the collected tales of the Brothers Grimm.

Ugly Duckling ❺

Andersen's story of the duckling that is bullied and despised by other snobbish birds, then grows into a **beautiful swan**, has all the power of a biblical parable. It is an allegory of Andersen's own life, but it contains a message of hope for anybody who has experienced hardship, been unfairly treated, or suffered despair.

DIFFERENT AND DESPISED The ugly duckling was not a duckling at all, but a cygnet hatched from a swan's egg laid in a duck's nest.

Thumbelina ❻

Andersen's take on the **Tom Thumb** theme has a girl as the hero of the story. She has many of the same adventures and encounters with animals as her male counterpart, but at the end of the story she is transported to a land populated by flower-spirits who are the same size as she is. She marries a prince of this land, and the king changes her name to **Maia** 'for Thumbelina is not a pretty name'.

Love story ❼

The **steadfast tin soldier** endures all manner of mistreatment for the love of a pasteboard dancer. He is thrown out of a window, dropped in a sewer and swallowed by a fish. Finally, he is thrown into a stove by a little boy: 'He felt extremely hot, whether this was the result of the fire or of the flames of love within him, he did not know.' His remains are found in **the ashes** in the form of a little tin heart.

★ 547

Rich song

In Andersen's 1844 tale ***The Nightingale***, the Emperor of China finds that the song of the nightingale, freely given, is worth more than all of his possessions – including a jewel-encrusted clockwork nightingale sent to him by the Emperor of Japan.

Fire starter ❽

In ***The Tinderbox***, a soldier kills a witch and steals her tinderbox. When the box is struck, three gigantic dogs appear to do his bidding. The soldier uses the dogs to meet a princess. He is caught, however, and condemned to death by the king. On the gallows, the soldier requests a last pipe. Using the magic box, he summons the dogs, who kill the king, allowing him to marry the princess and become king himself.

EARLY WORK *The Princess and the Pea* was one of the first of Andersen's fairy tales to be published, appearing in 1835.

The Princess and the Pea ❾

A girl is taken in for the night by a rather domestic king and queen. It turns out that she can feel the presence of a pea beneath 20 mattresses and 20 feather beds. This fact proves her sensitivity, and so her noble birth and suitability for marriage to the prince. *The Princess and the Pea* is one of Andersen's shortest tales. It is also one of the most class-conscious – a fact that has made it easy to ridicule: one musical burlesque based on the tale was entitled ***Once Upon A Mattress***.

The tellers of fables

QUESTION NUMBER

The numbers or star following the answers refer to information boxes on the right.

ANSWERS

QUESTION NUMBER	ANSWERS
1	**The tortoise** (3)
30	**Narcissus** (2)
259	**C: Ovid** (2)
267	**A wolf** (3)
288	**Echo** (2)
507	**Ichabod Crane** (4)
523	**Rudyard Kipling** (7)
583	**False** (it is by Aesop) (3) (7)
650	**Rip van Winkle** (4)
725	**A grasshopper** (1) (5)
738	***Just So Stories*** (7)
747	**Sour grapes** (3)
839	**True** (7)
854	**Ivan Krylov** (1) (6)
★ 861	**Washington Irving** (4)
924	***Just So Stories*** (7)

Core facts (1)

◆ A fable is a short story in prose or verse. The characters are usually animals or objects, and there is generally a one-line **moral** at the end.
◆ Fables have been a favourite kind of story since Greek times. Most European countries have a writer who adapted traditional fables and penned some more to suit his own country's culture – **La Fontaine** did this in France, for example, and **Ivan Krylov** in Russia.
◆ Fables look like nursery stories, and this innocent façade is often used to disguise a serious or even a sinister intent on the part of the writer. Much **political satire** has been written in the form of fables.

Ovid (2)

Ovid was a Roman poet writing at about the time of the birth of Christ. He wrote a number of folk tales drawn from classical mythology and Middle Eastern legends. Most of them involve mysterious transformations, hence the name by which they are known to us: ***Metamorphoses*** (Changes). Among the tales of Ovid is the story of Narcissus, who fell in love with his own reflection and was transformed into a flower. He also tells the related story of Echo, who loved Narcissus but was not loved in return.

UNWANTED Echo pined away to nothing, leaving just the faint sound of her voice.

Aesop's fables (3)

According to tradition, Aesop was a crippled slave. He is said to have lived in Phrygia in the 7th century BC. Aesop was the author of a collection of animal stories which satirise or highlight human foibles. He wrote the tale of the young shepherd who would cry out that wolves were attacking his sheep, only to laugh at the villagers who came running. One day he really was attacked by wolves, but the villagers ignored his screams – hence the expression '**to cry wolf**'. Aesop also tells of a fox who cannot reach some juicy grapes dangling above his head: when he gives up he declares that they were probably sour anyway – the origin of the expression '**sour grapes**'. Other proverbial expressions that derive from Aesop are 'to kill the goose that lays the golden eggs' and 'to be a dog in the manger'.

SLOW BUT SURE Aesop's tortoise beats the over-confident hare in a race, after the hare falls asleep.

Washington Irving

4

Washington Irving tried to give America its own folk-tale tradition. He did this by taking European themes and relocating them. His two best-known folk tales are ***Rip van Winkle*** and ***The Legend of Sleepy Hollow***. Rip van Winkle is an idle woodsman who goes on a trek to the Catskill mountains to escape his nagging wife. He falls asleep and wakes to find that many years have passed. When he comes down from the mountain, he finds that his wife is dead and he is forgotten. *The Legend of Sleepy Hollow* tells of a pompous teacher, **Ichabod Crane**, who comes to a provincial town and woos a landowner's daughter. He is scared off by a rival who poses as a headless horseman. Crane, it seems, is barely more sophisticated than the bumpkins he looks down on, and his pretensions are shown to be ludicrous.

SCREEN FABLE Johnny Depp starred as Ichabod Crane in Tim Burton's 1999 movie adaptation of *The Legend of Sleepy Hollow*.

La Fontaine

5

Jean de La Fontaine published over 240 fables between 1668 and 1694. His first works were elegant verse reworkings of **Aesop** and other ancient authors, but his later fables were the product of his own imagination. Each story ends with a moral – many of which have become French proverbs, such as 'Never sell the bear's skin before one has killed the beast' and 'A hungry stomach has no ears.'

Ivan Krylov

6

Ivan Krylov was a 19th-century Russian writer. His seemingly innocent animal tales are in fact biting satires, a fact which did not escape the Russian secret police. One of his 'political' stories concerns a lion (the tsar) who cannot abide multi-coloured sheep, but employs other animals such as the wolf to hunt them because he is too merciful to do it himself. Krylov's tales also make fun of human vices.

★ 861

American idol

Born in New York city in 1783, **Washington Irving** was perhaps the first American to gain global acclaim as a man of letters. As well as his fables, he wrote biographies of George Washington and Muhammad, and several other books dealing with subjects from 15th-century Spain to the lives of Native Americans.

WHALE TALE Rudyard Kipling's *Just So Stories* were first published in 1902.

Just So Stories

7

Rudyard Kipling's *Just So Stories*, are a series of fanciful tales about how various features of nature or civilisation came into being. They are deliberately written to have a mythic or fairy-tale quality, but with a non-European flavour. The leopard's spots, for example, are dabbed all over his body by the fingers of a friendly Ethiopian. The *Just So Stories* are:

How the Whale Got His Throat
How the Camel Got His Hump
How the Rhinoceros Got His Skin
How the Leopard Got His Spots
The Elephant's Child
The Sing-Song of Old Man Kangaroo
The Beginning of the Armadillos
How the First Letter Was Written
How the Alphabet Was Made
The Crab that Played with the Sea
The Cat that Walked By Himself
The Butterfly that Stamped

QUESTION NUMBER

The numbers or star following the answers refer to information boxes on the right.

ANSWERS

Question	Answer
★ 18	**Julius Caesar**
28	**Daniel** 5
109	**Cassandra** 4
121	**Revelation, or Apocalypse** 3
172	**Apollo** 6
178	**The Pythoness** 6
244	***Centuries*** 7
249	**Daniel** 1 5
321	**A: Four** 7
661	**A gypsy's** – to have your fortune told
698	**John Bunyan** 3
716	**Nostradamus** 7
731	**Sigmund Freud** (1856-1939)
750	**Belshazzar's** 5
864	**Belshazzar** 5
944	**Jacob** 8
959	**Israel** 8

Dreamers and soothsayers

Core facts (1)

◆ Dreams have always been one of the ways in which the gods have spoken to mankind. History is full of **visionaries** believed to have been able to interpret dreams.

◆ In the Old Testament, Daniel and Joseph are given the gift of **dream interpretation**, which they use to find favour with a great king.

◆ In the New Testament, the birth of Jesus is heralded by a series of dreams in which **angels** bring a message from God.

◆ The Greek myths teach that predictions of the future can be a lie. The truths of the oracle are always **deceitful**, or as confusing as the little occult quatrains of Nostradamus.

Joseph (2)

The Bible says that Pharaoh was troubled by a vision in which seven emaciated cows devoured seven fat cows. Joseph was in prison, where he had interpreted **the dreams** of two of his inmates. Now he was summoned to tell Pharaoh what the dream of the cows meant. He said that the dream foretold **seven years** of abundance followed by seven years of famine. Pharaoh was so impressed that he appointed Joseph to oversee the stockpiling of grain for the lean years.

WEIRD AND WONDERFUL (3)

Revelation, the last book of the Bible, contains a divine vision. This book inspired **John Bunyan** – sometimes called 'The Immortal Dreamer' because his *Pilgrim's Progress* also takes the form of a dream.

Cassandra (4)

In Greek myth Cassandra was the **daughter of Priam**, King of Troy. She was loved by Apollo, who gave her the gift of prophecy, but she refused his advances, and so Apollo spitefully decreed that her predictions would never be believed. So it was that Cassandra warned the Trojans in vain that the Wooden Horse was a trick, and that Troy would fall. Nowadays a person is called a Cassandra if he or she is an **outspoken pessimist**, always predicting a bad outcome.

Daniel (5)

Only Daniel could read the dream of king **Nebuchadnezzar**, predicting that it spoke of the end of his dynasty. Daniel later interpreted a second dream that foretold Nebuchadnezzar's seven years of madness. He also read the writing on the wall at the feast of **Belshazzar**, Nebuchadnezzar's son. The writing said: 'You have been weighed in the scales and found wanting.' Belshazzar died that very night.

ROYAL NIGHTMARE Nebuchadnezzar dreamed of a statue with a head of gold and feet of clay, which was destroyed by a great stone. Only the prophet Daniel understood its fateful meaning.

The Oracles (6)

There were many oracles in ancient Greece – **temples where the gods spoke** through priests (or priestesses) to answer enquiries about the future. These answers were nearly always unclear or even misleading. The wisdom of the oracle seems to be that it is not given to mankind to know what will be. The best-known oracle was the one at **Delphi** dedicated to Apollo – the so-called Delphic Oracle. The priestess at Delphi was known as the **Pythoness**.

Nostradamus

7

Born in Saint-Rémy, France, in 1503, Nostradamus was well-known in his lifetime as a physician and as an astrologer – he was court doctor to King Charles IX. In 1547, he began to write **prophetic four-line poems** about future events. All the verses are obscure, and open to divergent interpretations, but they seem to foretell such events as the rise of Adolf Hitler (who is misnamed 'Hister') and the assassination of President Kennedy.

FUTURE WORKS Michel de Notredame, known as Nostradamus, wrote two prophetic books under the title *Centuries*.

Jacob's ladder

8

The story of Jacob's ladder is one of the strangest tales in the Bible. One night, during a long journey, Jacob woke to see a ladder between Heaven and Earth. Angels went up and down it, and God stood on the top rung. Later in his life, Jacob had another mysterious encounter. He was set upon by a stranger who **wrestled him** through the night. At dawn the stranger 'touched Jacob's thigh', leaving him lame. He also gave Jacob a new name – **Israel** – meaning 'fights with God'.

STAIRWAY TO HEAVEN Jacob used his stone pillow to mark the spot where he saw the celestial ladder, illustrated here by William Blake. Tradition says that the Stone of Scone is this rock.

18

Ides of March

In the **Roman calendar**, the Ides are the 13th or 15th day of the month. According to the Roman historian **Plutarch**, Julius Caesar was warned by a soothsayer that danger threatened on the Ides of March. He was killed by Brutus, Cassius and the other conspirators on March 15, 44 BC.

QUESTION NUMBER

The numbers or star following the answers refer to information boxes on the right.

ANSWERS

38	*The Amityville Horror* 8
225	Poltergeist 6
265	Ouija board 3
334	*Ghostbusters* 7
396	C: May 1 2
420	Ebenezer 4
455	Exorcism 2
457	Medium 1 3
503	Parapsychology 7
590	True ★
610	*The Sixth Sense* 7
647	Mystery Inc. 7
784	*Hamlet* 4
788	Henrik Ibsen (1828-1906)
893	*Macbeth* 4
894	She is a ghost – written in 1941
900	*A Christmas Carol* 4
★ 956	Legion
973	Séance 1 3
987	Jacob Marley 4
996	*The Turn of the Screw* – novel published in 1898

Ghosts and spirits

Core facts 1

◆ Many people believe that the departed linger in ghostly form for a time 'beyond the veil', where they can observe the living.

◆ It sometimes seems that ghosts are the **souls of people** who have unfinished business, such as an injustice that needs to be put right.

◆ On the other hand, ghosts may be no more than the wishful thinking of the bereaved. It is no surprise that there was a **spiritualist boom** after the human losses of World War I.

◆ The author **Arthur Conan Doyle** was a great believer in ghosts and the spirit world. On the other hand, the escapologist **Harry Houdini** worked to expose mediums as frauds.

Exorcism 2

The practice of **expelling ghosts, unquiet spirits or diabolical presences** from a place or a person is known as exorcism. In the Middle Ages there was an official position of exorcist in the priesthood. Exorcism is still an accepted ritual of the **Roman Catholic Church**. But since new guidelines were issued in 1999, it has only been carried out on individuals after thorough psychological evaluations. In Central Europe the custom persists of exorcising towns on **Walpurgis Night** (May 1), when evil spirits are driven out using holy water, incense and loud noises.

FOUL MOUTH In medieval times, demonic possession was taken literally. Many cases would now be recognised as mental illness.

★ 956 ★

'My name is Legion'

The Bible tells that Jesus drove several **demons** out of a man who gave his name as Legion – 'for we are many'. On leaving the possessed man, the demons entered a herd of '**Gadarene swine**', which rushed over a cliff to their death.

Spiritualism
3

This is the belief that the dead can remain in contact with the world of the living. They do so via **mediums**, individuals who are tuned in to the 'spirit world'. Communication takes place at **seances**. The departed person may speak through the medium, or else spell out words on a wooden board marked with the letters of the alphabet. This board is called a **ouija**, a name based on a combination of the French and German words for yes – *oui* and *ja*.

Ghost theories
5

No ghost has ever been proved to exist. But enough people have had an experience of ghosts to make them a legitimate subject of study. Most theories account for ghosts in psychological terms – as figments of an excited imagination, or as 'wishful thinking' on the part of a bereaved person. Other theories hold that some type of **human energy** lingers in a place where horrific events have occurred.

Literature
4

Ghosts are a useful plot device – **Shakespeare** used ghosts more than once. At the start of ***Hamlet***, the ghost of Hamlet's father appears to his son and demands vengeance for his murder. In ***Macbeth***, the ghost of Banquo appears at a feast, but is visible only to the king who killed him. And in Dickens' ***A Christmas Carol***, the transformation of Ebeneezer Scrooge is brought about by visits from the ghost of his old business partner, Jacob Marley.

BAH HUMBUG! The joyless Scrooge is shown three visions: Christmas Past, Christmas Present and Christmas Future.

Famous ghosts
6

Queen **Anne Boleyn** is one of the world's most active ghosts. Sightings of her have often been claimed at the Tower of London, where she lost her head. Another notorious haunting occurred at Sampford Peverell in Devonshire in the 19th century, where a **poltergeist** (a spirit given to throwing things) caused all sorts of damage. A reward was offered for an explanation, but never claimed.

Ghosts at the movies
7

Perhaps the best known ghost film of all is *Ghost*, in which Sam, a murdered banker, uses a reluctant medium to warn his girlfriend of danger. In *The Sixth Sense*, a boy who 'sees dead people' is treated by a psychologist who is himself a damaged soul. Many ghost movies are comedies, among them *Beetlejuice*, starring Michael Keaton, and the *Scooby Doo* films.

UNQUIET SPIRITS Ghosts have featured in many films, including *Ghostbusters* (background) and *Poltergeist* (right).

WEIRD AND WONDERFUL
8

The film *The Amityville Horror* is based on a real event. In 1975 the Lutz family moved into a house in **Amityville**, New York, where a murder had taken place. They soon fled, driven out by demonic flying pigs and bleeding walls.

QUESTION NUMBER

The numbers or star following the answers refer to information boxes on the right.

ANSWERS

82 **False** (it is a branch of theology) ❸

87 **False** ❽

144 **St Peter** ❷

214 **Purgatory** ❼

226 **Limbo** ❼

245 **Hieronymus Bosch** ❽

247 **Traitors** ❻

317 **Dies Irae** (Day of Wrath) ❸

319 **The Tower of Babel** – intended to reach Heaven

★ 433 **Milton's *Paradise Lost***

560 **Conquest, War, Famine, Death** – Revelation 6

619 **At the entrance to Hell** ❻

649 **Halo** ❶

695 **Emanuel Swedenborg** ❺

800 **He raised Lazarus from the dead** – John 11

803 **Sulphur** ❽

813 **The Rapture** ❸

815 **Gehenna** ❽

948 **Paradise** (*pairi*=around + *daēza*=wall ❷

949 **7** – according to the Koran, there are seven heavens or levels of heaven

Heaven and Hell

Core facts ❶

◆ Many thinkers have tried to imagine what happens **after death**. Most agree that, as the Bible says, the sheep are sorted from the goats – some people go to Heaven, others to Hell.

◆ In folklore (though not in official Christian teaching), **souls in Heaven** wear a halo, have wings like angels and carry a harp.

◆ The **damned**, meanwhile, spend eternity in an underground Hell, where they are tormented by sadistic demons with tridents.

◆ In modern popular culture the medieval Christian view of Heaven and Hell has been reduced to a joke. People's ideas of an afterlife, if there is one, are likely to be more subtle.

Visions of Heaven ❷

According to the popular vision, the entrance to Heaven consists of a pair of **'pearly gates'**. To pass through these gates, one must first account for oneself to **Saint Peter**, who is said to hold the keys to Paradise. The word paradise is from the Persian for 'walled garden', and in Islamic thought, Heaven is a place of sensual delights. In the Bible, Heaven is described as the bosom of Abraham.

NEW JERUSALEM This vision of 'Heaven Opened' was painted by the 19th-century English artist George Jones.

Judgment Day ❸

Many cultures have stories that tell of a final judgment at the world's end. In Christian eschatology (study of the 'last days'), the Second Coming of Christ coincides with the **Dies Irae** (Day of Wrath). In some evangelical circles it is believed that on that day the righteous will be instantly transported to Heaven, leaving the ungodly behind. This gathering-up is known as the **Rapture**.

Nirvana ❹

Most religions and mythologies see Heaven as a spiritual goal, a reward for the souls of the righteous dead. But **Buddhists** believe that a departed soul returns to a different body and continues the cycle of death and rebirth. This process is called **samsara**. Only when enlightenment is achieved does the wheel of reincarnation stop, and the soul enter the blissful state called nirvana.

WEIRD AND WONDERFUL ❺

In 1758, the Swedish philosopher **Emanuel Swedenborg** wrote a book entitled *Heaven and Hell*. It reads like a detailed first-hand account of both places, even discussing the writing of angels and how marriage works in Heaven.

Dante's Inferno

6

The Divine Comedy is a trilogy describing Hell (Inferno in Italian), Purgatory and Heaven. Dante's Hell comprises nine circles, and has a sign above the gate: 'Abandon All Hope Ye Who Enter Here'. Each circle contains a different category of sinner. The first corresponds to Limbo; the lustful are in the second; heretics in the sixth, fraudsters in the eighth and traitors in the ninth.

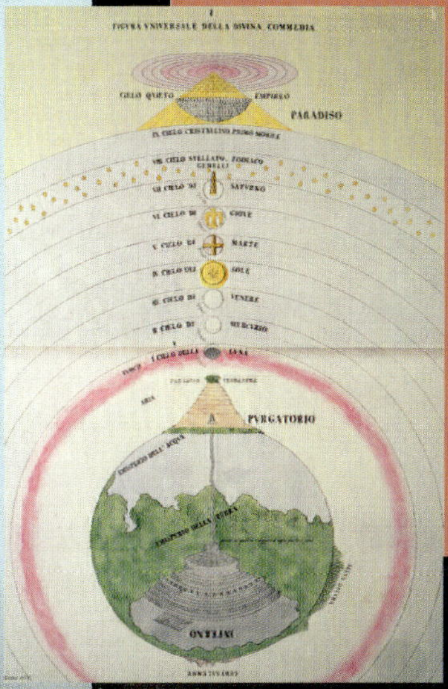

VICIOUS CIRCLES Dante's Hell was shaped like a funnel at Earth's centre.

IN-BETWEEN Limbo is the abode of good but unshriven souls.

Purgatory

7

Medieval Christian thought recognised that some people did not qualify for Heaven or Hell. This category included figures such as Moses, who could not go to Heaven because he was not a Christian, and also babies who died unbaptised. For them there was **Limbo**, a place of happiness, but not of bliss. **Purgatory**, on the other hand, was the place to which the souls of the dead went to be cleansed through suffering and punishment before they were fit for Heaven. The doctrine of purgatory was promulgated by the Pope in 1439, and rejected by the Church of England in 1562.

Visions of Hell

8

In **Christian** folklore, Hell is a place of **fire and brimstone** (the old word for sulphur). Jesus told of a poor man named Lazarus who went to Heaven, while the rich man in Hell longed for a drop of water. The **Koran** speaks of seven portals into Hell. In Chinese **Taoist** thought, meanwhile, there are 18 hells, each of which has its own torments. The **Hebrew** name for Hell is Gehenna.

HELL'S DEEP In the nightmarish vision of Dutch painter Hieronymus Bosch, Hell is a kind of infernal torture chamber.

433

Milton

John Milton's epic poem ***Paradise Lost*** is the story of the Fall, told from the point of view of Satan. The poem follows Satan on his journey from the 'burning lake' to the newly created Garden of Eden. Here he tempts Eve into sin as an act of pure revenge against God, who cast him out of Heaven.

QUESTION NUMBER

The numbers or star following the answers refer to information boxes on the right.

ANSWERS

138	B: A sea monster (3)
158	Abominable snowman (2)
164	*Alien* (6)
274	*The Hound of the Baskervilles* (1) (4)
309	North America (2)
335	Godzilla (1) (7)
340	King Kong (1) (5)
453	Yeti (2)
481	Loch Ness (1) (3)
516	D: A lake monster (3)
617	Edmund Hillary (2)
★ 721	A big cat
857	A ghostly hound (4)
961	Empire State Building (5)
978	Sasquatch (2)

Modern monsters

Core facts (1)

◆ While we know that most monsters are imaginary, there are some that lurk on the border between fiction and reality. For example, many people believe in the existence of the **yeti** and the **Loch Ness monster**, or claim to have seen them. Certainly no one has been able to prove that they do not exist.

◆ Some monsters that are undeniably fictional have a basis in reality, or in legend, as is the case with the **hound of the Baskervilles**.

◆ Even **Godzilla** and **King Kong** are no more than real animals magnified. We recognise that King Kong is a giant gorilla, and Godzilla an enlarged dinosaur that once walked the Earth.

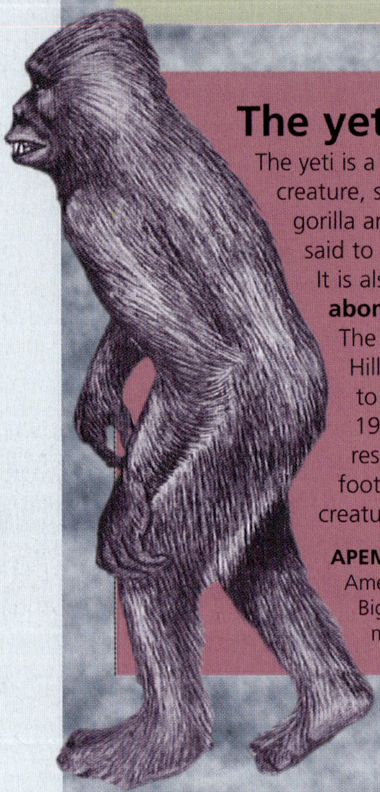

The yeti (2)

The yeti is a large hairy human-like creature, something between a gorilla and a bear, which is said to inhabit the Himalayas. It is also known as the **abominable snowman**. The mountaineer Edmund Hillary led an expedition to find the yeti in 1960. He found traces resembling a huge footprint, but not the creature itself.

APEMAN The yeti's North American cousin is known as Bigfoot, or Sasquatch (hairy man), to Native Americans.

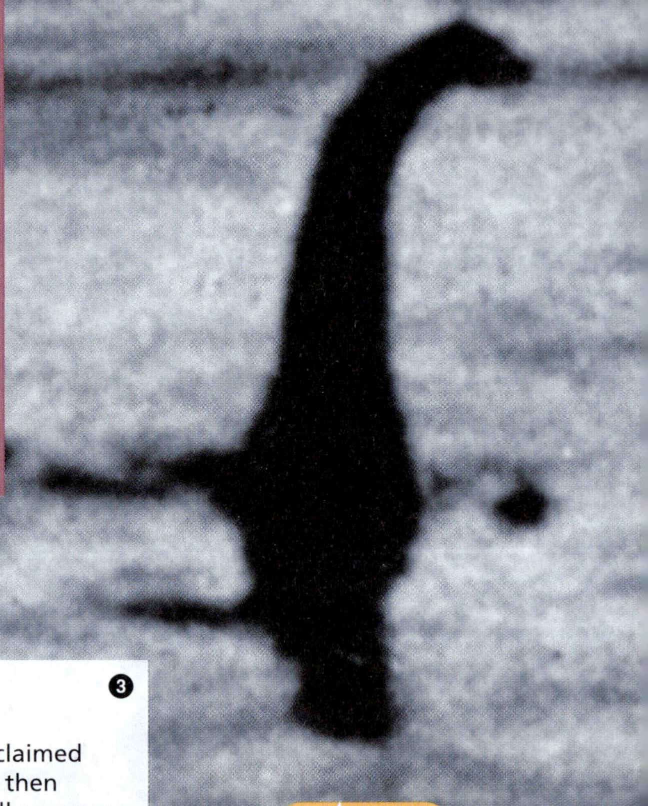

Lake monsters (3)

In 1933, a motorist driving past Loch Ness claimed to have seen the **Loch Ness monster**. Since then there have been countless sightings, as well as many scientific expeditions to find the animal, but it remains elusive. Nessie, as the creature is fondly known, is usually described as having a long neck and a humped back. One theory is that it is a surviving plesiosaur from the age of the dinosaurs, or that it is descended from one.

A similar creature is said to inhabit Lake Okanagan in British Columbia. **Ogopogo** has a long serpent-like body and a head shaped like that of a horse.

Havhest is a Norwegian sea creature. Its name means sea-horse, and reported sightings have come from sailors all along the Scandinavian coastline. Some of the reports date back to the Middle Ages.

HARD EVIDENCE? A London surgeon took this photo of Nessie in 1934, but it is now believed to be a hoax. Some say the monster was invented to bring tourists to the area.

★ 721

Exmoor beast

In the late 1970s there were many sightings of the **Beast of Exmoor**, a puma-like creature, with dark fur and green eyes. The stories peaked in 1983, when 80 sheep were found ripped to pieces. In 1988 Royal Marines searched the region, but found nothing. One theory is that the Beast is a **big cat** that has been released or escaped onto the moors.

The hound from hell

The fictional **hound of the Baskervilles**, the ghostly dog of Conan Doyle's story, is based on the legend of the **hell hound of Norfolk**. This tells of a large, spectral dog known as Black Shuck. It is the size of a calf and has large, blazing red eyes. Conan Doyle heard this story in Norfolk, but by the time he came to fictionalise it he had moved to Dartmoor, and found it more convenient to locate the action of his story there.

King Kong

The giant ape King Kong was first seen in the 1933 film of that name. The movie's success spawned many remakes and spoofs. The ape falls in love with beautiful blonde actress Ann Darrow (played by Fay Wray) and, in the climactic scene, is shot from the top of **the Empire State Building** by warplanes. An onlooker says: 'It wasn't the planes that got him, it was Beauty killed the Beast', a remark that betrays King Kong's link with the older monsters of fairy tales.

Alien

The space age brought a new breed of monster – the alien from outer space. Movie aliens range from the endearing creature of Steven Spielberg's *E.T. the Extra-Terrestrial* (1982) to the terrifying parasite of Ridley Scott's *Alien* (1979). *Dr Who* immortalised the daleks who first appeared on British TV screens in 1963.

TIME FOR A SNACK An inner extendible jaw was one of the alien's terrifying characteristics in the 1979 movie, starring Sigourney Weaver.

Godzilla

Godzilla (or **Gojira** in Japanese) made his debut in 1954. The monster, a giant mutated *Tyrannosaurus rex*, was dreamed up by a Japanese film studio called Toho. Fifty years later there have been 28 films in which the dinosaur battles with the **Smog Monster** and a greatly enlarged King Kong, among other enemies.

JAPANESE BEAST The word Gojira means 'gorilla whale'.

Symbols and signs

QUESTION NUMBER

The numbers or star following the answers refer to information boxes on the right.

ANSWERS

- **149** Israel (2)
- **313** Swastika (4)
- **341** St Peter (5)
- **378** Judaism (1)
- ★ **410** Five
- **577** Yang (3)
- **585** True (4)
- **688** The Star of David (2)
- **706** B: Wear it ★
- **806** Kaballah (2)
- **841** Mandalas (7)
- **850** Islam (1)
- **871** Ankh cross (8)
- **872** **Cross of Lorraine** (used by former dukes of Lorraine) (5)
- **873** **Tau cross** (T-shaped, after Greek letter *tau*) (5)
- **874** **Latin cross** (lower vertical arm longer than others) (5)
- **875** **Maltese cross** (used by Knights of Malta) (5)
- **877** **Russian cross** (three cross bars, Russian Orthodox) (5)
- **878** **Papal cross** (three cross bars, used by Pope) (5)
- **879** **Greek cross** (all four arms the same length) (5)
- **967** **Bethlehem** (where David was anointed king of Israel) (2)

Core facts (1)

◆ People have always believed that abstract signs possess magical power. **Charm bracelets**, **amulets**, the practise of **crossing fingers** for luck, all of these are remnants of a belief in the supernatural power of signs.

◆ Abstract signs still have the power to encourage or offend. The 'V for victory' sign in World War II was used to foster patriotism, and every culture has hand gestures that are considered obscene.

◆ Religions also have their defining signs: Christianity has its **cross**, Islam the **crescent moon**, and Judaism is often represented by the **menorah** (a seven-branched candlestick).

David's Star (2)

The **Star of David** is also known as **Solomon's Seal**. In Hebrew it is called the 'shield of David' and so is a symbol of **protection**. It is a relatively recent Jewish symbol and is rarely seen in a Jewish context before the Middle Ages, when it began to appear in the mystical texts of the ***Kaballah***. It was adopted by the Zionist movement in the 19th century and now features on **Israel's flag**. Christians associate the Star of David with the **Star of Bethlehem**.

Yin and yang (3)

The ancient **Chinese** idea that the Universe operates through two opposing but complementary forces is represented by the yin-yang symbol. Yin ('**dark**') is associated with the **Earth** and the **female** nature; it is passive and absorbing. Yang ('**bright**') stands for **heaven** and the **male** nature; it is active and penetrating. Where one force is greater, the other is lesser, but each contains the seed of the other (represented by the little circles), and together they make a unified whole.

IN BALANCE The central yin and yang symbol is surrounded by the eight trigrams or keys to knowledge.

The swastika (4)

In the 1920s the swastika was adopted as the symbol of the German **Nazi** party, and is now forever associated with the Hitler regime. But it is in fact a very ancient religious symbol, an emblem of **good luck**. At various times it has been thought to represent the Sun, the four winds and lightning. The word swastika comes from the Sanskrit for 'well-being'. The sign is also known as **gammadion**, **fylfot**, **cross cramponnée** and (in German) **Hakenkreuz**.

MOSAIC SWASTIKA A 2nd-century Roman floor shows a swastika being used decoratively in a representation of the four seasons.

★ 410 Pentagrams ★

A pentagram is a **five-pointed star** formed of five straight lines of equal length. It was used as a mystic symbol by the **Pythagoreans** in Greek times. In the Middle Ages it was used as a **charm** to ward off evil spirits. When worn as an amulet around the neck, it is called a '**pentacle**'. The pentagram symbol was used by **astrologers** and **necromancers**, and became associated with **witchcraft**.

The cross

5

The cross, a Roman instrument of torture, is now the pre-eminent symbol of **Christianity**. When the figure of Christ is depicted on the cross it is called a **crucifix**. There are many legends attached to the variations on the sign of the cross. St Andrew's cross is made up of two diagonals, because he is said to have been crucified on a cross of that shape; St Peter, according to legend, was crucified upside-down because he declared himself unworthy to die in exactly the same manner as Jesus. The Roman Emperor Constantine, a Christian believer, is said to have seen the sign of the cross before battle with the words '*In hoc signo vinces*' ('In this sign conquer'). The vision and his subsequent victory led him to issue an edict granting Christians religious toleration throughout the Roman empire.

CHRIST OVER RIO Perched on Corcovado Hill, the 40 m (130 ft) statue of Christ towers over Rio de Janeiro. Inaugurated in 1931, the statue was built by Brazilian engineer Heitor da Silva Costa.

WEIRD AND WONDERFUL

6

The earliest Christian symbol was the **chi-rho** made up of these two letters of the Greek alphabet superimposed on each other. The letters look like an X and a P and form the start of the word 'Christ'.

Mandalas

7

A mandala is a circular design, sometimes simple, sometimes complex, representing **wholeness**. The word comes from the Sanskrit for **circle**. Mandalas are used in **Buddhist** and **Hindu** religious practice as an aid to worship or as a focus for meditation. Some are a symbolic representation of the cosmos and they are also seen as the abode of the gods, or as power objects in their own right. In Tibetan Buddhism, monks create intricate mandalas out of coloured sand as an act of meditation and prayer. Once complete the **sand mandala** is destroyed to represent the impermanence of all things.

The ankh

8

The ankh takes the form of a T-shape with a loop on top. It was widely used in **ancient Egypt** as a symbol of **life**: as a hieroglyph in Egyptian texts it means 'to live'. It also signifies immortality or 'the life to come' and is often found in funerary contexts. **Maat** the Goddess of Truth is always depicted with the ankh in her hand. Later the symbol was adopted by the Christian **Coptic church** – because of its resemblance to the Christian cross. As a Coptic symbol the ankh is called the **'ansate cross'**.

FOR THE AFTERLIFE The ankh is often seen in Egyptian funerary goods, as in this mirror case retrieved from the tomb of Tutankhamun.

QUESTION NUMBER

The numbers or star following the answers refer to information boxes on the right.

ANSWERS

- **14** St Valentine ❻
- **227** Reiki – means universal life energy
- ★ **263** Samson
- **281** Cupid ❻
- **536** The palm of the hand ❷
- **537** The eyes ❽
- **538** The humerus – extends from shoulder to elbow
- **539** Lying ❺
- **615** The hand ❷
- **662** The USA's (adopted in 1782) ❽
- **791** His rib ❶
- **793** Delilah ★
- **818** Antaeus ❸
- **941** The Sun ❶

Magic symbols of the body

Core facts ❶

◆ The human body and all its parts are imbued with magical significance. Early humans revered the sexual organs and made **phallic** objects, which they linked with fertility.

◆ All mythologies make **anthropomorphic** connections between the body and the cosmos. The **Sun** is universally the **eye of Heaven**. In China hollows in the landscape were believed to be shaped by the **footprints** of gods and heroes.

◆ Legends are connected to parts of the body. The Bible says that Eve was fashioned from Adam's rib. The Greeks believed that the soul resided within the thymus gland of the brain.

The hand ❷

Aristotle called the hands **'the tool of tools'**. The right hand is associated with dexterity ('dexter' is Latin for 'right'), but left-handedness has always been looked on with suspicion: Latin for left is 'sinister'. It has long been believed that a person's life is prefigured in the lines on the hands and there is much symbolism attached to hand gestures. Crossing fingers for luck is actually an unobtrusive way of making the Christian sign of the cross. Many people believe that healing power can be transmitted through the hands.

VOTIVE HAND This bronze Roman hand has been embellished with various charms and symbols to avert the 'evil eye'.

The feet ❸

The feet represent a connection with the **Earth**, and the strength that can be drawn from it. In one of his adventures Heracles wrestled the giant **Antaeus**, who regained his strength whenever he touched the ground. Heracles defeated the giant by holding him aloft until he died. The Chinese believe that the whole body and its organs are connected to certain points on the feet – and this is the basis of **reflexology**.

★ 263

The hair ★

People's **strength** and life force is often associated with their hair. In the Bible, when **Delilah** cut **Samson**'s hair he lost all his strength. The **Buddah** is shown with orderly curls which represents his mastery over his life force and attainment of serenity and tranquility.

Tie-breaker ❹

Q On which part of the body, apart from the side and the feet, might one see the 'stigmata'?

A On the hands. Some Christians believe that these marks of Christ's wounds can be transferred to devout individuals. St Francis is said to have been the first to receive the stigmata.

The mouth

5

The mouth is the obvious symbol of **eloquence** and loquacity. In Egyptian funeral rites there was the ceremony of '**Opening the Mouth**', where the senses were re-animated so the soul could answer for itself in the Hall of Judgment. The mouth does not always tell the truth: '**to speak with a forked tongue**' is to lie.

MEDUSA'S POWER The severed head of the gorgon Medusa retained the ability to turn men into stone and was often depicted, complete with snakes for hair, on the shield of a Greek warrior.

The head

7

There are magical taboos concerning the head in many cultures. In **Polynesia** it is a grave offence to touch the head of a stranger. The **Yoruba** people of Africa believe that three spirits live in each body, and the first of them, called **Olori**, dwells in the head. In Greek mythology, Athena sprang from Zeus's head after he was plagued with a headache. She emerged from a wound made when Prometheus, or possibly Hephaestus, struck Zeus on the head with a bronze axe.

The heart

6

From time immemorial, the heart has been seen as the seat of the **emotions** and the source of the **life force**. In Egypt, the heart was the only organ left inside the body during mummification. People are said to fall in love when their heart is pierced by an arrow fired from the bow of **Cupid**, the babyish Greek god of love. The **Sacred Heart** of the Virgin Mary is often depicted pierced with seven swords (itself a mystical number) which represent her sorrows. Heart imagery is central to **St Valentine's Day** on February 14, which was thought to coincide with the start of the mating season for birds.

SWEETHEARTS The act of sending cards on Valentine's Day is a relic from the Roman sex festival of Lupercalia, held on February 15.

The eyes

8

The eyes have been called the '**windows of the soul**'. They are an almost universal symbol of knowledge. An eye inside a triangle is an old Christian symbol of the omniscience of the Trinity; to this day it appears on US banknotes. Paradoxically, **blindness** can also symbolise **wisdom**. Homer is said to have been blind. The statue of justice at London's Old Bailey is blindfolded to convey the idea of impartiality. St Paul was struck blind for three days after his divine encounter on the road to Damascus.

ALL-SEEING EYE The stylised eye of Horus, often seen in Egyptian hieroglyphs, is called the *udjat* and depicts strength and power.

Magical objects

QUESTION NUMBER

The numbers or star following the answers refer to information boxes on the right.

ANSWERS

56 **The olive tree** ❹

72 **Pumpkin** ❼

190 ***Alice in Wonderland*** ❸

292 **A peach tree** ❹

328 **C: A pomegranate** ❼

347 **The Mirror of Erised** ❸

371 **Hanukah** ❻

379 **St Lucia** ❻

★ **400** **C: The Holy Mandylion**

517 **B: A Buddhist staff** ❷

625 **On the doorframe** ❽

636 **C: Japan** ❻

744 **The pomegranate** ❼

792 **A snake** (Exodus chapter 4, verses 1-5) ❷

797 **He was struck dead** ❶

799 **Palm trees** ❹

912 **Lebanon** ❹

993 ***The Picture of Dorian Gray*** ❸

Core facts ❶

◆ All kinds of objects – man-made and natural – have been seen as sources of **magical power** by different cultures at various times.

◆ Sometimes the reverence is based on **symbolism** – the eight petals of the lotus, for example, stand for the eight cardinal directions of Buddhist thought.

◆ Sometimes the object has **holy power** in its own right. In the Bible, God strikes dead a man called Uzzah, who touched the Ark of the Covenant with unconsecrated hands.

◆ Some objects are **lucky**, such as a rabbit's foot or a four-leaf clover. Others bring misfortune, such as a broken mirror.

Staffs ❷

A staff is a **phallic symbol**, and so often stands for masculine power and authority. The royal sceptre is a stylised staff. Buddhist ceremonies make use of a metal rod called a **vadjra**, which represents a thunderbolt. Moses and later his brother Aaron used a staff to demonstrate God's power: both turned a staff into a snake and back again. The **magic wand** of witches and wizards is a kind of staff in miniature.

CEDARS OF LEBANON The wood from these cedar trees was considered sacred. Solomon used the wood in his temple and the pharaohs used it for their sarcophagi.

★ 400

The Mandylion

The Holy Mandylion was a miracle-working image of Christ, once venerated in Edessa in modern-day Turkey. According to one legend, the image formed when Christ wiped his face on a cloth or towel. He sent it to King Abgar of Edessa, who was healed by it. Some people believe that it is the same cloth we now know as the Shroud of Turin.

Mirrors ❸

Myth is full of magical mirrors which tell the **truth**. According to the Elizabethan poet Edmund Spenser, **Merlin's mirror** warned of **treason** and impending invasion. There are many magic mirrors in fiction: in the Harry Potter stories, the **Mirror of Erised** shows everyone who looks in it what they most **desire**. And in Oscar Wilde's fable, *The Picture of Dorian Gray*, the portrait is a true reflection of the sitter's soul: it grows uglier and more monstrous as he remains ever youthful.

ALICE'S LOOKING GLASS The magical power of mirrors is evoked when Alice goes through the looking glass and into another realm.

Tree lore

Many cultures have the concept of a **Tree of Life**. It appears in the Bible, along with the **Tree of the Knowledge of Good and Evil**. Australian Aboriginal belief has the **World Tree** that supports the sky while the stars rest in its branches. In Chinese mythology there is a **giant peach tree** that mortals may climb to paradise. In the ancient Middle East, the **cedar** was believed to be indestructible, and so was a symbol of immortality. The club of Heracles was said to be made of **oak**, a tree that was sacred to Zeus. The **olive** tree was sacred to Athena. The nuts of the **bodhi** tree (under which the Buddha achieved enlightenment) are sometimes made into prayer beads by Buddhists. Evergreen trees represent everlasting life because they remain green through the winter, one of the reasons why **yew** trees were held to be sacred by ancient Britons.

QUEEN OF LIGHT To celebrate St Lucia's day, Swedish girls wear white dresses with a red sash. One is chosen to be queen and wear a crown of candles.

WEIRD AND WONDERFUL

Long believed to have supernatural powers, the **mandrake**'s forked root makes it look like the lower half of a man. This resemblance has led to the idea that the plant screams when it is pulled from the ground.

Candles

The candle is a source of light, and so symbolises **spiritual illumination** and truth. Candles are used to ward off evil spirits: at Halloween, candles were carried from 11 o'clock till midnight. If they did not go out, that meant a year free from witchcraft. In Judaism, a candle is lit each night during **Hanukah**, the festival of lights. And in Sweden, girls wear crowns of candles on the feast of **St Lucia**. This is celebrated on December 13 and is a remnant of an older pagan midwinter festival. In Japan, candles in paper lanterns are used in the **Bon Festival** to welcome the spirits of the ancestors and then to speed them on their way.

Fruit

Fruit stands for **abundance and fertility**, but each fruit has its own significance. In China the pomegranate, peach and lemon are the '**three fortunate fruits**', offered to the household gods at New Year. At Halloween, a pumpkin is made into a **Jack O'Lantern**, which goes back to the story of an Irish blacksmith called Jack, who was forbidden to enter Heaven and wandered the Earth with a lantern made from the embers of Hell.

FAITHFUL FRUIT Pomegranates stand for marriage after a magical one was used to bind Persephone to Hades in the Underworld.

Doorways

There is much magic associated with doorways and thresholds. The Romans believed that **evil spirits** congregated in doorways, which is why brides are carried over the threshold – a custom still sometimes observed today. In Russia it is bad luck to **kiss** or **shake hands** across a doorway. In China at New Year, the doors of a house are locked as midnight approaches.

But doorways are also places of power. In Christian churches, the main ceremonial entrance usually faces the west, and is often highly decorated. Door frames in Jewish homes traditionally have a **mezuzah**, a phial containing a fragment of the Torah, which it is customary to touch as you pass through.

Superstitions

QUESTION NUMBER

The numbers or star following the answers refer to information boxes on the right.

ANSWERS

11	**Seven** (9)
20	**Friday 13th** (5)
★ 90	**False**
351	**A bride** (8)
397	**D: Stormy petrels** – family Hydrobatidae
513	**B: A black cat** (4)
535	**Acting** (1)
632	**A: Wood**
643	**Horseshoe** (3)
671	**Unlucky** (3)
701	**C: A rabbit's foot** (3)
740	**Magpie** – number of magpies predicts future
804	**13** (5)
830	**C: The albatross** (3)
890	**That person will be next to marry** (8)
899	**Lucky** (3)

Core facts (1)

◆ Superstition is universal. Superstitious beliefs have been called 'the workings of that religion natural to the human heart'.

◆ Many superstitions are intended to **confuse the forces of evil**. For example, some people will wish a friend bad luck while actually hoping for good. This is why actors say 'break a leg'. And in Russia hunters wish each other an empty bag with the words 'neither fur, nor feather'.

◆ In all cultures, superstitions tend to cluster around similar **objects and themes**: births, weddings, funerals, mirrors, numbers, strangers and domestic animals, to name but a few.

Salt (2)

It is said that a house short of salt will also be short of money – a superstition which may date back to **Roman** times, when salt really was money. It is bad luck to spill salt – when it happens one should throw a pinch over the left shoulder.

Lucky things (3)

Lucky	Unlucky
Horseshoe	Owl
Chimney sweep	Friday
Rabbit's foot	Albatross
Itchy hands	Stepping on cracks
Finding coal	Finding a knife

LUCKY CHARM Some people carry a rabbit's foot for good luck.

Cats (4)

Cats are linked with **witches** and are said to have **nine lives**. It is bad luck to see a cat in the morning, or for a black cat to cross your path. If, on the other hand, a cat comes towards you then walks away, that bodes well. In Ireland it was once the custom on entering a house to say: 'God save all here except the cat.'

Numbers (5)

In the Christian world the **number 13** is considered unlucky because there were 13 people at the Last Supper. Sometimes 13 is omitted from the numbering of a street or the storeys of a tall building. An irrational dread of the number 13 is called **triskaidekaphobia**.

There are also superstitions about the number **three**. For example, it is bad luck to light three cigarettes with the same match. Some say this dates to the trenches of World War I. A sniper would spot the first person lighting up, take aim with the second and shoot the third. Accidents and misfortunes are also said to occur in threes.

FATEFUL FEAST There were 13 people at the Last Supper, depicted here in a 14th-century fresco from San Gimignano, Italy.

WEIRD AND WONDERFUL (6)

In **Japan**, the number four (*shi*) is considered unlucky because it sounds the same as the word for death. It is also unlucky in Japan to cut your nails at night – if you do, you will not be with your parents when they die.

90

Ladders

The taboo against walking under ladders relates to the notion that a hanged man swings under the ladder that is placed up against the gibbet to tie the noose.

WORST LUCK In medieval times, ladders were often seen leaning against gibbets. They were used to place the noose and to cut the hanged man down.

Tie-breaker

7

Q Red, black and white are the most important colours in the traditions of which culture?

A Chinese. Red symbolises the positive aspects of life and is associated with good fortune. Black is linked with bad luck, while white is believed to harmonise all elements, hence its use at funerals.

Weddings

8

In British custom, a bride is supposed to wear something old, something new, something borrowed and something blue. In Somerset, to see a flight of birds on one's wedding morning means a big family to come. In Scotland it is unlucky for newlyweds to go home from church by the same route that they came. When newlyweds depart the festivities, the bride must throw her bouquet to the guests – the person who catches it is the next to be married. At Jewish weddings the bride and groom must stamp on a glass together for luck.

THE HAPPY COUPLE The marriage of Elvis and Priscilla Presley in 1967. According to superstition, the bride and groom should cut the first slice of the wedding cake together. It is also good luck to keep a piece of the cake – often the top layer – for the christening of the first child.

Mirrors

9

To break a mirror brings **seven years' bad luck**. If you look in a mirror for too long you will see the Devil at your shoulder. In Russia, you must look in the mirror if you return to your house to fetch something you forgot. Mirrors are sometimes covered if a person dies. In Scotland it is sometimes said you can see your future husband's face in a mirror if you eat an apple in front of it while holding a candle.

Names

10

There are many superstitions surrounding names. In Ireland it is sometimes considered unlucky to name a person after a living parent or a dead sibling. In Jewish homes, it was once common to change the name of a mortally ill child, so that the angel of death would not be able to find him. Christian parents of sick children would seek out a couple named Mary and Joseph and ask them to send their child a small gift. If three people with the same name or same initial sit at a table together, one of them, it is said, will be married within the year.

Nursery rhymes

QUESTION NUMBER

The numbers or star following the answers refer to information boxes on the right.

ANSWERS

71 **Four-and-twenty, or 24** ★

74 **Curds and whey** ❼

★ 75 **Simple Simon**

77 **Little girls** – boys: slugs, snails and puppy dog's tails

80 **Jack Horner** ★ ❼

184 **Struwwelpeter** ❺

293 **Mary, Mary, quite contrary** ❻

299 **Fall down** ❽

300 **Blue** – '... sugar is sweet, and so are you'

354 **Bells** – 'she shall have music wherever she goes'

403 **10 000** – a son of King George III (1763-1827)

411 **Humpty Dumpty** ❸

471 **Rich** ❷

612 ***Through the Looking-Glass*** ❸

618 **A mockingbird** ❷

620 **Peter Piper** – a traditional tongue-twister

664 **Sixpence** ★

767 **Little Miss Muffet** ❼

831 **The Moon** ❶

904 **Hubbard** – by Sarah Catherine Martin, 1805

931 **Old King Cole** – legendary Celtic British king

975 **'B'** – 'prick it and pat it and mark it with "B"'

Core facts ❶

◆ Many nursery rhymes date far back into history. Some scholars argue that a few may even originate in prehistoric times, having been passed on orally through the generations.

◆ The plots and the cast of characters in nursery rhymes are as colourful and diverse as in any mythology.

◆ Some rhymes are disguised commentaries on adult concerns: '**Pop Goes the Weasel**' is about poverty and pawnshops. Others, such as '**Eeny, Meeny, Miney, Mo**' are pure word-music.

◆ They can contain surreal wit or sad words: a cow vaults the Moon, and Solomon Grundy's bleak life is reduced to the events of a week.

Lullabies ❷

Cradle songs may be the oldest form of nursery rhymes. They are traditionally sung to lull babies and toddlers to sleep, but some contain frightening images, such as '... Daddy's gone a-hunting ...' and '... when the bough breaks the cradle will fall ...'. 'Rock-a-Bye Baby' may have been written in America, and some of the best-known cradle songs come from the New World. They include 'Hush Little Baby' ('... Momma's gonna buy you a mockingbird ...').

Taking a fall ❸

'Humpty Dumpty' is one of the most widespread nursery rhymes. Versions exist in most European countries, and in all of them Humpty is damaged beyond repair by his fall. In France he is called **Boule Boule**, and it is said 'no doctor in England can mend him'. In Germany he is known as **Hümpelkin-Pümpelkin**.

EGG HEAD In *Through The Looking-Glass* Humpty Dumpty declares: 'It's very provoking to be called an egg – very.'

★ 75

'Simple Simon' ★

Attempting to buy a pie when he has no money is just one of Simple Simon's foolish undertakings: he also tries to catch a whale in a bucket and find plums growing on a thistle. Pies often figure in nursery rhymes. There is **Jack Horner's** plum pie; and there is the pie containing four-and-twenty blackbirds, set before a king in his counting house.

NICE BUT DIM Simple Simon has long been an alliterative nickname for a simpleton.

4

'Oranges and Lemons ...

... say the bells of St Clements.' In the **City of London** there are two churches named after St Clement: both are near the wharf where citrus fruit was once unloaded. As for 'When will you pay me ...?', the debtors' prison was once close to the law courts on Old Bailey. All the churches mentioned are in London, including St Martin's, Shoreditch and the 'great bell at Bow' – that is St Mary le Bow, near St Paul's Cathedral.

5

Shock-headed Peter

Heinrich Hoffmann's **Struwwelpeter** stories were written in 1847 for the amusement of his son. They were intended to be a parody of cautionary tales, but immediately became a classic of children's scare-literature. Hoffmann's book contains the tale of the girl who plays with matches – and is entirely burned up except for her shoes. Then there is thumb-sucking Konrad. He will not stop, so his thumbs are snipped off by the tailor.

BONE IDLE Shock-headed Peter refuses to cut or comb his hair, or to trim his fingernails.

WEIRD AND WONDERFUL

6

There are different theories about 'Mary, Mary, Quite Contrary'. Mary may have been the Catholic queen 'Bloody' Mary, or Mary, Queen of Scots (a Catholic), or the Virgin Mary. Whichever way, the rhyme is anti-Catholic.

7

'Little Miss Muffet'

The Miss Muffet who sat on a tuffet may have been the daughter of an Elizabethan entomologist named **Thomas Muffet**. He was said to be a man 'whose admiration for spiders has never been surpassed'. But what is a 'tuffet'? The word may be related to 'tuft' (of grass) and mean a small mound, or it may be a three-legged stool of a type used by milkmaids. The form and metre of this rhyme are very similar to '**Little Jack Horner**'. It may be that both derive from a single source.

ARACHNOPHOBE Miss Muffet plays on children's deep fear of creepy-crawlies.

8

'Ring-a-Ring o' Roses'

It is often said that this rhyme contains a veiled description of the symptoms of **plague**: a rosy red rash, sneezing, and falling down dead. In fact, the words we now know became current in the 19th century, long after the era of plagues. Other versions suggest that this is an old dancing rhyme, and the falling-down is a curtsy gone comically wrong.

TRADITIONAL DANCE? The flowers and circular dance suggest a link with the spring maypole.

Fantasy fiction

QUESTION NUMBER

The numbers or star following the answers refer to information boxes on the right.

ANSWERS

- **24** **Sauron** 9
- **42** ***Chitty Chitty Bang Bang*** 4
- **148** **A monster** 2
- **166** **Daemons** 8
- **181** ***Le Petit Prince*** 3
- **262** **Hobbits** 5 9
- **279** **Draco Malfoy** 6
- **280** **Screwtape** – *The Screwtape Letters*, 1942
- **339** ***Monsters, Inc.*** 4
- **359** **The sorting hat** 1 6
- **415** **Smaug** 5
- **419** **Lewis Carroll** 2
- **486** ***The Dawn Treader*** 7
- **530** **Bilbo Baggins** 5 9
- **548** **Cair Paravel** 1 7
- ★ **733** **The *Gormenghast* trilogy**
- **768** **Joanna** 6
- **825** **C: A Cheshire cat** 2
- **852** **Ron Weasley** 6
- **901** **Cousin** 9
- **902** **Tweedledum** 2
- **926** **Characters in *The Lord of the Rings*** 9
- **976** **Elessar** 9

Core facts 1

◆ Many of the classics of fantasy fiction follow the same mythic pattern – Bilbo Baggins, the Narnia children, Harry Potter and Lyra Silvertongue are all sent on a **journey to another world**.

◆ Many of these characters, especially those in allegorical tales, fulfil some special destiny, or attain a special knowledge, which they then carry with them.

◆ So it is that Lyra Silvertongue saves her universe, the Narnia children become kings and queens of Cair Paravel, and Frodo Baggins, Bilbo's cousin, defeats the powers of Mordor and preserves Middle Earth.

The adventures of Alice 2

Alice in Wonderland and its sequel, ***Through the Looking-Glass***, were written by the Oxford University mathematician **Lewis Carroll** (real name: Charles Lutwidge Dodgson). The first book recounts the surreal adventures of Alice as she pursues a white rabbit underground. The second book has Alice pass through a mirror into a world where she encounters the Red and White Queens and Tweedledum and Tweedledee, among others. *Through the Looking-Glass* contains the poem '**Jabberwocky**', which uses a mass of newly coined words to recount the slaying of a monster. Both books make great play of Carroll's fascination with number and word games, and both are full of wit.

REAL GIRL *Alice in Wonderland* came about after Lewis Carroll made up the story for his young friend Alice Liddell.

LITERARY LEGACY Soon after *Le Petit Prince* was published in 1943, its author disappeared while flying on a reconnaissance mission over the Mediterranean Sea.

Little Prince 3

In this tale by **Antoine de Saint-Exupéry**, a downed pilot in the Sahara desert encounters a little prince. The prince tells the pilot about his travels to various planets, each inhabited by a single adult. The author uses this device to poke fun at the futility of aspects of adult existence. Yet the story remains tender and is made all the more so by the French author's beautiful illustrations.

Children's fantasy in film

4

Most films aimed at children contain elements of fantasy. Many are secret favourites of some adults, too.

Toy Story	Toys come to life when humans cannot see them.
The Wizard of Oz	Dorothy is transported from Kansas to Oz, and seeks the way back home.
Monsters, Inc.	Monsters harvest children's screams at night to fuel their own world.
Laputa: Castle in the Sky	Japanese cartoon classic in which a young boy and girl discover a magical floating island.
Mary Poppins	A saintly and magical nanny brings happiness to a stuffy Edwardian family.
Chitty Chitty Bang Bang	Children in a flying car overthrow the regime of a child-hating king.

CHIM, CHIM, CHER-EE Like *Chitty Chitty Bang Bang*, *Mary Poppins* was a 1960s musical film.

733

Gormenghast

The *Gormenghast* trilogy by **Mervyn Peake** is a dark but brilliant work of fantasy fiction. The three books, *Titus Groan*, *Gormenghast* and *Titus Alone*, weave a rich story full of characters far more complex than those usually found in this genre.

The Hobbit

5

This is the first book in which **J.R.R. Tolkien** presents **Middle Earth**, an invented world populated with characters drawn from European mythology – elves, dwarves, goblins and so forth. However, the timid little people called **hobbits** are a product of J.R.R. Tolkien's imagination. The hero of the book is a hobbit named **Bilbo Baggins**. With the connivance of the wizard **Gandalf**, he is co-opted by a band of dwarves on a quest to steal back their treasure from the dragon, **Smaug**. Along the way Bilbo is transformed into a resourceful adventurer. He also acquires a ring of invisibility that has long been in the possession of a sad creature named **Gollum**. This ring is central to the more ambitious and grown-up trilogy of Middle Earth, *The Lord of the Rings*.

Harry Potter 6

The Harry Potter stories by **J. (Joanna) K. Rowling** tell of a boy-wizard who is unaware of his gift until he is magically summoned to **Hogwarts**, a school for wizards in a hidden otherworld. At Hogwarts, he learns the wizard's craft while battling against various manifestations of **Voldemort**, the epitome of an evil wizard. The books draw heavily on the long tradition of boarding-school adventures in English fiction, while the magical remit of the school allows for much surreal humour. There are mythic elements in Harry's mysterious status as a 'chosen one', symbolised by the zigzag scar on his forehead. Like all mythical heroes, he has his helpers: on the one hand, the cool and knowledgeable **Hermione**, and on the other, the loyal and hotheaded **Ron Weasley**.

NEW SERIES
The fourth Harry Potter novel, *Harry Potter and the Goblet of Fire*, was first published in 2000.

The Narnia Chronicles

7

The best-known of **C.S. Lewis**'s Narnia books is *The Lion, the Witch and the Wardrobe*. Four children – **Peter**, **Susan**, **Edmund** and **Lucy** – find a magic gateway via a wardrobe to a fairy-tale world of talking animals. This world, Narnia, is ruled by a wicked **White Queen**. The children fight to overthrow the Queen, aided by the kingly and benevolent lion, **Aslan**. To save Edmund, Aslan hands himself over to the Queen and is put to death. But he is restored to life, and the Queen is defeated. The story is an allegory of the sacrificial death and resurrection of Christ. Christian values also permeate the other stories – including *Prince Caspian* and *The Silver Chair*.

His Dark Materials

8

This trilogy by **Philip Pullman** consists of *Northern Lights*, *The Subtle Knife* and *The Amber Spyglass*. The books portray a parallel universe in which everyone has a daemon – an animal that is a reflection of their personality, and which is always by their side. The daemon seems to be a personification of the soul. In this world, a wild young girl named **Lyra** becomes involved in a cosmic battle between **The Authority** (that is, a decrepit figure of God and his armies) and the rebels of the **Republic of Heaven**, who are led by her father. She is aided by a boy named **Will**, who is equipped with a knife that can cut windows between different universes.

The ultimate quest

9

The Lord of the Rings, like *The Hobbit*, is the story of a quest (a common genre in Nordic myths). The hero of the books is Bilbo's young cousin and heir, **Frodo Baggins**. He is charged with destroying Bilbo's ring, which turns out to be the focus of an ancient and evil force. With the help of the Merlin-like figure of **Gandalf**, and a kind of international alliance of elves, dwarves, hobbits and men, Frodo journeys to **Mordor**, the dark heart of the evil empire and the only place where the ring can be destroyed.

QUESTION NUMBER

The numbers or star following the answers refer to information boxes on the right.

ANSWERS

QUESTION NUMBER	ANSWERS
5	**The Mouse King** (4)
10	**Nana** (3)
58	**E.T.A. Hoffmann** (4)
141	**The Sugar Plum Fairy** (4)
195	**Peter Pan** (3)
218	**His shadow** (3)
290	**Columbine** (8)
356	**Harlequin** (8)
377	**Richard Wagner** (6)
413	**Darling** (3)
430	**The Lost Boys** (3)
468	***Twelfth Night*** – by Orsino who loves Olivia
781	**Prokofiev** – Sergei (1891-1953)
790	***The Magic Flute*** (6)
★ 814	**Mummers** (*mum* = silent)
819	**Pantaloon** (8)
887	**Pantomimes** (7)
925	***Commedia dell'arte* characters** (8)
968	**Dick Whittington** (born c.1350 and four times Mayor of London) (7)

Myths and tales on stage

Core facts (1)

◆ The earliest myths were narrated to groups of people by storytellers – and it is a short step from spoken tales to dramatic performances.

◆ Medieval **mystery plays** were an early form of popular theatre. Not for nothing are they also called miracle plays: they were intended to evoke wonder from their illiterate audiences.

◆ Even after theatre became a largely secular amusement, it aimed to inspire awe in the audience. The staging of fairy tales and magical stories allow for all kinds of **stagecraft**, such as trap doors, mirrors, smoke and resplendent scenery – to make myths visible and memorable.

Punch and Judy (2)

The slapstick character of Mr Punch grew out of **Pulcinella**, a stock *commedia dell'arte* figure. The diarist **Samuel Pepys** saw an Italian puppet show featuring the character in 1662. These puppets were stringed marionettes: the English hand puppet did not become popular until the end of the 19th century. By this time Punch had a wife named Judy. The standard plot involves a baby, a policeman, a priest and a hangman – and a finale in which Punch is eaten by a crocodile.

Peter Pan (3)

He is the little boy who **never grew up**, and it is this appealing idea that makes Peter Pan a mythic character. In the stage play by **J.M. Barrie**, Peter comes to the Darling household to retrieve his shadow. He entices **Wendy** and her siblings away to **Never Never Land**, where they join Peter's gang, the Lost Boys, to fight **Captain Hook** and his pirates.

The Nutcracker (4)

Tchaikovsky's ballet *The Nutcracker* is adapted from a fairy tale by the German writer and folklorist **E.T.A. Hoffmann**. It is a tale of toys coming to life. The nutcracker, in the form of a soldier, is a Christmas gift to a little girl Clara. Her brother spitefully breaks it. At the stroke of midnight Clara goes to look at her spoiled present, and finds herself shrinking to its size as the toys awaken. They fight a battle with the Mouse King, after which the nutcracker turns into a prince and transports Clara to the land of sweets where they are greeted by the **Sugar Plum Fairy**. There they celebrate the victory over the mice, until Clara wakes to find it has all been a dream.

TOY STORY Tchaikovsky's ballet for children was first performed in 1892. It is one of many tales in which magical things happen at Christmas.

The Magic Flute

This opera by Mozart is set in an imaginary, magical Egypt. The **Queen of the Night** asks a youth named **Tamino** to save her daughter **Pamina** from the evil **Sarastro**. He finds Sarastro, who turns out to be a goodly magus. He has Tamino undergo an initiation, after which he can claim Pamina's hand. The wicked Queen of the Night attacks Sarastro's temple, but is driven away by light. Finally, the lovers are united.

FIRM FAVOURITE
The captivating fantasy of *The Magic Flute* means it is often the first opera children are taken to see.

Wagner

Richard Wagner's **Ring cycle** consists of four operas: *The Rhinegold*, *The Valkyrie*, *Siegfried* and *The Twilight of the Gods*. Together they take more than 14 hours to perform. Wagner took his material from the medieval German epic known as the **Nibelungenlied**. From this he created a new kind of opera in which drama, myth and music were fused into a single grandiose narrative. A new theatre had to be built for the 1876 premiere in Bayreuth.

★ 814

Mummers' plays

Mummers were troupes of amateur actors – all men – who would go from house to house at Christmas. They performed light-hearted playlets such as ***Saint George and the Dragon***, which always involved mock swordplay and riotous scenes of slapstick between the minor characters.

Pantomimes

English pantomimes are stage versions of traditional fairy tales, spiced up with dance, comedy and song. They are a Christmas entertainment that grew out of the dumb shows of the Paris fairgrounds, fused with elements of Italian *commedia dell'arte*. In pantomime the **principal boy** is always played by a woman, and the **pantomime dame** by a man. There is noisy participation from the audience of children ('Look behind you!').

Among the most popular pantomimes are *Dick Whittington*, *Puss in Boots*, *Aladdin*, *Babes in the Wood* and *Cinderella*.

Commedia dell'arte

This is the name given to a particular genre of Italian theatre, popular in the 17th century. It featured a host of stock characters or 'masks' such as the beau **Harlequin**, his lover **Columbine**, the doddery old **Pantaloon**, the clownish **Pedrolino** (who developed into the lovelorn, white-faced **Pierrot**), and the bragging soldier **Scaramouche**. Performances were improvised around a skeleton plot in which the two lovers try to overcome the obstacles put in their way by the other characters.

SHARP DRESSER
Harlequin can always be recognised by his brightly coloured diamond-patterned silken suit.

Superheroes

QUESTION NUMBER

The numbers or star following the answers refer to information boxes on the right.

ANSWERS

- 27 **Mary Jane** ❹
- 57 **Alfred** ❼
- 150 **Bruce Wayne** ❼
- 198 **Robin** ❼
- 283 **Lois Lane** ❷
- 355 **Batman** ❼
- 414 **Wonder Woman** ❺
- 416 **Tarzan** (first novel: *Tarzan of the Apes*, 1914) ❹
- 472 **Jonathan and Martha Kent** ❷
- 562 **Spider-Man** ❹
- 576 **Kryptonite** ❷
- 579 **Jane** (daughter of US scientist) ❹
- 656 **Lord Greystoke** – the family surname is Clayton
- ★ 714 **Buffy the Vampire Slayer** ❶
- 719 **Gotham City** ❼
- 737 **George Bernard Shaw** – first performed 1905
- 763 **Peter Parker** ❹
- 766 **Bruce Banner** ❸
- 823 **C: The Riddler** (computer genius, loves riddles) ❻ ❼
- 851 **Green** ❸
- 957 **Spike** ★ ❶
- 963 **Sunnydale** ★ ❶
- 969 **Krypton** ❷

Core facts ❶

◆ Many of the best-known superheroes first appeared in the comic books of the 1930s.

◆ New superheroes are still being created. ***Buffy the Vampire Slayer*** began life in a humorous film made in 1992.

◆ Many superheroes are **orphans**. The mother of Bruce Banner is murdered by his father; Superman's parents die in the destruction of Krypton, and Batman's parents are murdered.

◆ It is as if superheroes have to be free of attachments to do their duty. They also often reject the women who love them.

IS IT A BIRD? ❷ Superman first appeared in *Action Comics* in 1938. Since then, several films and television series have been based on the character.

Superman

A native of the planet **Krypton**, Superman lives on Earth under the pseudonym **Clark Kent** (adopted son of Jonathan and Martha Kent), and works in Metropolis at a newspaper named the ***Daily Planet***. He is in love with his fellow reporter **Lois Lane**. His powers include great strength, the ability to fly and X-ray vision. These abilities derive somehow from the Earth's yellow sun – under a red sun he is powerless. Superman has one weakness, rather like Achilles' unprotected heel. He can be laid low by exposure to fragments of **kryptonite** from his home planet. Though he is an international superhero, dedicated to protecting the world, his motto is 'Truth, Justice and the American way'.

The Hulk ❸

The real name of the Hulk is **Bruce Banner**. In a laboratory accident he is exposed to radiation that changes his genetic makeup. Whenever he is enraged, he turns into the giant, muscle-bound, green hulk. Unlike other superheroes, he does not channel his powers towards fighting crime, though in the event it is usually the forces of evil who are on the receiving end of his wrath.

Spider-Man

4

Spider-Man is the superhero alter ego of **Peter Parker**, who is bitten by a radioactive spider (in recent films, the spider is 'genetically modified'). This gives Parker spider-like powers: he has great agility; he can climb walls, leap long distances, spin webs to catch criminals and shoot web-ropes from his wrists, allowing him to swing like Tarzan through the urban jungle. As with Superman, the burden of his special powers prevents him from declaring his love for **Mary Jane** who, like Lois Lane, is in love with his mysterious super-persona.

Wonder Woman

5

Rooted in Greek mythology, Wonder Woman is **Diana**, a princess of the tribe of female warriors called the Amazons. In Greek stories the Amazons are descended from **Ares**, the god of war, but in the *Wonder Woman* tales Ares is the enemy, whom Diana defeats in combat before entering the world of men.

POWER JEWELLERY Wonder Woman wears a pair of bracelets that can deflect bullets.

Antiheroes

6

All heroes have enemies. Naturally, those of superheroes are far worse than most.

Character	Description
Green Goblin	Enemy of Spider-Man. Alter ego of Peter Parker's college roommate.
Lex Luthor	Enemy of Superman. Uses his great intelligence to try to outsmart the superhero.
Penguin	Enemy of Batman. Waddles like a penguin, chews on a cigarette-holder, and carries an umbrella.
Joker	Enemy of Batman. Cackles wildly as he commits his crimes.

HARLEQUIN The Joker's lover, Harleen Quinzel is another of Batman's many enemies.

714

Buffy

Buffy Summers is a schoolgirl in the town of **Sunnydale**. But she also happens to be the chosen Slayer, the one whose destiny it is to protect Earth from vampires and demons. Sunnydale, it turns out, is sited on a gateway to the netherworld. Buffy goes out nightly to take on demons with a combination of magic and martial arts.

Batman

7

Unlike most superheroes, Batman does not have otherworldly powers. His real name is **Bruce Wayne**, and to the world he is a bored and immensely rich playboy. He uses his wealth to fund his fight against crime in **Gotham City**, accompanied by his sidekick, **Robin**, the Boy Wonder. Batman is known as the Caped Crusader: Batman and Robin together are the Dynamic Duo. Wayne's butler, Alfred, is the only person who knows their secret.

HERO AND ANTIHERO Batman's first outing was in *Detective Comics* in 1939. Catwoman appeared in the first issue of *Batman* in 1940.

Space fantasy

QUESTION NUMBER

The numbers or star following the answers refer to information boxes on the right.

ANSWERS

13 **The tardis** ❼

23 ***Blade Runner*** – directed by Ridley Scott

34 ***AI*** ❾

★ 45 ***The Time Machine***

89 **True** ❻

153 **Extraterrestrial** ❺

231 **H.G. Wells** (published 1898) ★

268 **A close encounter of the first kind** ❹

286 **Dale Arden** ❸

338 **Obi-Wan Kenobi** ❽

372 **The Jedi** ❽

543 **Ming** ❸

586 **False** ❹

607 **The daleks** ❼

611 **'To infinity and beyond'** ❸

657 **Jean-Luc Picard** ❻

658 **Buster Crabbe** ❸

717 **Luke Skywalker** ❽

761 **Spock** ❻

780 **Light-sabre** ❽

848 **Dr McCoy** ❻

881 **Unidentified Flying Object** ❹

884 **Buzz Lightyear** ❸

Core facts ❶

◆ A decline in religious belief in Western societies has not led to any decrease in the role of myth and legend. We still need tales of heroes and strange countries, only now they are usually located in the future or outer space.

◆ The **unexplored Universe** has taken the place once occupied in the human imagination by places such as Atlantis. Few people are now tormented by demons, but some individuals believe that they have been abducted by aliens.

◆ Fictional tales such as ***Star Wars*** and ***Star Trek*** provide a gallery of mythical warriors and adventurers every bit as potent as Hercules, Woden or Robin Hood.

Alien visitors ❷

The reports of alien sightings gathered over the past 50 years seem to agree on the visitors' appearance. The aliens who have supposedly visited this planet are short and bald with reptilian nostrils. They have large, dark almond-shaped eyes and a grey or greenish hue to their skin. They go naked. They can communicate telepathically between themselves. This image has been reinforced by countless depictions in film and fiction.

Flash Gordon ❸

In this popular film and serial of the 1930s, Flash was played by **Buster Crabbe**. The storyline concerns an empire ruled by the evil **Ming**. Flash, along with his girlfriend **Dale Arden** and other rebels, is fighting the empire. Flash Gordon and similar characters, such as **Buck Rogers**, lead directly to *Star Wars*' **Luke Skywalker**. They are all parodied in *Toy Story* in the person of **Buzz Lightyear**, with his unscientific war cry: 'To infinity and beyond'.

UFO sightings ❹

The terms **UFO** (Unidentified Flying Object) and **flying saucer** were coined as a result of the same incident in 1947. An American pilot saw some strange objects in the sky, which he described as moving like 'saucers skipping across the water'. The investigating officer coined the acronym UFO, and newspapers came up with flying saucer. Such a sighting is sometimes called 'a close encounter of the first kind'. The third kind is a face-to-face meeting with an alien: no such incident has ever been proved to have happened.

E.T. ❺

The first portrayals of alien visitors cast them as hostile invaders. But in 1982, Steven Spielberg's film *E.T.* drew a picture of an 'extra-terrestrial' something akin to an angel. E.T. performs small miracles of healing, and despite a powerful intelligence is naive and childlike. Pursued and persecuted as a dangerous outsider, E.T. apparently dies, and comes back to life. So the story can be read as a **Christian allegory** as well as a space-age fairy tale.

Star Trek

6

The adventures of the crew of the starship ***Enterprise***, which began in 1966, were like a series of parables. They dealt with issues of race, violence, greed and power. The central characters were the bold **Captain Kirk**, the Vulcan **Spock** who lived by logic and abjured emotion, and **Dr McCoy,** whose temper was the mirror image of Spock's cool imperturbability. In 1987, *The Next Generation* continued the journey beyond the 'final frontier', with the wise and diplomatic **Jean-Luc Picard** as captain. *Voyager* introduced a female captain of the starship *Voyager* and a common mythic situation: the Long Journey Home. The crew of this ship were as lost and homesick as Odysseus after Troy.

TO BOLDLY GO *Star Trek* is in a tradition of fabulous voyages that encompasses Sinbad the Sailor, Jason and the Argonauts, and the Irish hero Brendan the Navigator, who sailed to the Land of Promise.

Dr Who

7

An enigmatic hero akin to a wizard or a magus, Dr Who's very name sounds like a question. The Doctor is a **time lord** and so virtually immortal. He travels back and forth through the aeons in a **tardis**. This time machine has the outward form of a police box: a puzzling and old-fashioned piece of street furniture even when the series began. Like a genie's lamp, it is much bigger on the inside than on the outside – a source of constant wonder to new visitors. Doctor Who makes it his business to protect our world from enemies such as **daleks** and **cybermen**.

45 ★

H.G. Wells

The Time Machine by H.G. Wells was one of the first works of science fantasy. An unnamed 'Traveller' goes forward into the 800th century. He encounters the **Morlochs**, a race of subterranean savages. Throughout the adventure, the machine never leaves the spot: the only travel is temporal.

Star Wars

8

The success of the *Star Wars* films is due in part to the way that they tap directly into familiar ideas from folklore. **Luke Skywalker**, the orphaned hero, is like a young King Arthur: he is given a sword (his light-sabre) and a knightly code (the way of the Jedi) by his Merlinesque mentor **Obi-Wan Kenobi**. **Leia** is instantly recognisable as a fairy-tale princess. And the struggle between The Force and the Dark Side, between Good and Evil, is the deepest and most ancient preoccupation of mythology.

COMPANIONS IN ARMS *Star Wars'* cast of characters includes loveable robots, such as the ever-anxious 'droid' C-3PO ('See-Threepio').

WEIRD AND WONDERFUL

9

The film ***AI*** depicts a world of Pinocchio-like androids who are used as servants and as surrogate children. The screenplay is based on a short story by **Brian Aldiss** entitled *Supertoys Last All Summer Long.*

Quiz 0 (page 8)

1 The tortoise
2 A dog
3 A gryphon
4 Pan
5 The Mouse King
6 Friday
7 The nightingale
8 The mermaid
9 A bull
10 Nana

Quiz 1 (page 8)

11 Seven
12 100 years
13 The tardis
14 St Valentine
15 Midnight
16 Midsummer's night
17 Thor
18 Julius Caesar
19 The dragon
20 Friday 13th

Quiz 2 (page 8)

21 Clyde Barrow
22 Dionysus
23 *Blade Runner*
24 Sauron
25 Gary Oldman
26 Hans Christian Andersen
27 Mary Jane
28 Daniel
29 Pontiac
30 Narcissus

Quiz 3 (page 8)

31 *Monty Python and the Holy Grail*
32 Danny Kaye
33 *Westworld*
34 *AI*
35 Dracula
36 A mermaid
37 *Company of Wolves*
38 *The Amityville Horror*
39 Charlton Heston
40 *Crouching Tiger, Hidden Dragon*

Quiz 4 (page 9)

41 St Christopher
42 *Chitty Chitty Bang Bang*
43 St Brendan the Navigator
44 Baba Yaga
45 *The Time Machine*
46 Walkabout
47 A gremlin
48 Walter Raleigh
49 *Seven Years in Tibet*
50 Richard Burton

Quiz 5 (page 9)

51 Rumpelstiltskin
52 Vishnu
53 Hope
54 One
55 Bluebeard
56 The olive tree
57 Alfred
58 E.T.A. Hoffmann
59 The Toltecs
60 Thoth

Quiz 6 (page 9)

61 A
62 C
63 A
64 B
65 C
66 A
67 C
68 A
69 D
70 D

Quiz 7 (page 10)

71 Four-and-twenty, or 24
72 Pumpkin
73 William Tell
74 Curds and whey
75 Simple Simon
76 The Salmon of Knowledge
77 Little girls
78 Garlic
79 Snow White
80 Jack Horner

Quiz 8 (page 10)

81 True
82 False
83 False
84 True
85 False
86 False
87 False
88 False
89 True
90 False

Quiz 9 (page10)

91 October
92 Nine
93 100
94 Five
95 Ten
96 Four
97 12
98 Nine
99 30
100 12

Quiz 10 (page 10)

101 Jason
102 Janus
103 The Hydra
104 Mercury
105 Chaos
106 They turned to stone
107 Hector
108 Romulus and Remus
109 Cassandra
110 Daedalus

Quiz 11 (page 11)

111 Sleeping Beauty
112 Finland
113 'November Rain'
114 Confucius
115 The Wandering Jew
116 Finn MacCool
117 Maui
118 North America
119 A race of dwarves
120 Shiva

Quiz 12 (page 11)

121 Revelation, or Apocalypse
122 Greek
123 Seamus Heaney
124 James Hilton
125 Geraint
126 His burden of sin
127 The Book of the Dead
128 Peter Carey
129 Bruce Chatwin
130 The *Mahabharata*

Quiz 13 (page 11)

131 B
132 B
133 B
134 C
135 B
136 C
137 A
138 B
139 D
140 B

Quiz 14 (page 12)

141 The Sugar Plum Fairy
142 Elf
143 A sheep's
144 St Peter
145 Dice
146 Buddha
147 Jesus
148 A monster
149 Israel
150 Bruce Wayne

Quiz 15 (page 12)

151 Little John
152 Pandora
153 Extraterrestrial
154 Urban myth
155 Romulus
156 Papyrus
157 Glastonbury
158 Abominable snowman
159 Astrology
160 Merlin

Quiz 16 (page 12)

161 Puss in Boots
162 A wolf
163 The peacock
164 *Alien*
165 Africa
166 Daemons
167 A baboon
168 The dragon
169 The Aztecs
170 Anubis

Quiz 17 (page 12)

171 Achilles
172 Apollo
173 The Fates
174 To bring up Cerberus from the Underworld
175 Hestia
176 Polyphemus
177 Eos
178 The Pythoness
179 The Graces
180 Sisyphus

Quiz 18 (page 13)

181 *Le Petit Prince*
182 *Thumbelina*
183 *Goblin Market*
184 *Struwwelpeter*
185 *Uncle Remus*
186 *The Wizard of Oz*
187 *Frankenstein*
188 *Puss in Boots*
189 *Animal Farm*
190 *Alice in Wonderland*

Quiz 19 (page 14)

191 Halloween
192 Goldilocks
193 Moses
194 Gandalf
195 Peter Pan
196 Aquarius
197 Beauty and the Beast
198 Robin
199 The Holy Grail
200 Babylon

Quiz 20 (page 14)

201 True
202 Mount Fuji
203 Mount Sinai
204 St Bernard
205 Mount Caucasus
206 Ireland
207 Mount Ararat
208 Mount Etna
209 Mount Kilimanjaro
210 Silbury Hill

Quiz 21 (page 14)

211 Woe
212 Esther and Abi Ofarim
213 Little Red Riding Hood
214 Purgatory
215 Valhalla
216 Styx
217 Geniuses
218 His shadow
219 Passion play
220 Flora

Quiz 22 (page 14)

221 Shaman
222 Leprechaun
223 Beelzebub
224 Miracle plays
225 Poltergeist
226 Limbo
227 Reiki
228 Prometheus
229 Nefertiti
230 Hagiography

Quiz 23 (page 15)

231 H.G. Wells
232 The Valkyries
233 March
234 Odin, or Woden
235 Mebd of Connacht
236 Ares
237 Valencia
238 The Philistines
239 Paris
240 The Zulus

Quiz 24 (page 15)

241 The *Odyssey*
242 Brueghel the Elder
243 St Luke
244 *Centuries*
245 Hieronymus Bosch
246 *Primavera*
247 Traitors
248 Canova
249 Daniel
250 Iceland

Quiz 25 (page 15)

251 B
252 D
253 C
254 A
255 D
256 B
257 A
258 B
259 C
260 B

Quiz 26 (page 16)

261 Once upon a time
262 Hobbits
263 Samson
264 St Catherine
265 Ouija board
266 A pumpkin
267 A wolf
268 A close encounter of the first kind
269 A snake, or serpent
270 A broomstick

Quiz 27 (page 16)

271 Mary Shelley
272 Exodus
273 Jonathan Swift
274 *The Hound of the Baskervilles*
275 Uncle Remus
276 John Bunyan
277 Arthur
278 The Bible
279 Draco Malfoy
280 Screwtape

Quiz 28 (page 16)

281 Cupid
282 Maid Marion
283 Lois Lane
284 *The Hunger*
285 Aphrodite
286 Dale Arden
287 *The Steadfast Tin Soldier*
288 Echo
289 Pygmalion
290 Columbine

Quiz 29 (page 16)

291 Gnome
292 A peach tree
293 Mary, Mary, quite contrary
294 The Green Man
295 The lotus
296 Druids
297 Lancelot
298 Japan's
299 Fall down
300 Blue

Quiz 30 (page 17)

301 St Andrew
302 New Zealand
303 Wales
304 Turkey
305 Finland
306 Lilliput
307 Denmark
308 Egypt
309 North America
310 St George

Quiz 31 (page 17)

311 No place
312 Karel Čapek
313 Swastika
314 Cape Finisterre
315 Dreamtime
316 Cistercian
317 Dies Irae
318 Werewolf
319 The Tower of Babel
320 The Alamo

Quiz 32 (page 17)

321 A
322 B
323 A
324 C
325 B
326 C
327 C
328 C
329 B
330 D

Quiz 33 (page 18)

331 Doc
332 *Thriller*
333 Arnold Schwarzenegger
334 *Ghostbusters*
335 Godzilla
336 Kevin Costner
337 Data
338 Obi-Wan Kenobi
339 *Monsters, Inc.*
340 King Kong

Quiz 34 (page 18)

341 St Peter
342 Jinn, or genie
343 Roxy Music
344 Works hard
345 Man-like
346 *The Princess and the Pea*
347 The Mirror of Erised
348 *The Little Mermaid*
349 A bull
350 *My Fair Lady*

Quiz 35 (page 18)

351 A bride
352 Invisibility
353 Glass
354 Bells
355 Batman
356 Harlequin
357 Joseph
358 Ruby slippers
359 The sorting hat
360 *The Emperor's New Clothes*

Quiz 36 (page 18)

361 Mecca
362 Tintagel
363 Lhasa
364 The Tiber
365 Bodh Gaya
366 Santiago de Compostela
367 Oberammergau
368 Medina
369 Calcutta
370 The Incas

Quiz 37 (page 19)

371 Hanukah
372 The Jedi
373 The first
374 Prometheus
375 Japan
376 Serafina Pekkala
377 Richard Wagner
378 Judaism
379 St Lucia
380 Diwali

Quiz 38 (page 19)

381 'Circle of animals'
382 A dog
383 A lion
384 A stag
385 Human beings
386 Taurus the Bull
387 An ape
388 Satyrs
389 *The Insect Play*
390 The cockerel

Quiz 39 (page 19)

391 D
392 B
393 A
394 C
395 C
396 C
397 D
398 B
399 B
400 C

Quiz 40 (page 20)

401 12
402 Seven
403 10 000
404 One
405 He rested
406 Two
407 Three
408 40
409 12
410 Five

Quiz 41 (page 20)

411 Humpty Dumpty
412 Mars
413 Darling
414 Wonder Woman
415 Smaug
416 Tarzan
417 Ned Kelly
418 Hinduism
419 Lewis Carroll
420 Ebenezer

Quiz 42 (page 20)

421 Playful
422 Run away
423 Mercury
424 *Camelot*
425 Persephone
426 D.H. Lawrence
427 Paris
428 Buddha
429 Vesta
430 The Lost Boys

Quiz 43 (page 20)

431 Ariel
432 *The Epic of Gilgamesh*
433 Milton's *Paradise Lost*
434 Geoffrey of Monmouth
435 Blind Harry
436 *The Winter's Tale*
437 The Roman state
438 From a snake bite
439 Oisin
440 John Keats

Quiz 44 (page 21)

441 Simorgh
442 Bast, or Bastet
443 Anubis
444 Cernunnos
445 Hanuman
446 Horus
447 Tawaret
448 Nandi
449 Ganesha
450 Sebek

Quiz 45 (page 22)

451 Satan
452 Scarab
453 Yeti
454 Camelot
455 Exorcism
456 Vlad
457 Medium
458 Carp
459 Angel
460 Noah

Quiz 46 (page 22)

461 Igor Stravinsky
462 Australia
463 The Pied Piper
464 Orpheus
465 Bremen
466 Mick Jagger
467 Nirvana
468 *Twelfth Night*
469 Joseph Haydn
470 Kraftwerk

Quiz 47 (page 22)

471 Rich
472 Jonathan and Martha Kent
473 Uranus
474 Odysseus
475 Isis
476 Morgan le Fay
477 Queen Maya
478 Odin, or Woden
479 Hades
480 Frigg

Quiz 48 (page 22)

481 Loch Ness
482 The *Argo*
483 Scylla and Charybdis
484 The Nile
485 Mermaid
486 The *Dawn Treader*
487 The Inuit
488 Orion
489 Atlantis
490 Poseidon

Quiz 49 (page 23)

491 Heracles
492 Helios
493 Caligula
494 Odysseus
495 The Titans
496 Three
497 Heinrich Schliemann
498 Erato
499 The Harpies
500 Tartarus

Quiz 50 (page 23)

501 Lindisfarne
502 Taoism
503 Parapsychology
504 Beatification and canonisation
505 Jean Sibelius
506 Osiris
507 Ichabod Crane
508 *Goblin Market*
509 The Maya
510 Savannah, Georgia

Quiz 51 (page 23)

511 B
512 C
513 B
514 C
515 B
516 D
517 B
518 B
519 A
520 C

Quiz 52 (page 24)

521 Genesis
522 Homer
523 Rudyard Kipling
524 Matthew, Mark, Luke and John
525 Santa's reindeer
526 *Wonderful Wizard of Oz*
527 Pinocchio
528 Its maker
529 Kubla Khan
530 Bilbo Baggins

Quiz 53 (page 24)

531 Heel
532 The heart
533 His head
534 Little Red Riding Hood
535 Acting
536 The palm of the hand
537 The eyes
538 The humerus
539 Lying
540 Through the nose

Quiz 54 (page 24)

541 Helen
542 Augustus
543 Ming
544 Zeus
545 Rapunzel
546 Titania
547 A clockwork nightingale
548 Cair Paravel
549 Europa
550 Sheherezade

Quiz 55 (page 24)

551 Rossini
552 Playing cards
553 *Nosferatu*
554 The Chinese
555 Phaethon
556 Witchfinder General of England
557 False
558 Edward Elgar
559 Joseph
560 Conquest, War, Famine, Death

Quiz 56 (page 25)

561 Jason
562 Spider-Man
563 Hercules
564 William Tell
565 Achilles
566 Lancelot
567 Perseus
568 Thor
569 William Wallace
570 Robin Hood

Quiz 57 (page 26)

571 *Terminator*
572 The Garden of Eden
573 Virgo
574 Thursday
575 Merlin
576 Kryptonite
577 Yang
578 The pipe of peace
579 Jane
580 *Snow White and the Seven Dwarves*

Quiz 58 (page 26)

581 False
582 True
583 False
584 True
585 True
586 False
587 True
588 False
589 False
590 True

Quiz 59 (page 26)

591 A swan
592 The owl
593 The ostrich
594 A raven
595 The pelican
596 The phoenix
597 A falcon
598 St Francis of Assisi
599 Icarus
600 The goldfinch

Quiz 60 (page 26)

601 A banshee
602 *The Little Match Girl*
603 The Black Death
604 St Lawrence
605 Mordred
606 Lazarus
607 The daleks
608 Voodoo
609 Hel
610 *The Sixth Sense*

Quiz 61 (page 27)

611 'To infinity and beyond'
612 *Through the Looking-Glass*
613 Jack and the Beanstalk
614 Tuesday
615 The hand
616 Vespasian
617 Edmund Hillary
618 A mockingbird
619 At the entrance to Hell
620 Peter Piper

Quiz 62 (page 27)

621 St Thomas More
622 Death of the firstborn
623 Shinto
624 A self-playing harp
625 On the doorframe
626 A shower of gold
627 The Furies
628 A tinderbox
629 St Matthew
630 Winged horses

Quiz 63 (page 27)

631 B
632 A
633 B
634 B
635 C
636 C
637 B
638 B
639 C
640 A

Quiz 64 (page 28)

641 Tooth
642 *Fantasia*
643 Horseshoe
644 Golden eggs
645 Great Sphinx
646 Stonehenge
647 Mystery Inc.
648 Jupiter
649 Halo
650 Rip van Winkle

Quiz 65 (page 28)

651 Jean Sibelius
652 The Styx
653 Wicca
654 The creation of the world
655 The Shangri-Las
656 Lord Greystoke
657 Jean-Luc Picard
658 Buster Crabbe
659 China
660 Leo

Quiz 66 (page 28)

661 A gypsy's
662 The USA's
663 The Golden Fleece
664 Sixpence
665 El Dorado
666 St Nicholas
667 The Prodigal Son
668 Midas
669 Pluto
670 Evil

Quiz 67 (page 28)

671 Unlucky
672 The sky
673 A silver coin
674 A snake
675 Buddha
676 Thanatos
677 Cowherds
678 The Slavonic god of thunder
679 Old Master
680 A goblin

Quiz 68 (page 29)

681 They all built arks
682 Trolls
683 Woodworkers
684 Phidias
685 Winchester
686 Lhasa
687 Abraham
688 The Star of David
689 The Great Pyramid at Giza
690 Nara

Quiz 69 (page 29)

691 The Book of Changes
692 Anne Rice
693 The Grimm Brothers
694 Friedrich Schiller
695 Emanuel Swedenborg
696 Hesiod
697 *Frankenstein*
698 John Bunyan
699 Ptolemy
700 Clio

Quiz 70 (page 29)

701 C
702 C
703 B
704 D
705 B
706 B
707 C
708 C
709 C
710 A

Quiz 71 (page 30)

711 Big Friendly Giant
712 Pixie
713 Cinderella
714 Buffy the Vampire Slayer
715 Mr Hyde
716 Nostradamus
717 Luke Skywalker
718 Monday
719 Gotham City
720 Brother

Quiz 72 (page 30)

721 A big cat
722 An elephant
723 The Sphinx
724 A snake
725 A grasshopper
726 Toto
727 A monkey
728 A cat
729 Centaur
730 George Orwell

Quiz 73 (page 30)

731 Sigmund Freud
732 Robert Browning
733 The *Gormenghast* trilogy
734 'In the beginning …'
735 *The 1001 Nights*
736 *The Water-Babies*
737 George Bernard Shaw
738 *Just So Stories*
739 Bram Stoker
740 Magpie

Quiz 74 (page 30)

741 'Isle of Apples'
742 Circe
743 Cockaigne
744 The pomegranate
745 Osiris
746 Currants
747 Sour grapes
748 A horn of plenty
749 Dionysus
750 Belshazzar's

Quiz 75 (page 31)

751 Dionysus
752 Vishnu
753 Amaterasu
754 Venus
755 Apollo
756 Avalokitesvara
757 Diana
758 Shou Lao
759 Odin
760 Bes

Quiz 76 (page 32)

761 Spock
762 Christian
763 Peter Parker
764 Adam
765 Thumbelina
766 Bruce Banner
767 Little Miss Muffet
768 Joanna
769 Hansel and Gretel
770 Tinkerbell

Quiz 77 (page 32)

771 Excalibur
772 Mistletoe
773 The trident
774 A silver bullet, or silver arrow
775 The boomerang
776 Sagittarius
777 The Garden of Eden
778 A hammer
779 A bolt of lightning
780 Light-sabre

Quiz 78 (page 32)

781 Prokofiev
782 Prospero
783 Rossini
784 *Hamlet*
785 Dvořák
786 Richard Wagner
787 *Macbeth*
788 Henrik Ibsen
789 Harrison Birtwistle
790 *The Magic Flute*

Quiz 79 (page 32)

791 His rib
792 A snake
793 Delilah
794 A swarm of bats
795 Job
796 Goliath
797 He was struck dead
798 Noah's Ark
799 Palm trees
800 He raised Lazarus from the dead

Quiz 80 (page 33)

801 The Blarney Stone
802 Cusp
803 Sulphur
804 13
805 Karma
806 Kaballah
807 Butsudo
808 Wanderer
809 Samsara
810 Leviathan

Quiz 81 (page 33)

811 Culture Club
812 Gaia
813 The Rapture
814 Mummers
815 Gehenna
816 Krishna
817 Brownie
818 Antaeus
819 Pantaloon
820 Morrigan

Quiz 82 (page 33)

821 A
822 B
823 C
824 D
825 C
826 B
827 C
828 A
829 B
830 C

Quiz 83 (page 34)

831 The Moon
832 A swan
833 The crocodile
834 True
835 Aries
836 A snake
837 The narwhal
838 Reindeer
839 True
840 The unicorn

Quiz 84 (page 34)

841 Mandalas
842 Van Helsing
843 The Milky Way
844 Rob Roy
845 A dragon
846 Witch
847 Toto
848 Dr McCoy
849 Donner and Blitzen
850 Islam

Quiz 85 (page 34)

851 Green
852 Ron Weasley
853 Snow White
854 Ivan Krylov
855 Lincoln green
856 White
857 A ghostly hound
858 Sir Gawain
859 The Slaughter Stone
860 Chernobog

Quiz 86 (page 34)

861 Washington Irving
862 Yama
863 Medea
864 Belshazzar
865 Castor
866 Kali
867 Zephyrus
868 Adonis
869 John Keats
870 Mary Magdalene

Quiz 87 (page 35)

871 Ankh cross
872 Cross of Lorraine
873 Tau cross
874 Latin cross
875 Maltese cross
876 St Andrew's cross
877 Russian cross
878 Papal cross
879 Greek cross
880 Celtic cross

Quiz 88 (page 36)

881 Unidentified Flying Object
882 Merlin
883 Capricorn
884 Buzz Lightyear
885 Wednesday
886 Friar Tuck
887 Pantomines
888 Professor Dumbledore
889 Tom Thumb
890 That person will be next to marry

Quiz 89 (page 36)

891 Puck
892 Juno
893 *Macbeth*
894 She is a ghost
895 The Inca
896 A forest spirit
897 In a field
898 Samantha
899 Lucky
900 *A Christmas Carol*

Quiz 90 (page 36)

901 Cousin
902 Tweedledum
903 Jocasta
904 Hubbard
905 Gepetto
906 Joseph
907 Hermaphroditos
908 Orestes
909 Menelaus
910 Apollo

Quiz 91 (page 36)

911 St Patrick
912 Lebanon
913 Germany
914 Brobdingnag
915 St Nicholas
916 Greece
917 Tibet
918 Danish
919 Georgia
920 St David

Quiz 92 (page 37)

921 Knights of the Round Table
922 Signs of the Chinese zodiac
923 Greek wind gods
924 *Just So Stories*
925 *Commedia dell'arte* characters
926 Characters in *The Lord of the Rings*
927 Titans
928 Wagner's *Ring* cycle
929 Polynesian gods
930 Fairies in *A Midsummer Night's Dream*

Quiz 93 (page 37)

931 Old King Cole
932 Uther Pendragon
933 Oberon
934 Oedipus
935 Edward I
936 Robert the Bruce
937 *The Faerie Queene*
938 Prince of Dyfed
939 Alfred the Great
940 Solomon

Quiz 94 (page 37)

941 The Sun
942 Orion
943 Atlas
944 Jacob
945 Cancer
946 The Sun
947 Andromeda
948 Paradise
949 7
950 Babylon

Quiz 95 (page 37)

951 Lemuel
952 Galahad
953 Shangri-La
954 Lethe
955 El Cid
956 Legion
957 Spike
958 Quetzlcoatl
959 Israel
960 Minerva

Quiz 96 (page 38)

961 Empire State Building
962 Tokyo
963 Sunnydale
964 Nottingham
965 The Tower of London
966 Troy
967 Bethlehem
968 Dick Whittington
969 Krypton
970 Zion

Quiz 97 (page 38)

971 Warlock
972 Basilisk
973 Séance
974 Salamander
975 'B'
976 Elessar
977 Goblin
978 Sasquatch
979 Pageant
980 Armageddon

Quiz 98 (page 38)

981 Venus
982 Loki
983 St Joseph
984 Saul
985 Lyonnesse
986 The Dalai Lama
987 Jacob Marley
988 Selene
989 John Wayne
990 R2-D2 (or Artoo-Detoo)

Quiz 99 (page 38)

991 100
992 Brahma, Shiva and Vishnu
993 *The Picture of Dorian Gray*
994 A hippopotamus
995 Ariadne
996 *The Turn of the Screw*
997 *Tales of Mother Goose*
998 St Martin
999 *Into the Woods*
1000 Ilium

Question sheet

Quiz Number **Quiz Title**

Questions	Answers
1	1
2	2
3	3
4	4
5	5
6	6
7	7
8	8
9	9
10	10

Answer sheet

Name

Quiz Number **Quiz Title**

Answers

1

2

3

4

5

6

7

8

9

10

Total score

PICTURE CREDITS

Abbreviations: T = top; M = middle; B = bottom; L =left; R =right
BPK = Bildarchiv Preussischer Kulturbesitz
BAL = Bridgeman Art Library
Front Cover: BAL/Private Collection
Back Cover: The Art Archive/Dagli Orti

1 Art Archive/British Library, London. **2-3** BAL/Gavin Graham Gallery, London. **4-5** BAL/Corbally Stourton Contemporary Art, London. **13** Left to right and top to bottom: Antoine de Saint-Exupéry, *Le Petit Prince*, © Editions Gallimard/Photography John Meek, 1; *Tommelise*, illustration by W. Heath Robinson from *Hans Anderson Fairy Tales*, Constable, 1913/Photo John Meek, 2; Illustration by Dante Gabriel Rossetti from *Goblin Market and Other Poems*, by Christina Rossetti, Macmillan, 1862/Photo John Meek, 3; *The* 'Story of The Inky Boys', from *Struwwelpeter* by Heinrich Hoffmann, Keagan Paul/Photo John Meek, 4; *Brer Rabbit and Brer B'ar*, illustration by A.H. Frost from *Uncle Remus and His Friends* by J.C. Harris, J.R. Osgood, McIlvaine, 1893/Photo John Meek, 5; Kobal Collection/MGM, 6/Universal. 7/Joseph Shaftel Productions,10; Illustration by Cruikshank, from Brothers Grimm/Photo John Meek, 8; © The Halas and Batchelor Collection Limited, 9. **21** Left to right and top to bottom: akg-images/Gerard Degeorge, 1; Michael Holford/British Museum, London, 2, 8, 10; Michael Holford, 9; BPK/Pelizaeus Museum, Hildersheim, 3; Werner Forman Archive/National Museum Copenhagen, 4; BAL/Dinodia Picture Agency, Bombay, 5; BPK/Margarete Büsing, 6; Werner Forman Archive, 7. **25** Left to right and top to bottom: The Art Archive/Museo del Prado, Madrid/Dagli Orti,1; Spider-Man: TM & © 2004 Marvel Characters Inc. SUPER HEROES is a jointly owned trademark of Marvel and DC Comics. Used with permission/Photography John Meek, 2; BAL/Kunsthistorisches Museum, Vienna, 3; Art Directors/T Gognar, 4; Michael Holford/ British Museum, London, 5; Illustration by Roy Morgan, from *Stories of King Arthur and his Knights*, by B.L. Picard, OUP, 1955/Photo John Meek, 6; Art Archive/Dagli Orti, 7; THOR and the character likeness shown herein: TM & © 2004 Marvel Characters Inc. Used with permission/Photography John Meek, 8; Illustration by J.R. Skelton, from *Scotland's Story* by H.E. Marshall, Thomas Nelson, 1906/Photo John Meek, 9; Illustration by S Van Abbé, from *Robin Hood, the Prince of Outlaws* by Carola Oman, J.M. Dent, 1959/Photo John Meek, 10. **31** Left to right and top to bottom: Michael Holford/British Museum, London, 1; BPK/Staatliche Museen, Berlin/Jürgen Liepe, 2; Michael Holford/Victoria & Albert Museum, London, 3, 6; BAL/Giraudon/ Galleria degli Uffizi, Florence, 4; BPK/Vatican, Rome, 5; BPK/Staatliche Museen, Berlin/Jörg P. Anders, 7; BAL/ National Museums Liverpool, 8; BAL/Royal Library, Copenhagen, 9; BPK/Staatliche Museen, Berlin/Jürgen Liepe, 10. **35** Left to right and top to bottom: Art Archive/ Dagli Orti, 1; BAL/Armoury Museum, Kremlin, Moscow, 2; Art Archive/ Archaeological Museum, Madrid/Dagli Orti, 3; BAL/St. Michael's, Doddiscombsleigh, Devon, 4; Art Archive/Dagli Orti, 5; BAL/Musée des Tapisseries, Angers, 6; V & A Images/ Victoria and Albert Museum, 7; The Art Archive/Museo della Civita Romana, Rome/Dagli Orti, 8; Art Archive/Russian Historical Museum, Moscow/Dagli Orti, 9; Art Archive/Dagli Orti, 10. **40** Michael Holford/British Museum, London, T. **40-1** *Creation of Adam*, detail from fresco by Michelangelo Buonarroti, Sistine Chapel, Vatican, Rome/BPK (background). **41** akg-images/Henning Bock, TL; BAL/*Izanami and Izanagi Creating the Japanese Islands*, Meiji era, Japan, c.1885 (hanging scroll: ink & colour on silk) by Kobayashi Eitaku/Museum of Fine Arts Boston, Massachusetts, USA, William Sturgis Bigelow Collection, TR. **42** BAL/Giraudon/ National Museum, Aleppo, Syria, BL. **42-3** BAL/*The Animals Entering the Ark*, detail from panel by Jacob Savery II/Christie's Images, London, (background). **43** BAL/*Sirens holding a cornucopia*, detail from painting c.1724 by Francois Boucher on the State Carriage of Peter the Great/Hermitage, St. Petersburg, T; BPK/ Dietmar Katz, B. **44** akg-images/Museo Egizio, Turin/Nimatallah, L; BPK/Staatliche Museen, Berlin/Jürgen Liepe, R. **45** BAL, T; BPK/Staatliche Museen, Berlin/Jürgen Liepe, M; Jürgen Liepe/Egyptian Museum, Cairo, B. **46** akg-images/National Museum, Cairo/Erich Lessing. **47** BAL, T; BAL/ Oriental Museum, Durham University, M; Michael Holford/British Museum, London, B. **48** Michael Holford/Horniman Museum, London, T; Michael Holford/Musée Guimet, B; **48-9** BAL/ Stapleton Collection/Victoria & Albert Museum, London (background); **49** Michael Holford/Musée Guimet, T; Michael Holford/Victoria & Albert Museum, London, MR. **50** Art Archive/Musée Guimet, Paris/Dagli Orti, M, B. **50-1** akg-images/Jean-Louis Nou (background). **51** Michael Freeman, BL, MR. **52** BAL/ Oriental Museum, Durham University, L; BAL/Victoria & Albert Museum, London, BR. **52-3** Michael Freeman (background). **53** BAL/Bonhams, London, T. **54** The Art Archive/Bodleian Library, Oxford/Ashmole 304 folio 2v, T; The Art Archive/Real Biblioteca del Escorial/Dagli Orti, B. **54-5** Science Photo Library/John Chumack (background). **55** BAL, T; BAL/Private Collection, MR. **56** BAL/The De Morgan Centre, London, BL; BAL/Collegio del Cambio, Perugia, BR. **57** Michael Holford, T; Michael Holford/British Museum, London, B. **58** BAL/British Museum, London, MR; BAL/*Psyche Giving the Coin to the Ferryman* (oil on canvas) by Sir Edward Burne-Jones/Birmingham Museums and Art Gallery, B. **58-9** Art Archive/Galleria Borghese, Rome/Dagli Orti (background). **60** Art Archive/Museo Civico Orvieto/Dagli Orti, T; Art Archive/ Museo Nazionale Taranto/Dagli Orti, B. **60-1** Art Archive/Dagli Orti (background). **61** BAL/Museo Nazionale, Taranto, Puglia, T; Art Archive/Archaeological Museum Piraeus/Dagli Orte, B. **62** The Art Archive/Galleria degli Uffizi, Florence/Dagli Orti. **62-3** Illustration by G Doré from *La Divina Commedia* (Inferno) by Dante Alighieri/Photo John Meek (background). **63** BAL/*The Naiad* by Emil Gustav Adolf Clockner/Roy Miles Fine Paintings, TL; BPK/Staatliche Museen, Berlin/Jürgen Liepe, BR. **64** Michael Holford/British Museum, London, L; BAL/Vatican Museums and Galleries, Vatican City, Italy, BR. **65** BAL/*Phaeton and Apollo* by Giovanni Battista Tiepolo (Giambattista)/ Akademie der Bildenden Kunste, Vienna,T; BAL/*Europa Being Carried off by Jupiter Metamorphosed into a Bull*, c.1700, by Pierre Gobert/Victoria & Albert Museum, London, B. **66** Michael Holford/British Museum, London, B; BPK/Vatican, Rome, MR. **67** BAL/*The Fall of Icarus*, 1731, (engraving) by Bernard Picart/Stapleton Collection, TL; BAL/Galleria Doria Pamphilj, Rome, MR; BAL/Hermitage, St Petersburg, BL. **68** BAL/Museum of Fine Arts, Boston, Massachusetts, USA, gift in honour of Edward W. Forbes from his friends, T; Art Archive/Archaeological Museum, Florence/ Dagli Orti, B. **68-9** *Juno and Argus*, 1611 (oil on canvas) by Peter Paul Rubens/ Wallraf Richartz Museum, Cologne, (background). **70** BAL/Bibliotheque Municipale, Dijon, ML; BAL/Museo Capitolino, Rome, B. **70-1** Art Archive/Dagli Orti (background). **71** Art Archive/British Museum, London, T. **72** THOR and the character likeness shown herein: TM & © 2004 Marvel Characters, Inc. Used with permission. **72-3** naturepl.com/Asgeir Helgestad (background). **73** Art Archive/Bodleian Library, Oxford, TL; Werner Forman Archive/National Museum, Copenhagen, TR; BAL/*The Ride of the Valkyries* by William T. Maud/Gavin Graham Gallery, London, BL. **74** BAL/*The Death of Cuchulain*, c.1940 (pen and ink) by John Yunge-Bateman/Private Collection. **74-5** Robert Harding/Michael Jenner (background). **75** Art Archive/British Library, London, MR. **76** Kobal Collection/ Orion/Warner Bros, BM. **76-7** Robert Harding Picture Library/Michael Jenner (background). **77** BAL/Bibliothèque Nationale, Paris,TL; BAL/British Library, London, BM; BAL/*The Last Sleep of Arthur in Avalon*, 1881-98, by Sir Edward Burne-Jones/Museo de Arte, Ponce, Puerto Rico, West Indies, BR. **78** BAL/*Seppo Llmarinen Ploughing the Field of Snakes* by Joseph Alanen/Private Collection, T; BAL/Sketch for the set of the opera, *Russalka* by Aleksandr Sergevich Dargomyzhsky (w/c on paper)/Novosti/Private Collection, B. **79** *Prince Astrach on His Horse*, illustration by De Rosciszewski, from *The Russian Garland*, edited by R. Steel, published by A. M. Philpot, 1922/Photo John Meek (background); Baba Yaga, from book of Russian folktales, 1899/Photo John Meek, BR. **80** Michael Holford/British Museum, London, R. **80-1** BAL/*Warnampi Tingari*, 1980 (acrylic) by Dick Pantimas Tjupurrula/ Corbally Stourton Contemporary Art, London. **81** Art Archive/Antenna Gallery Dakar Senegal/Dagli Orti, TM; BAL/Ken Welsh, BR. **82** BAL/Coloured engraving by Jacques Le Moyne after, *Sun Worshipping Ritual with an Offering of a Deer*, from Brevis Narratio, engraved by Theodore de Bry 1563/Service Historique de la Marine, Vincennes, France, BR. **82-3** BAL/ *Medicine Mask Dance* (oil on canvas) by Paul Kane/Royal Ontario Museum Toronto, (background). **83** Kobal Collection/20th Century Fox, BR. **84** BAL/*St Francis of Assisi Preaching to the Birds*, (oil on panel) by Giotto di Bondone/Louvre, Paris,TL; Art Archive/Saint Sebastian Chapel Lanslevillard Savoy/Dagli Orti, BL. **84-5** BAL/*St George and the Dragon*, c.1470, (oil on canvas) by Paolo Uccello/National Gallery, London, (detail and phased out background). **86** BAL/detail from *The Lady and the Unicorn: Sight* (tapestry)/Musée National du Moyen Age et des Thermes de Cluny, Paris. **87** BAL/Stapleton Collection, T; BAL/detail from *Behemoth and Leviathan*, from the Book of Job (pl.15) c.1793 (hand-tinted line engraving) by William Blake/Fitzwilliam Museum, University of Cambridge, UK, MR; BAL/*St Michael and his Angels Fighting the Dragon*, no.36 from *The Apocalypse of Angers* (tapestry) by Nicolas Bataille/Musée des Tapisseries, Angers, France, BL. **88** Illustration by Arthur Rackham, 1911, from *Siegfried and the Twilight of the Gods*. From *Arthur Rackham, His Life and Work* by D. Hudson, published by Heinemann, 1974/Photo John Meek/© The Arthur Rackham pictures are reproduced with the kind permission of his family. **88-9** Allied Artists/Kobal Collection (background). **89** Corbis Images/Reuters, BR. **90** BAL/*The Fall*, detail from the Grabow Altarpiece (tempera on panel) by Master Bertram of Minden/Hamburg Kunsthalle, Hamburg, German, MR. **90-1** Kobal Collection/ Lucasfilm/20th Century Fox (background, B). **91** Ronald Grant Archive/Nero Film, TL; Art Archive/*The Devil Taking a Child* by Francesco Melanzio/Pinacoteca-Museo Comunale Montefalco/Dagli Orti, TR. **92** BAL/Victoria & Albert Museum, London. **92-3** *Animal Farm* 1951-54. © The Halas & Batchelor Collection Limited. Produced and directed by John Halas and Joy Batchelor for DeRochemont Films Inc. (background). **94** Art Directors/T. Bognar, BL. **94-5** Kobal Collection/Warner Bros (detail and phased-out background). **95** Corbis/Bettmann, TR; Photo John Meek, BR. **96-7** BAL/Illustration from *The Pied Piper of Hamelin*, 1912 (w/c, pencil on paper) by Margaret Tarrant/Chris Beetles Ltd, London/Private Collection. **97** BAL/*A Sailor Boy Begs for his Life from an Ogre* (litho)/Collection Kharbine-Tapabor, Paris, TL; BAL/Hanson Collection, BR. **98** Corbis/Inume Pass in Kai Province, by Hokusai/Burstein Collection, TR; Corbis/Adam Woolfitt, BL. **98-9** Corbis/ Paul A. Souders. B. **99** Corbis/Craig Lovell, T. **100** BAL/*Land of Cockaigne*, 1567 (oil on panel) by Pieter the Elder Brueghel/Alte Pinakothek, Munich, Germany, B. **100-1** Art Archive/*El Dorado the Golden Man New Muisca Leader Anointed with Gold Dust*, 1599 (engraving) by Theodore De Bry, (background). **101** Art Archive/*Spies returning from the Land of Canaan* from Biblia Sacra Germanica Nurnberg Koberger, 1483/Victoria & Albert Museum, London/Graham Brandon, B. **102** Kobal Collection/Walt Disney, B. **103** Kobal Collection/MGM, (background); BAL/ *Morgan Le Fay: Queen of Avalon* by Anthony Frederick Augustus Sandys, B. **104** *Little Tom Thumb*, Illustration by G. Dore from *Les Contes de Perrault* by Charles Perrault, published by Hetzel, 1867/Photo John Meek, BL; *Snow White and the Seven Dwarfs*. Illustration from *Bruder Grimm Kinder-Marchen*, published by Ferdinand Carl, Stuttgart, 1910/Photo John Meek, BR. **105** Scala Picture Library/ Museo Nazioale, Naples, TL; BAL/ Illustration from *Les Voyages de Gulliver* (colour litho) by Frederic Lix/Archives Charmet/Private Collection, MM; Ronald Grant Archive/Allied Artists Picture Corp, R. **106-107** BAL/*Titania Awakes*, 1793-94, (oil on canvas) by Henry Fuseli/Kunsthaus, Zurich, Switzerland. **107** Title page from *The Water Babies*, by Charles Kingsley, published by Macmillan, 1872/Photo John Meek, TL; BAL/Louvre, Paris, R; BAL/*The Troll and the Boy* (w/c on paper) by John Bauer/Nationalmuseum, Stockholm, B. **108** BAL/Front cover of *Dracula* by Bram Stoker, 1920 (litho) by Pierre Falke/ Bibliotheque Nationale de France/Archives Charmet, M. **108-9** Kobal Collection/ MGM. **109** BAL/Hammer, BL; BAL/Roger Perrin/Private Collection, BR. **110** Illustration by Carlo Chiostri from *Le Aventure di Pinocchio* by C. Collodi published by R Bemporad, 1924/Photo John Meek, L; Ronald Grant Archive/ courtesy Universal Pictures, R. **111** Illustration by W. W. Denslow from *The Wonderful World of Oz* by L F Baum, first published 1900/Photo John Meek, TL; BAL/*Galatea and Pygmalion* by Agnolo Bronzino/Galleria degli Uffizi, Florence, TR; Kobal Collection/Carolco, B. **112** Illustration by John Austen from *Tales of Passed Times* by C. Perrault, published by Selwyn & Blount, 1922/Photo John Meek, TR, BL. **112-3** Bradbury and Williams (background). **113** Illustration by G Doré from *Les Contes de Perrault* by Charles Perrault, published by Hetzel, 1867/Photo John Meek, T; Illustration by E.V. Boyle from *Beauty and the Beast*, published by Sampson Low, 1875/Photo John Meek, B. **114** Illustration by G. Cruikshank from *German Popular Stories* by the Brothers Grimm, 1823-26/Photo John Meek. **115** Illustration by G. Doré from *Les Contes de Perrault* by Charles Perrault, published by Hetzel, 1867/Photo John Meek (background); Illustration by Arthur Rackham, 1912, for *Mother Goose*, from *Arthur Rackham, his Life and Work* by D. Hudson, published by Heinemann, 1974/Photo John Meek/©The Arthur Rackham Pictures are reproduced with the kind permission of his family, TR; Illustration by A. H. Frost from *Uncle Remus and His Friends* by J.C. Harris, published by J.R. Osgood, McIlvaine, 1893/Photo John Meek, B. **116** Illustration from *The Little Mermaid* by Honor C Appleton, from *Fairy Tales* by Hans Christian Andersen, published by Thomas Nelson, 1922/Photo John Meek, T; **116-7** *The Emperor's New Clothes*, and *The Ugly Duckling*. Illustrations by W. Heath Robinson from *Hans Andersen's Fairy Tales*, published by Constable, 1913/ Reproduced by permission of Polinger Limited and the proprietor/Photos John Meek, B, TL; BAL/Illustration from *The Princess and the Pea* by Hans Christian Andersen, c.1911 by Edmund Dulac/ Victoria & Albert Museum, London. Used by permission of Hodder & Stoughton, MR. **118** Illustration by C.H. Bennett from *Bennett's Fables from Aesop* published by Chatto and Windus, 1978, first published 1857/Photo John Meek, T; BAL/*Echo and Narcissus*, 1903 (oil on canvas) by John William Waterhouse/Walker Art Gallery, Liverpool/National Museums Liverpool, B. **118-9** Kobal Collection/Paramount Pictures/Mandalay Pictures/Clive Coote (background); **119** Illustration from *Just So Stories* by Rudyard Kipling, published by Methuen Children's Books, 1989/ (w/c) by Jonathan Langley/Chris Beetles Ltd, London, BL. **120** BAL/*Daniel Interpreting Nebuchadnezzar's First Dream* (oil on canvas) by Mattia Preti (Il Calabrese)/Private Collection, B; **120-1** *Jacob's Ladder* (pen and w/c on paper) by William Blake/British Museum, London, (background); **121** *Michel Nostradame* (coloured engraving) by French School (19th century)/Musée Nat.des Arts et Traditions Populaires, Paris, T. **122** Art Archive/Museo Diocesano Orta/Dagli Orti. **123** Art Archive, TR; Kobal Collection/Columbia, M; Kobal Collection/MGM/SLA Entertainment, B. **124-5** BAL/*Heaven Opened* (w/c on paper) by George Jones/Birmingham Museums and Art Gallery. **125** BAL/*Dante's Vision of Heaven, Purgatory and Hell*, by M. Caetari, Rome 1855/British Library, London, TL; BAL/*Panel of the Descent into Limbo*, from the altarpiece of the convent of Santo Sepulchro, Zaragoza (tempera on panel) by Jaume Serra/Museo Provincial de Bellas Artes, Zaragoza, Spain, TR; BAL/*Hell* (oil on panel) by Hieronymus Bosch (school of)/Hermitage, St.Petersburg, Russia, B. **126-7** Fortean Picture Library, L, (background). **127** Kobal Collection/20th Century Fox, L; Kobal Collection/Toho, BR. **128** Michael Holford/Wellcome Collection, T; akg-images/Gilles Mermet, B. **128-9** Corbis/David Pollack (background). **129** BAL/Egyptian National Museum, Cairo, BR. **130-1** Michael Holford/British Museum, London, BL, (background). **131** The Art Archive/Private Collection, TR; BAL/ Egyptian National Museum, Cairo, BR. **132** Illustration by Tenniel from *Through the Looking-Glass* by Lewis Carroll, published by Macmillan, 1927/Photo John Meek. **132-3** BAL/*View of the Cedar Forests of Lebanon* seen from the Tripoli Road, c.1800 (ink and w/c on paper) by Louise Francois Cassas/Bibliothèque Mazarine, Paris, (background). **133** Corbis/Bo Zaunders, T; Corbis/*Proserpine* by Dante Gabriel Rossetti/Christie's Images, B. **134** Corbis/Thom Lang, T; BAL/*The Last Supper*, from a series of scenes of the New Testament (fresco) by Barna da Siena, B. **135** Art Archive/Musée Condé Chantilly/ Dagli Orti, T; Rex Features/Everett Collection, B. **136** Illustration by Tenniel from *Through the Looking-Glass* by Lewis Carroll, published by Macmillan, 1927/Photo John Meek, T; Illustration from *Mother Goose's Book of Nursery Rhymes and Songs*, edited by E and G Rhys, published by J.M. Dent (now a division of the Orion Publishing Group), 1910/Photo John Meek, B. **137** Illustration from Struwwelpeter by Heinrich Hoffmann, Kegan Paul/Photo John Meek, TR; BAL/*Little Miss Muffet* (w/c over pencil on drawing board) by Rosa Petherick/York Art Gallery, UK/York Museums Trust, BL; BAL/*Ring-a-Ring-a-Roses-Oh* (oil on canvas) by Frederick Morgan/Towneley Hall Art Gallery and Museum, Burnley, Lancashire, BR. **138** *Le Petit Prince*, written and illustrated by Antoine de St Exupéry, 1943/©Editions Gallimard/Photography John Meek, TR; Illustration by Tenniel from *Alice's Adventures in Wonderland* by Lewis Carroll, Macmillan/Photo John Meek, BL. **139** Kobal Collection/Walt Disney Pictures ©1964, T; *Harry Potter and the Goblet of Fire* by J.K. Rowling. Illustration by Giles Greenfield, publisher, Bloomsbury/Photo John Meek, B. **140** Alina Cojocaro in *The Nutcracker*, Royal Opera House, London, 12 December 2001/Photo Dee Conway. **140-1** ArenaPal/*Die Zauberflote* by Mozart/Glyndebourne Festival Opera, May, 2004 with Pavol Breslik as Tamino/Photo Clive Barda (background). **141** BAL/Tamara Karsavina as Columbine and Vaslav Nijinsky as Harlequin in Fokine's *Carnaval* in 1910, (pochoir print) by Georges Barbier, pub.1914/Private Collection, BR. **142-3** "Wonder Woman" #203 TM & © 2004 DC Comics. All Rights Reserved. Used with Permission. SUPERMAN, BATMAN, CATWOMAN & HARLEY QUINN TM & © 2004 DC Comics. All Rights Reserved. Used with permission. **144-5** Kobal Collection/Paramount. **145** Kobal Collection/Lucas films/20th century Fox, BR.

Myths, Legends and Folk Tales was published by The Reader's Digest Association Ltd, London. It was created and produced for Reader's Digest by Toucan Books Ltd, London.

Researched and written by
Jonathan Bastable

For Toucan Books:
Editors
Jane Chapman
Helen Douglas-Cooper
Andrew Kerr-Jarrett
Picture researchers
Cynthia Frazer
Christine Vincent
Proofreader
Ron Pankhurst
Indexer
Laura Hicks
Design
Bradbury and Williams

For Reader's Digest:
Project editor
Christine Noble
Project art editors
Heather Dunleavy
Louise Turpin
Pre-press accounts manager
Penny Grose

Reader's Digest, General Books:
Editorial director
Cortina Butler
Art director
Nick Clark

Colour origination
Colour Systems Ltd, London

Printed and bound
in Europe by Arvato, Iberia

ISBN 0 276 42941 9
BOOK CODE 625-009-01
CONCEPT CODE UK0095/G/S
ORACLE CODE 355500009H.00.24

The Reader's Digest Association Ltd,
11 Westferry Circus,
Canary Wharf,
London E14 4HE
www.readersdigest.co.uk

We are committed to both the quality of our products and the service we provide to our customers. We value your comments, so please feel free to contact us on 08705 113366 or via our web site at **www.readersdigest.co.uk**

If you have any comments or suggestions about the content of our books, you can email us at **gbeditorial@readersdigest.co.uk**